grow fruit

LONDON, NEW YORK, MUNICH, MELBOURNE, DELHI

Project Editor Anna Kruger
Project Art Editor Alison Gardner

Senior Editor Helen Fewster
Managing Editor Esther Ripley
Managing Art Editor Alison Donovan
Associate Publisher Liz Wheeler
Production Editor Joanna Byrne
Production Controller Sophie Argyris
Picture Researcher Ria Jones
Jacket Designer Mark Cavanagh
Publisher Jonathan Metcalf
Art Director Bryn Walls

Special photography at West Dean Gardens, West Sussex

First published in Great Britain in 2010
by Dorling Kindersley Limited
80 Strand, London WC2R 0RL

A Penguin Company

2 4 6 8 10 9 7 5 3 1

Copyright © 2010 Dorling Kindersley Limited
Text copyright © 2010 Alan Buckingham

A CIP catalogue record for this book is available from the
British Library

ISBN 978-1-4053-3739-7

Printed and bound in Singapore by Star Standard

Discover more at
www.dk.com

grow fruit

ALAN BUCKINGHAM

Specialist consultant JO WHITTINGHAM

CONTENTS

Why grow your own?

There are many, many reasons why it's worth growing your own fruit. Freshness, flavour, good health, and choice are all part of the equation, but so too are concerns about the industrialization of commercial food production and the feeling that we want to know more about where our food comes from, how it is grown, and what is done to it before it reaches us. That, and the fact that many are rediscovering a very simple truth: it is not only delicious but also extraordinarily satisfying to eat food we have grown ourselves.

Perfectly ripe, perfectly fresh

All fruit reaches a peak of perfection, a moment when it is perfectly ripe. Usually – though not always – it is still on the tree, bush, or vine and the trick is to harvest it and enjoy it as close to that moment as possible. If you grow your own, you'll have a good chance of anticipating and then tasting this perfect ripeness. If you buy fruit from the supermarket you'll certainly miss out. Commercially grown fruit is almost always picked before it is ripe so that it can be transported without the fruit being damaged, and it may then be stored in climate-controlled warehouses to stop it from going off. The idea is that it ripens either when it reaches the supermarket shelf or when you get it home. In any case, it never tastes as good as fruit that has been left on the plant to ripen naturally.

Seasonal and local

Strawberries in February. Redcurrants at Christmas. Apples and pears in May. How does that work? The answer is obvious: these are fruits grown on the other side of the world that have travelled thousands of miles before they reach us. But at what cost to quality and flavour? And what about their carbon footprint? We're so accustomed to everything we want being available all year round that we've lost touch with how much better fruit tastes if it is grown locally and eaten in season.

A perfectly ripe peach: meltingly soft, sweet, aromatic, juicy, picked and eaten straight from the tree. Can you imagine a better reason for growing your own?

Choice and variety

An aisle of well-stocked supermarket shelves may give the impression of choice, but what you are looking at is a mere drop in the ocean compared to the real choice you have if you decide to grow your own. Even modest garden centres and plant nurseries offer a surprising range of fruit varieties, and a specialist supplier will have literally hundreds. Some will be modern cultivars, bred for particular attributes such as size, colour, flavour, or resistance to various pests and diseases. Others are likely to be heritage varieties, often unusual, and sometimes rediscovered after being forgotten for decades or more. You'll also find unusual fruits that you will probably never see on sale commercially because they are simply impossible and too expensive to transport – mulberries, for example.

The organic option

This book does not take sides in the debate over the pros and cons of organic gardening. Using chemicals is a sensitive issue, and most of us would rather eat food that is as natural and unadulterated as possible, but fruit is prone to numerous pests and diseases, and treatments are sometimes called for. At the end of the day, whether you use organic or synthetic fertilizers, pesticides, fungicides, and weedkillers is a decision only you can take. At least when you grow your own, the choice is one you make yourself.

(below, left to right) **Spring blossom** can be so spectacular that it's almost reason enough to plant fruit trees. Apple blossom is irresistible to bees and other pollinating insects. **Clusters of young grapes** begin to form in May or June once flowering is over. Then slowly, over the course of the next few months, they swell and the bunches become denser. (opposite) **Picking cherries** and eating them straight from the tree, sun-warmed and ripe, is one of the high moments of summer.

The fruit gardener

How difficult is it to grow your own fruit? How much know-how do you really need? How much time and effort are involved? These are difficult questions to answer, because it all depends on where you live, what sort of garden or allotment you have, and what fruit you want to grow. Some are certainly easier than others. Plenty of apples and pears will grow almost anywhere. So, too, will most gooseberry and currant bushes, strawberries, blackberries, and raspberries. Others need a bit more care and attention – grapes, for example – or the right sort of soil, as do blueberries. And tender fruits such as peaches, apricots, melons, and citrus demand a warm, sunny spot protected from frost and wind. Otherwise, although they may grow, fruit is unlikely to ripen at all.

The bottom line is that none of the fruits in this book are hard to grow, but you are likely to have much more success if you read up about what they like, choose the right varieties for the growing conditions you can offer, look after them attentively, and gently coax them into producing a good crop of fruit.

Picking developing fruitlets in early summer and throwing them away may seem wasteful but thinning is vital. The remaining apples will grow larger and tastier if the tree is not overburdened.

What fruit can I grow?

To answer this question meaningfully, you need to start with your climate. That, of course, will depend on where you live. At what latitude? At what altitude? Is your plot exposed or sheltered, inland or near the coast, north- or south-facing? These elements all help to determine the climatic conditions in which your plants grow. The nature and composition of your soil is important too. So are feeding, mulching, watering, training, pruning, and so on. But the climate – or, to be specific, the microclimate – is almost certainly the most important factor.

The north-south divide

In the UK, we have what's called a cool temperate climate, and we are able to grow a wide variety of fruit fairly successfully. That said, there are real differences from one part of the country to another. An imaginary line drawn from the Bristol Channel to the Wash is often said to more-or-less indicate the divide between north and south. Cool-climate tree fruits such as apples, pears, plums, and cherries, and soft fruits such as raspberries, blackberries, gooseberries, and currants can be grown pretty much anywhere, although they are all likely to flower earlier, and fruit will ripen and be ready to pick sooner, south of this line. Fruits whose natural habitat is a warm temperate or Mediterranean climate will struggle north of the line. It's not impossible, but it's certainly a challenge to grow outdoor peaches, nectarines, apricots, citrus fruit, melons, and grapes in Wales, the Midlands, and farther north.

Fruit varieties and cultivars

A quick look at the catalogue of a specialist plant nursery – or, indeed, at a few of the pages that follow in this book – will give you an immediate idea of just how many different varieties or cultivars there are of each major type of fruit. There are literally thousands of different apples, and scores if not hundreds of pears, plums, cherries, grapes, strawberries, melons, and so on. Choosing a variety is not merely about size, shape, colour, and flavour. It's also about its suitability for your climate. Many of the

Must-grow fruit

1 Strawberries
Difficulty *Easy to grow*
Protect fruit against birds and slugs, and replace plants after two or three years.
■ See p.183.

2 Grapes
Difficulty *Tricky to grow well*
In cool climates, grapes for winemaking are easier than grapes for eating. Even so, you may need a greenhouse.
■ See p.264.

3 Plums
Difficulty *Easy to grow*
Plums are notorious for having good years and bad years. A lot depends on whether blossom is pollinated in spring.
■ See p.103.

4 Cherries
Difficulty *Easy to grow*
Nets to protect fruit against birds are an absolute must.
■ See p.121.

5 Quinces
Difficulty *Very easy to grow*
Almost maintenance-free and a good choice if you want to try something slightly unusual.
■ See p.158.

6 Blackberries
Difficulty *Very easy to grow*
Cultivated varieties produce better fruits than wild brambles. Try some of the unusual hybrids too.
■ See p.209.

7 Blueberries
Difficulty *Very easy to grow*
Given the right sort of acid soil, blueberries couldn't be easier.
■ See p.247.

8 Redcurrants
Difficulty *Very easy to grow*
Grow upright cordons if space is limited. Try the slightly sweeter whitecurrants too.
■ See p.231.

9 Apples
Difficulty *Easy to grow*
Teach yourself how to prune. You'll get better fruit and heavier crops if you do.
■ See p.41.

named cultivars have been bred – and many of the traditional ones are still grown – because they to do well in particular regions. Sometimes there's a clue in the name: 'Worcester Pearmain', 'Cornish Aromatic', or 'Norfolk Beauty', for example. These are all local apples attuned to their local climates. Even if you are growing fruit that's from farther afield, it's best to choose varieties that share similar requirements. So, if you are attempting outdoor grapes in the UK, go for a variety from Germany or northern France, not one from Italy or Spain.

Microclimates

Most gardens contain microclimates. Usually, they're a good thing: a patio that acts as a late-afternoon suntrap, a warm sheltered corner, or a south-facing fence or wall can make all the difference to what you're able to grow. They may offer just the right site for, say, a container-grown fig, a dwarf peach, or a wall-trained apricot, all of which might survive but not produce ripe fruit elsewhere.

Unfortunately, the corollary is true, too. Gardens sometimes have the kind of microclimates that you'd prefer not to have. A low-lying spot at the foot of a slope that acts as a frost trap, for example, or a patch of soil that's in what's called a "rain shadow", overhung by a nearby wall or fence and therefore prone to drying out even when the rest of the garden is damp.

Growing fruit under cover

You can exploit greenhouses, conservatories, polytunnels, and even cold frames to extend the range of fruit you can grow. They allow you to create microclimates over which you are in complete control. If you live in a cool temperate region such as the UK, they provide a warm, frost-free environment for sheltering tender, container-grown fruit such as citrus during the worst of the winter months. And a heated greenhouse or polytunnel is really the only means of growing subtropical and tropical fruit.

There is a long tradition, at least in Europe, of growing fruit in large, custom-built glasshouses, so that tender and exotic fruit such as grapes, oranges, peaches, apricots, melons, figs, and even pineapples could be served almost all year round. Orangeries were designed with tall glazed doors that opened directly onto wide terraces, so that heavy container-grown citrus trees could be wheeled outside in summer and back inside in winter where they continued to receive plenty of light from the huge windows. In the 19th century, greenhouses were heated not just by coal furnaces that fired hot-water systems but also by the warmth that emanated naturally from decomposing farmyard manure, sometimes piled in special "pineapple pits".

10 Peaches and nectarines
Difficulty *Moderate*
These stone fruits need a warm, sheltered site and plenty of sun in order to ripen.
■ See p.145.

11 Citrus fruit
Difficulty *Moderate*
In cool climates, grow citrus in containers and bring them under cover in winter.
■ See p.285.

12 Gooseberries
Difficulty *Very easy to grow*
Given the right conditions, and barring attack by mildew, plants are almost indestructible. Pruning and netting are all that's required.
■ See p.219.

13 Raspberries
Difficulty *Easy to moderate*
Autumn-fruiting varieties are much easier than summer-fruiting. They're less trouble to support and to prune, and may not need nets.
■ See p.197.

14 Figs
Difficulty *Easy to moderate*
Trees are not hard to grow, but figs need sun and warmth so the amount of fruit you get may be variable.
■ See p.167.

15 Apricots
Difficulty *Easy to moderate*
In cool climates, choose an appropriate variety and grow in a sheltered, sunny spot.
■ See p.137.

16 Blackcurrants
Difficulty *Very easy to grow*
It's hard to think of a site where blackcurrants won't grow, but they do need pruning once a year to go on cropping well.
■ See p.239.

17 Pears
Difficulty *Easy to grow*
Pears are slightly fussier than apples, but easier to prune. The hardest thing is knowing the best moment to harvest them.
■ See p.81.

18 Melons
Difficulty *Moderate*
In warm climates, melons are easy to grow. In cool climates, they are trickier and best grown under cover.
■ See p.295.

Growing fruit in small gardens

A small garden should not prevent you from growing your own fruit. Admittedly, if space is limited you're hardly going to be planting an orchard of full-sized fruit trees, and a large walk-in fruit cage is also likely to be off the agenda. But with a little ingenuity and careful thought about how to make the best use of the space you have, there are plenty of other crops you can grow.

Dwarfing and compact fruit trees

One of the achievements of specialist fruit breeders during the last few decades has been the production of smaller trees. It's something we now take for granted, but not so long ago cherries and pears, in particular, grew into very large trees. Apples and plums, too. They were hard to prune and care for, and difficult to harvest. Everything had to be done using ladders. It was, therefore, very much in the interests of commercial growers to develop smaller trees that could be planted more closely, cropped more heavily, and were easier to pick. Their success has led to the development of a wide range of modern varieties grown on dwarfing rootstocks to restrict their size (see p.52). Home growers have benefited, too. There's now a good choice of fruit trees ideally suited to the small garden.

Space-saving tree forms

The way you train and prune your fruit trees plays a big part in controlling how large they grow. For a small garden, traditional "restricted" forms are a good choice. A short row of vertical or oblique cordons takes up very little space and allows you to grow a number of different varieties. The same goes for minarettes, which produce fruit from clusters of spur systems all the way up a single vertical trunk. They can be planted very closely together indeed. Miniature horizontal stepovers make good edgings for flower borders. And walls and fences can be used to train espaliers and fans against. If they are

(clockwise, from top left) **A row of dwarf pear cordons** not only makes a fruitful use of space but will grow into a fashionable designer hedge. **A redcurrant grown as a standard** frees up planting space at ground level for a short-term crop of salad leaves and onions. **Grape vines** climb naturally over pergolas and arches, though they will crop better if pruned regularly. **Apple stepovers** are single cordons bent over horizontally at about knee or waist height. Along with minarettes, they are the most compact of all the tree forms. (right) **A hanging basket** for strawberries saves on valuable ground space and should protect the fruit from all but the most athletic of slugs.

south-facing, even better; they may allow you to grow tender fruits, such as peaches, apricots, figs, and citrus, which would struggle in an open, unsheltered spot in the garden.

If you have room to plant only one tree of each sort of fruit, buy a self-fertile variety that will pollinate itself without needing a partner. A family tree, which has more than one cultivar grafted onto a single rootstock, is a way of broadening the range of fruit you grow (see p.53). If it's an apple, for example, it may give you both eating apples and cooking apples, some for harvesting early in the season and some for later on.

Growing fruit in containers

All but the largest, most vigorous fruits can be grown in pots. In a few cases, it may even be better to grow them in containers than in the open ground. Figs positively thrive and will produce more fruit and less foliage if their roots are constrained (see p.171). Blueberries will grow only in very acid soils, so if your garden soil is neutral or alkaline, a large pot filled with special ericaceous compost is the perfect solution (see p.252). Tender fruits that won't tolerate frosts become movable when grown in containers: they can be carried or wheeled indoors or under cover during winter and out into a spot in full sun in the summer.

There are a few simple rules to follow if you are growing fruit in containers. In the case of trees, choose dwarfing varieties that won't grow too large. However, don't overdo the size of the pot to start with; it's better to begin with a small or medium one and pot on into incrementally larger ones every couple of years. Use the right soil: usually a mix of all-purpose loam-based compost mixed with sand or gravel to ensure that it drains freely. Thereafter, water regularly, much more often in the summer than in the winter, and feed as necessary.

(left) **Container-grown plants** are the ultimate in mobile fruit gardening. They are perfect for making the best use of a restricted space and, provided they do not become too large and heavy, they can be moved from one microclimate to another. You can give them a sheltered, frost-free corner over winter, then move them out into full sun to ripen their fruit in summer.

Traditional kitchen gardens

Historically, a separate area of the garden was reserved for growing vegetables, fruit, and herbs. It was quite distinct from lawns, flowerbeds, and other ornamental areas. The reasons were largely practical. The first was to provide shelter and to create a warm microclimate by enclosing the whole kitchen garden within walls or tall hedges. The second was to conceal the sheds, storerooms, glasshouses, bins for compost and manure, and other working outbuildings that were deemed better kept out of sight. Few of us have gardens large enough for such luxury nowadays, but there are still benefits to be had from dedicating an area to growing your own.

Kitchen garden layouts

Because most fruits are long-lived plants and most vegetables are grown as annuals, fruit trees and bushes have always tended to form the main structural components or "bones" of the kitchen garden. Cordons planted on either side of main paths can be trained up and over to form arches and fruit tunnels, and rows of espaliered fruit

(below) **A formal grid** of beds planted with fruit, vegetables, flowers, and herbs, all hedged with clipped box, and neat paths arched with fruit cordons – these are all hallmarks of a traditional potager.

trees can form a series of living fences or screens. These help divide up the garden into beds in which vegetable crops can be grown in rotation from one year to the next.

Potager gardens took this idea to a highly stylized level. The word is French and the literal translation is "a vegetable stew or soup", although potagers are much more formal than that implies. They divide the kitchen garden into strict geometric units, usually squares, rectangles, or triangles. Each of these is planted with different vegetables, fruit, herbs, and even flowers, and the neat paths separating the beds are bordered by low hedges, espaliers, or stepover fruit trees. The effect is wonderful, but there's no getting away from the fact that they involve a lot of painstaking work.

The art of espalier

The technique of training fruit trees into espalier forms dates back centuries, certainly to medieval Europe, and perhaps even to the Romans or ancient Egyptians. The variety of forms is astonishing, as is the terminology – from elaborate candelabras to palmettes, and from curvilinear fans to three-dimensional spiral vases or goblets. It's true that espaliered trees are sometimes dismissed as the fruit grower's version of topiary, but they serve a practical purpose as well as an ornamental one. First, espalier trees are space-saving. They can be grown where there would not otherwise be room. Second, they are more productive. The way they are pruned and trained is designed to get them to produce the maximum yield of fruit. Third, they are healthier, because they are, quite simply, nurtured and fussed over. Fourth, they are easier to harvest. And lastly, when you grow espaliered peaches, nectarines, apricots, and other tender fruits against a warm, sunny, sheltered wall, the microclimate they enjoy can mean you may be as successful with these fruits as you are with apples and pears.

It's quite possible to train your own espaliers, starting from scratch with young maiden whips or feathered maidens. You'll find instructions on how to do so in the following pages, but it's increasingly common to find pre-trained young trees for sale even in regular garden centres. It seems that the espalier may well be the new designer fruit tree.

(right, top to bottom) **A fruit tunnel** is created by training two parallel rows of pear cordons up and over a pathway to form a series of arches. **An apple espalier** in full blossom brings welcome colour to the kitchen garden early in the year. **Three-dimensional shapes** require a high level of expertise. At West Dean, a pear has been trained on a wire frame into a "vase" or "goblet" form.

(left) **A multiple cordon** apple tree has been skilfully trained against an old brick wall in the restored kitchen garden at West Dean in Sussex.

Large gardens, allotments, and orchards

If you're lucky enough to have a large plot of land you can devote to a fruit garden or even a small orchard, then your growing options are wide open. Be wary of large fruit trees, though. It's far better to grow small trees on modern dwarfing rootstocks; they're easier to care for and you can plant more of them in the space, while at the same time trying lots of different varieties. For soft fruit, a fruit cage can't be recommended too strongly. It will certainly mean you eat much more of your fruit, instead of sharing it with the birds. And if you have the space for a good-sized greenhouse or polytunnel, you can grow even more.

Planning an orchard

The secret to designing and planting an orchard lies in choosing the right mix of trees. Let's assume you want apples, pears, plums, and cherries. Perhaps you want some more unusual fruits, too: quinces, medlars, mulberries, crab apples, and – at least in warmer regions – peaches and apricots as well. The first thing is to think about whether the trees are self-fertile or not. If not, they will need pollinating partners nearby. Then think about whether they will flower at the same time. Pollination charts elsewhere in this book will provide the information you need. Next, find out when the fruit will be ready to harvest. Ideally, you want a mix of early-, mid- and late-harvest fruit, to extend the season for as long as possible. Finally, try to select a good balance of dessert and culinary varieties, including some that are best eaten soon after picking and others that will store well.

The fruit cage

There are few things more satisfying than stepping inside a large, walk-in fruit cage. If you've ever experienced the loss of a whole year's crop of strawberries, summer raspberries, redcurrants, gooseberries, cherries, or plums to a flock of voracious, hungry birds, then you'll think you've died and gone to heaven. Unlike scarecrows, wires, strings, windmills, and all manner of other less-than-useful bird scarers, the fruit cage offers total protection – and total peace of mind. Just remember to remove the nets in late autumn. Winter is when you actually want the birds inside the cage, so that they pick off and eat any lurking insects as well as their eggs.

(left) **A newly planted** apple orchard. (right, clockwise from top) **A fruit cage** strong enough to withstand a tempest, let alone birds. **Harvest time** in an established orchard. **Wire frames** support young trees being trained into formal pyramids.

The fruit grower's year

The gardening year has its own rhythm. In fact, one of the pleasures of growing your own produce, especially for desk-bound city-dwellers, is that it gets you back in tune with the changing seasons. It's partly about knowing what tasks need doing at different times of the year, but it's just as much about heightened sensibility, about being more aware of what is happening around you outdoors as the seasons change, and of how your plants are growing, flowering, fruiting, and ripening.

Winter

Winter is the dormant season. Apart from certain tropical and subtropical species, most fruit trees and bushes enter a period of shut-down. Deciduous plants drop their leaves, and their metabolism slows to a crawl. In fact, temperate fruit trees and bushes actually need this period of winter chill – not just by way of a rest but also because a certain length of time at a low temperature produces a hormonal trigger that jump-starts dormant winter buds into growth again, and results in better-quality fruit the following year. Most apples, for example, are thought to need 1,000–1,400 hours below 7°C (45°F) each winter. The figures vary according to variety, however; apples bred to grow in warm regions such as the Mediterranean and the southern states of the USA may need as few as 300–500 hours of chilling per year. Other fruits differ. Cool-climate raspberries, currants, and gooseberries are happy with longer, colder winters and do not require particularly hot summers for fruits to ripen; in fact, they don't do well in warm climates at all.

(below, left to right) **Truly hardy plants** such as this blackcurrant can withstand most hard winters. They are tougher than you think, and once dormant will survive sub-zero temperatures. **The symmetrical form** of an expertly pruned pear espalier is clearly revealed in winter. **Prune** most fruit trees and bushes in winter when they are dormant. Not plums, cherries, and other stone fruit, though; they should be pruned in summer.

Spring

Spring is a crucial time, and if you live in an area prone to frost it can be an anxious one, too. It's exciting to see buds burst, new leaves start to unfurl, and blossom begin to open, but plants are at their most vulnerable now. Frost can strike at almost any time. The first trees to flower are usually apricots, peaches, and nectarines – and they are the ones most likely to need some kind of protection. They are closely followed by pears and plums, then cherries and apples, and all the soft fruits as well.

Spring is also a critical time for pollination. Successful fertilization and fruit set depend on compatible flowers being open at the same time and also on the weather being warm enough for pollinating insects such as bees to be out and about, doing their job. It's often said that the deciding moments governing whether or not the year will produce a successful autumn crop take place during the course of just a few days in spring.

(clockwise, from right) **An apple bud** bursts into leaf as spring temperatures rise and days begin to lengthen. **Redcurrant blossom** doesn't last for long but its tresses of pale yellow-green flowers are unexpectedly beautiful. **A bee collects pollen** from a cluster of blueberry flowers. **Sowing melon seeds** under cover early in spring ensures that young seedlings will be ready to plant as soon as the weather is warm enough. **Spring blossom opens** on a row of apple cordons.

Summer

The first ripe fruit of the year is always eagerly, impatiently awaited. To walk in from the garden with a dish of fragile, freshly picked strawberries and raspberries, a full bowl of gooseberries and currants, or a handful of early-season cherries is confirmation that summer has arrived.

The summer months are not a time for idleness, however. Certain tasks still need doing. Watering is the most important of all. Don't let your plants dry out, especially young, recently planted ones, those growing in containers, and any that are close to fences and walls in potential "rain shadows". Feed plants that need it, thin fruit so plants are not overburdened, and keep a watchful eye for insect pests, for scavenging birds, and for any early warning signs of disease.

(clockwise, from right) **Thinning plums** from June onwards stops the tree from being too heavily ladened and produces better quality fruit. **Freshly picked strawberries** perfectly encapsulate the taste of summer. **Whitecurrants** are naturally sweeter than the better known red types. **Modern blackcurrant varieties** are being bred so that when ripe they are sweet enough to be eaten raw. **All container-grown fruits** need regular watering in the summer months, as fruits swell and ripen.

Autumn

If all has gone to plan, late summer and early autumn should overlap in one long continuous harvest, as summer berries and tender fruits such as peaches, apricots, and melons give way to plums, apples, and pears. To grapes too, of course – as well as more unusual fruits such as quinces, damsons, mulberries, medlars, kiwifruit, and Cape gooseberries.

Before the year comes to an end, it's time to start thinking about the next one. Autumn is the season to order new fruit trees and bushes, to plant them while the soil is still slightly warm, to clean up and tidy the garden, and to begin winter pruning.

(clockwise, from right) **Autumn** is usually the best time for planting. Here, new raspberry canes are bundled up ready to go. **The apple harvest** can last for three months or more, depending on the varieties you grow. Early apples are for eating immediately, while later ones can be stored. **Late-season grapes** may still be ripening on outdoor vines until well into October if the autumn weather is mild. **Quinces** are the perfect example of why you should grow your own: slightly out of the ordinary, they are rarely available in the shops. **'Conference' pears** are one of the most popular home-grown varieties: easy, reliable, and delicious.

Tree fruit

At the risk of stating the obvious, tree fruits are fruits that grow on trees. They're also known as "top fruits", to distinguish them from those that grow lower down, on bushes, canes, or vines. Apples, pears, plums, and cherries grow successfully throughout the UK and in most other temperate climates too, though certain varieties are better suited to long, hot, dry summers and others to short, cool, damp ones. Peaches, nectarines, apricots, and figs are mostly hardy enough to withstand cold winters but they really require a warm temperate climate for their fruit to ripen fully. In cool northern regions, they can be coaxed into fruiting if they are grown in sunny, sheltered spots, usually trained against a wall or fence, in containers, or under cover.

In addition, there are a few somewhat more unusual tree fruits – quinces, medlars, mulberries, damsons, mirabelles, and so on – most of which have a long history. They are all worth trying if you have the space for them. Nuts such as almonds, walnuts, pecans, chestnuts, and cobnuts are all strictly speaking tree fruits too, but they are beyond the scope of this book.

Apples for storing must be picked and handled carefully, as any bruising or splits in the skin will cause them to rot. Gather windfalls and use them straight away – for cooking if they are no longer appetizing enough to eat raw.

Growing tree fruit

In truth, most fruit trees pretty much take care of themselves. As long as they're planted somewhere broadly suitable, and provided they receive the essentials they need to keep them alive – light, air, warmth, water, and nutrients from the soil – they should get along just fine, with the minimum amount of intervention. That said, the more care you do give them, the better they will grow. If you feed, water, weed, mulch, prune, and protect them against pests and diseases, then they will repay you with more reliable, more generous crops of better-looking, better-tasting fruit.

Buying fruit trees

The first decision to make when buying a new fruit tree is whether to go for one that has bare roots or one that is potted up in a container. Young trees for sale in garden centres are usually sold container-grown and can be bought all year round. Specialist nurseries, on the other hand, usually sell their trees bare-root. They are dug up to order when dormant, and are therefore only available from about November to March. After being uprooted from the nursery bed, most of the loose soil is shaken from their roots, and the trees are bagged up, usually in plastic. It's

important that the roots are kept moist and that a bare-root tree is planted as soon as you get it home or, if you've bought it online or via mail-order, as soon as it is delivered.

The advantages of buying a bare-root tree are that you will have a much wider choice of varieties and the tree you choose is likely to be in better condition, since it will have been lifted from the ground only very recently. The disadvantages are that you can only plant in the autumn or winter. Container-grown trees are easier to obtain and can, in theory, be planted at any time of the year, regardless of whether or not they are dormant. However, it's always wise to avoid the hot, dry summer months.

Whenever or wherever you buy fruit trees, always obtain them from a source that can guarantee the plants are officially certified disease-free.

How young trees develop

Most young trees are sold as one- or two-year-olds. One-year-old trees that have just a single stem without any sideshoots are called maiden whips. One- or two-year-old trees that have had time to develop sideshoots are called feathered maidens. Both are suitable for all of the major tree forms – although a maiden whip will take a little longer to establish itself and start bearing fruit.

It's also possible to buy pre-trained trees. These are usually three years old, and will have already been pruned and trained by the nursery into the formative shapes of espaliers, fans, or multiple cordons. They are a good choice if you want to get off to a quick start with wall- or wire-trained trees.

(opposite, left to right) **Container-grown trees** are available all year round, and are therefore often bought when in leaf. **A maiden whip** is a one-year-old tree. At this age, it is nothing more than a single stem or leader growing from the point where it was originally grafted on to the rootstock. **A feathered maiden** may be one or two years old. By now, a few sideshoots (or feathers) will have appeared. It's likely that some of these will grow on to form the main branches.

BUYER'S CHECKLIST

Bare-root trees
■ Look for a strong stem that has been trained vertically, without excessive kinks.
■ If the tree is feathered, it should have up to half a dozen strong, well-spaced laterals forming wide V-shaped angles with the main stem. They should be capable of eventually forming the main framework branches.
■ Be wary of trees with overlong, spindly growth.
■ Roots should be healthy and vigorous, radiating evenly all around the base of the tree.
■ The union should be strong and undamaged.

Container-grown trees
■ Choose a tree with a straight main stem or central leader, clean of sideshoots at the base.
■ Look for a healthy root system, with a balance of strong main roots and plenty of thinner, white, feeding roots. Avoid plants that are pot-bound with roots that coil round the sides or grow out of the bottom of the container.
■ Potting compost should be moist, not dried out, and should have no weeds or moss growing on the surface.
■ If the tree is in leaf look for discoloured or distorted foliage, any signs of dieback or weak growth, and infestations of aphids, mites, or other insect pests.
■ Check the union, where the scion has been grafted onto the rootstock (see p.32). It should be strong and clean, with no signs of splitting or other damage.

When choosing container-grown trees, always examine the rootball. The tree on the left has a healthy root system whereas the roots of the tree on the right are congested and will struggle to spread out into the planting hole.

Rootstocks

Most fruit trees are propagated by grafting a bud or shoot (called the "scion") from the original tree onto the roots from a different one (called the "rootstock"). Sometimes, the best rootstocks aren't even from the same species. Pears, for example, are usually grafted onto quince rootstocks, and peaches are grown on plum rootstocks.

(right, far right) **The "union"** is the join where the scion from one tree was grafted onto the rootstock of another. It's visible as a knobbly joint. Keep it above soil level or the scion may start to root. **Evidence of grafting** can still be seen on mature trees – even on the trunk of this thirty-five-year-old apple.

FRUIT TREE FORMS

Fruit trees can be grown in a wide variety of different shapes and sizes. Free-standing, free-growing forms are the most natural, though they all involve a certain amount of pruning and shaping. They include open-centred trees such as bushes, standards, and half-standards and central-leader trees such as pyramids and spindlebushes. Wall- or wire-trained trees, are much more strictly trained and pruned. They include cordons, espaliers, and fans.

Bush trees have a short trunk just 75–90cm (30in–36in) tall. The central leader will have been removed early in the tree's life to create an open centre. Evenly spaced branches form a low, spreading head.

Half-standards are similar to the bush but with a taller, clear trunk of about 1.5m (5ft) tall. Their average height is 4–5m (12–16ft) and, like the bush, they have a fairly open centre that allows in light and air.

Standards are the largest tree form with a clear trunk of about 2m (6ft) and a large, spreading canopy. Grow a standard form only if you have a big garden and it's practical for you to pick the fruit.

Stepovers are single cordons that have been bent over at a right angle close to the ground to form a low, horizontal tree. They are ideal for small gardens and can make a decorative edging to a border.

Cordons comprise a single central leader with short fruiting spurs along its length. It may be upright (vertical) or oblique (trained at an angle). All cordons need regular summer and winter pruning.

Double ("U") cordons are formed by cutting back the central leader and then training two laterals upwards as vertical arms. They are economical on space and best grown against a fence or wall.

Multiple cordons have three or four vertical arms. Sometimes, each of these arms is divided or "bifurcated" yet again, slightly higher up, to create ever more complex trained forms.

It's the rootstock that largely determines how big the tree will eventually grow. Today, there is a much wider choice of rootstocks than previously, including many more that produce small, more manageable trees better suited to gardens and allotments, and even to container growing. These are called dwarfing or semi-dwarfing rootstocks.

Pollination

All trees need pollinating in order for fruit to be produced. The process involves pollen from the male parts of a flower (the stamen) being transferred to the female parts (the stigma) – sometimes by insects such as bees, sometimes by the wind. With luck, fertilization then takes place and fruits start to form. Most flowers contain both male and female parts, but in some cases separate male and female flowers exist on the same tree, and in one or two instances (kiwifruits, for example) a single tree has either male or female flowers, not both. Figs are an exception; they do not produce flowers in the normal way at all.

Some fruit trees can fertilize themselves with their own pollen. They are called self-fertile. Others need pollen from nearby trees. Indeed, as a general rule, it's always better if trees are cross-pollinated,

Spindlebush forms are productive and widely used by commercial growers. The branches are relatively few in number and radiate out from the central leader to form a low, conical shape.

Pyramids are freestanding trees with branches that require regular summer pruning to maintain the shape. The arrangement of the branches allows sunlight to reach most parts of the tree.

Dwarf pyramids are, as you would expect, smaller versions of the pyramid and are grown on a more dwarfing rootstock. They are neat, compact trees and their small size makes for easy harvesting.

Minarettes are short vertical cordons that consist of a single stem or central leader that fruits on short spurs. Known as columns or ballerina trees, they can be planted as close as 60cm (24in) to one another.

Espalier trees have tiers of evenly spaced horizontal arms, which radiate outwards to the left and right from a main stem or central leader. On a perfectly trained espalier, the arms are all of the same length, and the tree is completely symmetrical.

Fans usually have a short trunk from which two main ribs radiate. Each of these ribs then produces sub-laterals which are spread out evenly and tied in to wire supports. This creates the classic fan shape, one of the most attractive trained forms.

Palmettes are a cross between an espalier and a fan – a combination of two very decorative tree forms. Like an espalier, they retain a main stem or central leader. Like a fan, the lateral arms are trained at an angle rather than horizontally.

whether they are self-fertile or not. However, not all trees will pollinate each other: some are simply incompatible. The whole issue of cross-pollination and compatibility can get complex, especially with pears and cherries, but specialist nurseries will be able to advise you if necessary.

With pollination, timing is everything. Not all fruit trees flower at the same time, and of course no insect on earth is able to transfer pollen from blossom that's open to blossom that's not. For this reason, fruit trees are often put into pollination groups to help you choose trees that flower simultaneously.

There are further potential problems with trees that flower very early in the year or that are grown under cover – apricots, peaches, and nectarines, for example. When the blossom opens, it may be too early for pollinating insects to be around. If so, hand pollination may be required (see p.148).

Even if pollination does take place, it doesn't guarantee fertilization. A certain minimum temperature is required, because fruits just won't form if it's not warm enough.

Most fruit growers are used to crops varying from one year to the next. In some years there's a really bumper yield, in others a tree may produce next to no fruit at all. Often, the cause goes right back to that crucial week or two in the spring, when the weather will have determined whether pollination was successful and whether or not there was a good fruit set.

Planting fruit trees

Arguably, the most important thing that happens to a fruit tree during its lifetime is the way it's planted. If you plant it properly and get it off

Wooden tree stakes should be pressure-treated or steeped in preservative to keep them from rotting for as long as possible.

to a good start, there's a strong chance that it will be trouble-free from then on.

Choosing the right site is crucial, of course. But preparing the ground is important too. A few weeks beforehand, weed the whole area very thoroughly. Perennial weeds such as bindweed and couch grass are hard to remove once trees are established. Dig over the soil and incorporate plenty of well-rotted manure or garden compost. You may also want to add some general fertilizer, and balance the pH of the soil if necessary. Don't dig the actual hole for the tree until just before you are ready to plant.

When is the best time to plant a new tree? In most cases, the answer is November or thereabouts, when the soil is still warm enough for the roots to start getting established. December, January, and February may be too cold, especially if the ground is likely to be frozen. Better to wait until March. All bare-root trees must be planted when they are dormant, between November and March. It's possible to plant container-grown trees at any time of year, but November and March are the best months for them, too. July and August, when it's likely to be hot and dry, are the worst.

Staking and supporting fruit trees

New, young, stand-alone trees need supporting with a stake after planting, certainly until their roots have a strong enough foothold to secure them in strong winds. For vigorous bush, standard, and half-standard trees, all of which will grow quite tall, use a short stake 1.2m (4ft) long driven vertically into the ground to a depth of about 60cm (2ft) if it is bare-root, or a stake 1.5m (5ft) long driven in at an angle if it is container-grown, to avoid damaging the rootball. The stakes can be removed after four or five years. For pyramids, spindlebushes, and

Oblique pear cordons take up relatively little space and can be trained on galvanised wires held taut between sturdy wooden posts. Mesh tree guards protect the stems from grazing animals.

minarettes on dwarfing or semi-dwarfing rootstocks, use longer 2.5m (8ft) stakes and be prepared to leave them in place permanently. Position the stake so that it is on the side of the prevailing wind.

Trees that are trained as cordons, espaliers, or fans all need supporting on wires strung between vertical posts or attached to a wall or fence. Wooden posts, treated with preservative, should be 8cm (3in) or 10cm (4in) in diameter. Sink them into the ground to a depth of at least 60cm (2ft) and brace them with diagonal supports at each end. Use heavy-gauge, galvanized wire strong enough to support the branches of the tree when fully grown and laden with fruit. Attach horizontal lengths of wire with eye bolts or vine eyes, and tension them with straining bolts to keep them taut.

(opposite, left to right) **Special tree ties** are available for securing the tree to its stake. All allow for adjustment so that they do not become too tight as the trunk grows. **If rabbits,** badgers, deer, or other animals are a problem, protect young trees by encircling the trunk and stake with a mesh tree guard. **Fix wire supports** to walls, fences, or posts with eye bolts or vine eyes. Leave a space of at least 5–8cm (2–3in) between the wire and the wall or fence, to allow air to circulate freely. Use 12-gauge wire for cordons and espaliers, and 14-gauge for fans.

Pruning and training fruit trees

In terms of pruning, there are two stages in a tree's life. In the first few years, the aim is to train the tree into the desired shape or form. This stage is called formative pruning. Thereafter, the aim is to keep the tree tidy and healthy, and to encourage it to produce fruit as reliably and generously as possible. Depending on the tree, this stage may be referred to as regulative or renewal pruning. If a tree has been neglected and left unpruned for several years, it's likely to need renovation pruning to get it back into shape (see p.76).

(left, top to bottom) **Diseased** branches should be cut out before infection can spread. **Damaged** branches allow bacteria and fungal growths to take hold. **Crossing,** touching, or crowded spurs and branches must be removed. If they rub against each other, wounds open up that become infected.

When to prune

Freestanding apple and pear trees are pruned in autumn and winter, when they are dormant. Stone-fruit trees such as plums, cherries, apricots, peaches, and nectarines, however, are pruned in spring and summer, when they are actively growing, in order to reduce the risk of infection from silver leaf and bacterial canker.

Wire-trained or "restricted" trees such as cordons, espaliers, and fans are an exception to this rule. They need controlling and shaping much more strictly, so they all require pruning during spring and summer, either to encourage the new growth that you do want or to remove the growth you don't.

What to prune

Let's start with what's easy. At least once a year, inspect your trees carefully and prune out any stems or branches that are dead, damaged, or diseased – sometimes known as "the three Ds". Once you've done that, look for areas that are crowded and congested or where branches are touching or crossing. Thin those out so that light can get in and air can circulate freely. Cut back any branches that are hanging too low or touching the ground. Check the overall height, spread, and form of the tree and adjust it to keep it balanced and well-shaped.

Next, turn your attention to the pruning that will ensure your trees produce as much fruit as possible. For this you first need to understand that trees bear fruit in different ways. Most, though not all, apples and pears fruit on wood that is two years old or older. Peaches, nectarines, and acid cherries fruit on shoots that are younger – those that grew the previous year. And plums, apricots, and sweet cherries fruit on a mixture of wood that is one and two years old. Fruit is sometimes borne on clusters of stubby spurs, sometimes along the length of branches, and sometimes mostly at the tips (see p.67). The aim of pruning is to remove old wood that is no longer fruitful and to stimulate new growth that is.

Beware of over-pruning. Removing too much wood in one go tends to propel the tree into rapid growth, but it will produce mostly foliage at the expense of fruit.

How to prune

There's an art to knowing where and how to cut. It's hard to generalize about what you should and shouldn't remove because everything depends on the type of tree, its age and size, and the form in which it is being grown. But here are a few simple guidelines to follow.

Cutting back to a bud

If possible, identify a healthy growth bud and cut back to that. Select one that is pointing in the direction you want the new growth to go, usually outwards from the tree, not into the centre.

Cutting back to a shoot

If you are removing overlong stems or old wood that no longer produces much fruit, cut back to a younger sub-lateral or sideshoot – one that is strong and healthy, and already growing in the right direction.

Cutting back to a branch or trunk

Use loppers or a pruning saw to cut substantial lateral or sub-lateral

(top to bottom) **Prune** close to a healthy growth bud. **Make clean, angled cuts** parallel with the shoot to which you are cutting back.

REMOVING A HEAVY BRANCH

Heavy branches have a tendency to tear under their own weight if you try to remove them with a single cut. It is safer to prune them in stages.

The first cut is made on the underside, about 30cm (12in) from the trunk. Saw only about a quarter way through.

Make a top cut straight down and about 2cm (³⁄₄in) further along the branch from the undercut.

The branch should now fall to the ground safely. It shouldn't tear but if it does it won't damage the trunk.

Cut away the branch stump from the top, sawing just beyond the collar, where the branch meets the trunk.

The correct cut is sloping and parallel with the bud so that rainwater drains away from it. Cut close but not too close.

Cut too close and you will slice through the base of the bud, leaving a large surface area that will be slow to heal.

Cut too far away and the stub left above the bud will die back and may become infected with disease.

A torn and jagged cut made with a blunt tool produces a large, ragged wound that won't heal well.

Cut at the wrong angle and you will leave an unecessary stub. Water will drain towards the bud instead of away.

(clockwise from top) **Loppers** are ideal for cutting out old or damaged stems, and for those that are hard to reach. **Pruning saws** must be kept sharp. To avoid rust and maintain sharpness, wipe them with an oily rag after use. **Clean secateurs** by removing any dried-on debris with wire wool, and always disinfect them if you've been pruning diseased material.

branches. Cut at a very slightly sloping angle to the main branch or trunk, leaving the collar encircling the join intact so that the wound will heal cleanly.

Good cuts and bad cuts

Always use a sharp, clean pair of secateurs and ensure that the thinner of the two blades is the one closest to the bud, even if this means coming in at a different angle or turning the secateurs upside down. That way you'll be able to make a more precise cut.

Pruning tools

The most important tools are a pair of secateurs, loppers, and a pruning saw.

Use secateurs to cut pencil-thick stems – up to 1.5cm (½in) in diameter. Bypass secateurs are the best kind. Their blades cross over when they cut, like scissors. Anvil secateurs have a sharp cutting blade that presses down onto the flat metal edge of the lower blade, like a knife on a chopping board.

For stems or branches up to about 4cm (1½in) thick, use loppers. And for anything thicker, use a pruning saw. For tall trees, long-armed loppers and saws are available. A sharp garden pocket knife is also useful – not for pruning as such but for neatening and smoothing the edges of pruning cuts.

All pruning tools should be kept sharp, otherwise cuts will be ragged, and wounds will take longer to heal. They must be kept clean, too. To reduce the risk of spreading infection, sterilize them.

FRUIT TREE ANATOMY

The vocabulary for the different parts of a tree can be confusing. Trunks, branches, and twigs we're all familiar with, of course. But professional fruit growers talk of leaders, laterals, sub-laterals, and spurs. Here's a guide to what the jargon means.

(far left) **The central leader** is the main trunk or stem. In the case of pyramids, spindlebushes, and single cordons, it is allowed to grow to the full height of the tree. In the case of bushes and standards, it is removed to create an open centre. Large branches on established trees may be called branch leaders. (left) **Laterals** are shoots or stems coming off the main trunk or off branch leaders. (above) **Sub-laterals** are sideshoots that come off laterals. They are secondary branches.

Spurs are knobbly clusters of fruit buds that grow each year on short, stubby lengths of wood. In time, they may become so overcrowded that they need thinning.

Fruit buds are fatter than growth buds because they contain the embryo flower. If this flower is successfully pollinated and fertilized it will grow and develop into a fruit.

Growth buds, sometimes called vegetative buds, are usually thinner and more pointed than fruit buds. They produce new shoots that carry leaves but not fruit.

Apples

Apples are believed to have originated in Central Asia, in the mountains of what is now Kazakhstan. From there they spread, and there are written accounts of Roman apple growers propagating new varieties using grafting techniques. Settlers then took the apple to North and South America and to Australasia, where extensive cross-breeding took place. Indeed, 'Golden Delicious' and 'Granny Smith' originated in the US and Australia, respectively.

There are literally thousands of named cultivars and new apple varieties are continually being introduced. From time to time long-lost, traditional varieties are also rediscovered. Choose your varieties wisely and you'll not only experience a much wider range of wonderful flavours than any supermarket will ever offer, but you could well be eating your own home-grown fruit for six months of the year or more – from the first early-season apples of late summer through to fruit you've stored over winter to eat in spring the following year.

When choosing a dessert apple, decide whether you want a variety for early picking and eating or one to keep. Many late-harvest varieties store well and you can savour their delicious flavour during the winter months.

Which forms to grow

- **Bushes and standards** The dwarf bush, bush, half-standard, and standard all have the same open-centre form but the main stem or trunk varies in height.
- **Spindlebush and pyramid** Freestanding trees with a central leader.
- **Cordon** Wire-trained single or multiple stems that produce fruits on short sideshoots.
- **Minarette** A short, vertical stem – good for small spaces.
- **Espalier and fan** Wire-trained forms with arms growing either side of a central stem or radiating from a short trunk.
- **Stepover** A knee-high, horizontal cordon often used as a decorative edging to a border.

Must-grow dessert apples

1 'James Grieve'
Pollination group B
A Scottish variety that flowers early but is hardy and frost resistant – so it is fine for cooler regions. Good yield and good flavour. Does not grow well in humid conditions, which can encourage canker and scab. Spur-bearer.
■ **Harvest** September
■ **Eat** September–October

2 'Falstaff'
Pollination group B
A modern English variety that is a cross between 'James Grieve' and 'Golden Delicious'. Very heavy cropping, good flavour, and easy to grow. There is a 'Red Falstaff' too. Spur-bearer.
■ **Harvest** October
■ **Eat** October–December

3 'Ashmead's Kernel'
Pollination group C
Reputedly bred by Dr Ashmead in Gloucestershire in about 1700 – and still rightly popular after 300 years. A late-harvest, russet eating apple with a wonderful flavour – though can be unreliable and prone to frost damage. Spur-bearer.
■ **Harvest** October
■ **Eat** December–March

4 'Court Pendu Plat'
Pollination group D
Written records of this apple go back to 1613, although it is rumoured to have been grown in Roman times or even earlier. It was a Victorian favourite. Late flowering, medium-sized, sweet, and aromatic, with a slight pineapple flavour. Spur-bearer.
■ **Harvest** October
■ **Eat** December–April

5 'Laxton's Superb'
Pollination group C
Traditional, 19th-century English variety still grown for its flavour, frost resistance, and keeping qualities.

Sometimes biennial, spur-bearer.
- **Harvest** October
- **Eat** November–January

6 'Mother'
Pollination group D

Sometimes known as 'American Mother' owing to its 19th-century USA origin. Sweet, juicy apples with a distinctive, aromatic flavour. Spur-bearer.
- **Harvest** October
- **Eat** November–March

7 'Ellison's Orange'
Pollination group C

Sometimes know as 'Red Ellison'. Juicy, slightly soft flesh with a rich taste that has a hint of aniseed when fully ripe. Sometimes biennial, spur-bearer.
- **Harvest** September
- **Eat** September–October

8 'Cox's Orange Pippin'
Pollination group B

Grow this one for its outstanding, justly famous flavour – it is one of the very best. But be warned: it's not easy to grow. Easily damaged by frost, it is prone to disease, and needs optimum growing conditions. Spur-bearer.
- **Harvest** October
- **Eat** October–January

9 'Golden Delicious'
Pollination group C

Contrary to most preconceptions, this is not a modern apple but one that dates back to around 1890 and comes from Virginia in the USA. A favourite of commercial growers – it is heavy cropping, reliable, and stores well. In warm climates, it ripens to a honeyed sweetness; in cooler regions it may disappoint. Spur-bearer.
- **Harvest** October
- **Eat** November–February

10 'Elstar'
Pollination group B

A mid-20th-century Dutch variety bred from 'Golden Delicious'. Generous crops of sweet, juicy, well-flavoured apples. Sometimes biennial, spur-bearer.
- **Harvest** October
- **Eat** October–January

11 'Jonagold'
Pollination group B

Derived from one of the best-known and most popular American apples, 'Jonathan'. Now grown all over the world. Crisp, juicy, with a rich, sweet-acid flavour. Triploid, spur-bearer.
- **Harvest** October
- **Eat** November–March

12 'Greensleeves'
Pollination group C

Like 'Falstaff', a cross between 'James Grieve' and 'Golden Delicious'. It has similar qualities: heavy cropping, hardy, reliable, good balance of sweetness and acidity. Tip- and spur-bearer.
- **Harvest** September
- **Eat** September–November

13 'Gala'
Pollination group C

From New Zealand, this cross-breed of 'Golden Delicious' and 'Kidd's Orange Red' is crisp and juicy. Best eaten soon after picking, even though it will keep into the new year. Spur-bearer.
- **Harvest** October
- **Eat** October–January

14 'Adams's Pearmain'
Pollination group A

Traditional variety that dates back to the early 19th century. Aromatic fruits with a nutty flavour. Biennial, tip- and spur-bearer.
- **Harvest** October
- **Eat** November–March

15 'Discovery'
Pollination group B

A heavy cropper with brightly coloured yellow-red fruits that ripen early. Sweet and aromatic with a good flavour. Easy to grow. Tip- and spur-bearer.
- **Harvest** August
- **Eat** August–September

16 'Sunset'
Pollination group B

Like 'Fiesta', this apple is bred from 'Cox's Orange Pippin' but is easier to grow. Retains a traditional Cox-like flavour, tolerates a wider range of growing conditions and is less susceptible to disease. Spur-bearer.
- **Harvest** September
- **Eat** October–December

17 'Worcester Pearmain'
Pollination group B
Traditional English apple with a distinctive, strawberry-like flavour. Best left to ripen fully before picking and then eaten promptly. Tip-bearer.
- ■ **Harvest** September
- ■ **Eat** September–October

18 'Pixie'
Pollination group C
Late-harvest variety that is best stored for a while before eating. Outstanding rich, aromatic flavour. Compact and easy to grow. Spur-bearer.
- ■ **Harvest** October
- ■ **Eat** December–March

19 'Kidd's Orange Red'
Pollination group B
Not the easiest apple to grow, as it is prone to disease, needs sunshine, and requires careful thinning, but outstanding flavour. Originally bred in New Zealand as a cross between 'Cox's Orange Pippin' and 'Red Delicious'. Spur-bearer.
- ■ **Harvest** October
- ■ **Eat** November–January

20 'Lord Lambourne'
Pollination group A
Early flowering but hardy and easy to grow. Compact habit, so good for small gardens. Excellent flavour. Tip- and spur-bearer.
- ■ **Harvest** September
- ■ **Eat** September–November

21 'Queen Cox'
Pollination group B

A self-fertile strain of 'Cox's Orange Pippin'. Crisper, tastier, more colourful, and heavier cropping. Spur-bearer.
- **Harvest** October
- **Eat** October–December

22 'Scrumptious'
Pollination group B

Modern variety that is frost hardy and easy to grow. A good choice for beginners. Juicy, sweet, and aromatic with excellent flavour. May even be ready for picking in August. Spur-bearer.
- **Harvest** September
- **Eat** September–October

23 'Ribston Pippin'
Pollination group A

A traditional apple that, in Europe, dates back to at least the 17th century. Not the easiest apple to grow but worth searching out for its sweet, aromatic, old-fashioned flavour. Triploid, spur-bearer.
- **Harvest** September
- **Eat** October–January

24 'Egremont Russet'
Pollination group A

Perhaps the best-known and most popular russet. Very firm with a sweet, nutty flavour. It flowers very early, so may need frost protection in some areas. Spur-bearer.
- **Harvest** September
- **Eat** October–December

25 'Braeburn'
Pollination group C

A relatively modern variety that originates from New Zealand. Needs a warm, sunny climate to ripen successfully. Crisp, juicy, aromatic, with good acidity. Spur-bearer.
- **Harvest** October
- **Eat** December–March

26 'Tydeman's Late Orange'
Pollination group C

A crossbreed of 'Laxton's Superb' and 'Cox's Orange Pippin'. Needs thinning or the fruits will be small. Only moderate yields, but flavour is outstanding and apples will store right through into spring. Spur-bearer.
- **Harvest** October
- **Eat** December–April

27 'Fiesta'
Pollination group B
Also known as 'Red Pippin'. Bred from 'Cox's Orange Pippin', it has inherited some of its flavour but is much easier to grow. Spur-bearer.
■ **Harvest** September
■ **Eat** October–January

'Cobra' (not illustrated)
Pollination group B
A new English variety, crossbred from a 'Cox' and a 'Bramley' – hence its name. Sweet enough to eat raw if fully ripe and also sharp enough to use as a cooker. Spur-bearer.
■ **Harvest** September
■ **Eat** September–March

'Katy' (not illustrated)
Pollination group B
Sometimes spelled 'Katja', it originates from Sweden. Average flavour but a useful early-season apple for cool, northern regions. Best eaten soon after picking. Spur-bearer.
■ **Harvest** September
■ **Eat** September–October

'Limelight' (not illustrated)
Pollination group B
A modern English apple, the result of a cross between 'Greensleeves' and 'Discovery'. It has almost luminous, bright, yellow-green fruits. Compact, heavy cropping, and disease-resistant. Perfect for a small garden. Tip- and spur-bearer.
■ **Harvest** September
■ **Eat** September–November

'Peasgood's Nonsuch' (not illustrated)
Pollination group C
Crisp, juicy, and refreshing when eaten ripe, this large apple also cooks well. Raised by Mrs Peasgood in Lincolnshire and described by the RHS in 1872 as "one of the most handsome apples in cultivation". It certainly is. Spur-bearer.
■ **Harvest** September
■ **Eat** September–December

'Winter Gem' (not illustrated)
Pollination group B
Relatively modern variety. Ripens late and stores well. Crisp, juicy, and aromatic. Spur-bearer.
■ **Harvest** October
■ **Eat** November–March

Must-grow culinary apples

'Emneth Early' (not illustrated)
Pollination group B
Also known as 'Early Victoria' and, as its names suggest, one of the earliest to ripen of all the cooking apples. Good sweet-sharp flavour. Usually biennial, spur-bearer.
■ **Harvest** July
■ **Eat** July–August

'Grenadier' (not illustrated)
Pollination group B
Long-standing favourite amongst early cooking apples. Crisp, white flesh with a good, sharp flavour. Does not keep, so eat soon after picking. Spur-bearer.
■ **Harvest** August
■ **Eat** August–September

'Lane's Prince Albert' (not illustrated)
Pollination group B
Hardy, reliable, and reasonably compact – a good tree for a small garden. Fine sharp flavour. Spur-bearer.
■ **Harvest** October
■ **Eat** November–March

'Rev. W. Wilks' (not illustrated)
Pollination group A
Compact but heavy cropping. Crisp, juicy, white flesh that cooks down to a smooth, fine-tasting puree. Biennial, spur-bearer.
■ **Harvest** September
■ **Eat** September–November

Must-grow culinary apples

1 'Edward VII'
Pollination group D
Late-flowering, so good for northern regions or frost-prone sites. Fruits will store all through winter until spring. Spur-bearer.
- **Harvest** October
- **Eat** December–April

2 'Arthur Turner'
Pollination group B
Heavy crops of large apples – perfect for baking. Good for cool, northern regions. Spectacular pink blossom. Spur-bearer.
- **Harvest** September
- **Eat** September–November

3 'Bramley's Seedling'
Pollination group B
Traditional cooker with excellent flavour, and fluffy texture. Very vigorous but can be grown on dwarfing rootstocks. Triploid, tip- and spur-bearer.
- **Harvest** October
- **Eat** November–March

4 'Newton Wonder'
Pollination group D
Popular, late-flowering cooker. Yellow-green fruits turn increasingly red as they ripen and can be eaten uncooked late in the season. Biennial, spur-bearer.
- **Harvest** October
- **Eat** November–March

5 'Howgate Wonder'
Pollination group C
Very large apple with juicy flesh that cooks to a smooth puree. Hardy, vigorous and stores well. Spur-bearer.
- **Harvest** October
- **Eat** October–March

6 'Golden Noble'
Pollination group C
Yellow-green 19th-century English apple. Excellent flavour and texture. Hardy and heavy cropping. Tip- and spur-bearer.
- **Harvest** October
- **Eat** October-December

1
2
3
4
5
6

Must-grow dual-purpose apples

1 'Bountiful'
Pollination group B
A cross between 'Cox's Orange Pippin' and 'Lane's Prince Albert'. A compact, reliable tree with large, sweet, fruit that can be eaten uncooked after storing for a couple of months. Spur-bearer.
■ **Harvest** September
■ **Eat** September–January

2 'Idared'
Pollination group A
An American apple originating from Idaho. Crisp, juicy, and sweet if rather bland. Useful as a dual-purpose cooking and eating apple. It stores exceedingly well. Spur-bearer.
■ **Harvest** October
■ **Eat** November–May

3 'Charles Ross'
Pollination group B
Large, beautifully shaped apples with a lovely flavour – especially if eaten raw, soon after picking. If stored for more than a few weeks, they are best used for cooking. Spur-bearer.
■ **Harvest** September
■ **Eat** September–December

4 'Blenheim Orange'
Pollination group B
An 18th-century apple worth searching out for its distinctive, nutty flavour. Triploid, sometimes biennial, tip- and spur-bearer.
■ **Harvest** October
■ **Eat** November–January

'Broadholme Beauty' (not illustrated)
Pollination group B
A large, smooth-skinned apple that is disease resistant and easy to grow. Fruits contain enough natural sugars not to require additional sweetening when cooked. Spur-bearer.
■ **Harvest** September
■ **Eat** September–March

Choosing and buying apple trees

Before buying an apple tree of any kind, there are four things to consider. First, what form of tree do you want? The answer will probably depend on how much space you have. If you have plenty of room, then you might choose a freestanding tree such as a half-standard or spindlebush. If space is limited, then consider a dwarf bush or pyramid, or a wire-trained form such as a cordon or espalier. The size to which the tree will grow is determined by the second factor: the rootstock. Certain rootstocks produce small or "dwarfing" trees; others are much more vigorous and can end up very tall. The third factor to consider is the cultivar or variety you'd like to grow, and the fourth is when the flowers appear – which is crucial for pollination.

Choosing a tree form

Freestanding trees are either open-centred or have a central leader. Open-centred trees have had their central leader cut out, in order to create a shape rather like a goblet or a cupped hand, palm upwards with the fingers outspread. They include, in ascending order of size: the dwarf bush; bush; half-standard; and standard. Central-leader trees, which include the spindlebush and dwarf pyramid, are usually smaller and more conical in shape.

Trees trained against walls, fences, or wire supports are called restricted forms. They can vary in size from large-scale arches and espaliers to tiny, knee-high stepovers, and their shape can be as simple as single minarettes or as complex as traditional zig-zag and diamond cordons. It's possible to train apples as fans, but it's perhaps less common in practice.

(left) **Many garden centres** will stock a range of container-grown trees but specialist nurseries will offer a much wider choice. Buying bare-root trees from nurseries in autumn or winter is the cheapest option.

(opposite clockwise from top) **A mature espalier** takes several years to reach its full potential and is a beautiful sight in blossom. **Modern dwarfing rootstocks** ensure small trees that may produce fruit just a year or two after planting. **A row of cordons** is an efficient way to use space in a small garden.

CHOOSING A ROOTSTOCK

Apples are never grown on their own roots. Instead, they are always grafted onto a special rootstock by the fruit nursery where they are raised. In most cases, grafting restricts their size to manageable proportions, and it encourages them to start cropping relatively early. It also makes them less prone to disease.

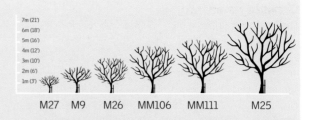

7m (21')
6m (18')
5m (16')
4m (12')
3m (10')
2m (6')
1m (3')

M27   M9   M26   MM106   MM111   M25

Apple rootstocks are classified according to a mysterious system of alphanumeric codes. The "M" stands for Malling – the East Malling Research Station in Kent where, during the 20th century, much of the early work on developing dwarfing rootstocks was done. "MM" stands for Malling–Merton and denotes rootstocks that came from a collaboration between East Malling and the John Innes Institute in Merton. There is no hidden horticultural logic to the numbers: they refer to the position in the nursery where the trees originally grew.

M27

- **VIGOUR** Very dwarfing
- **CHARACTERISTICS** Very small trees ideal for town gardens and patios. Even after 15 years, they may not be much more than head-high. M27 rootstocks suit vigorous, strong-growing apple varieties and need rich, fertile soil. Keep them free of weeds and surrounding grass.
- **FIRST CROP** At 2–3 years old.
- **SUPPORT** Stake permanently.
- **FORMS** Dwarf bush, spindlebush, pyramid, cordon, stepover.
- **HEIGHT** 1.5–2m (5–6ft).

M9

- **VIGOUR** Dwarfing
- **CHARACTERISTICS** The best choice for a small garden or an intensively cultivated allotment. Will grow best in good soil. Weed, water, and feed regularly and keep grass away from the trunk.
- **FIRST CROP** At 3–4 years old.
- **SUPPORT** Stake permanently.
- **FORMS** Dwarf bush, spindlebush, pyramid, cordon, stepover.
- **HEIGHT** 2–3m (6–10ft).

M26

- **VIGOUR** Semi-dwarfing
- **CHARACTERISTICS** A slightly larger, stronger tree than M9, producing heavier crops and larger apples. Less demanding in terms of growing conditions, though it will establish quicker in good, fertile soil. A good choice for gardens and allotments.
- **FIRST CROP** At 3–4 years old.
- **SUPPORT** Stake for the first 3–4 years.
- **FORMS** Bush, spindlebush, pyramid, cordon, espalier.
- **HEIGHT** 2.5–4m (8–12ft).

MM106

- **VIGOUR** Semi-vigorous
- **CHARACTERISTICS** A good all-round choice. Will grow well on most sites and in most soils – although the better the soil and the more vigorous the variety, the larger the tree.
- **FIRST CROP** At 4–5 years old.
- **SUPPORT** Stake for the first 4–5 years.
- **FORMS** Bush, half-standard, standard, spindlebush, pyramid, espalier, fan.
- **HEIGHT** 4–5.5m (12–17ft).

MM111

- **VIGOUR** Vigorous
- **CHARACTERISTICS** Unless grown in poor soil conditions, will produce a tree too large for all but the biggest gardens. Takes several years before fruiting begins, and then pruning and harvesting require ladders.
- **FIRST CROP** At 6–7 years old.
- **SUPPORT** Stake for the first 4–5 years.
- **FORMS** Bush, half-standard, standard, espalier.
- **HEIGHT** 5.5–6.5m (17–21ft).

M25

- **VIGOUR** Very vigorous
- **CHARACTERISTICS** Uncommon nowadays, even in orchards, as trees are so large that pruning and harvesting are extremely difficult.
- **FIRST CROP** At 6–7 years old.
- **SUPPORT** Stake for the first 4–5 years.
- **FORMS** Half-standard, standard.
- **HEIGHT** 6.5–8m (21–25ft).

Choosing a variety

The choice of varieties or cultivars is bewildering. Even your local garden centre will probably offer a reasonable selection, and specialist nurseries may have a catalogue listing hundreds of different apples. Some of the names you will recognize – 'Cox', 'Discovery', 'Golden Delicious', and so on. Others may be less familiar – 'Ashmead's Kernel', 'Newton Wonder', or 'Worcester Pearmain', perhaps. How to choose? Here are some criteria to bear in mind when making your selection.

■ Do you want the apples for eating fresh or for cooking? Varieties are classified according to sweetness–acidity, and are described as either dessert or culinary. There are a few hybrids too, which can be used for either purpose.

■ Do you want the apples for eating straight away or for storing through the winter? Apples that are ready to pick early in the summer don't keep well and should be eaten within a few days of picking. In contrast, apples that ripen later in the season may actually need storing for a while before they are ready to eat.

■ What sort of climate do you have? Apples don't all flower at the same time. In early-flowering varieties, the blossom can appear by mid-April. So, if you are prone to severe frosts in spring, choose a late-flowering or frost-resistant variety instead. And if you suffer from cold, damp winters, avoid varieties such as 'Cox's Orange Pippin', which need more favourable growing conditions.

■ What other apples are you growing or do you plan to grow? Apples are not usually self-fertile. For pollination to be successful they need to be grown close to compatible trees that flower at the same time. Choosing varieties from the same flowering or pollination group should help ensure this.

Insect pollinators can only transfer pollen from tree to tree when flowers are open, so ensure that neighbouring trees are from the same pollination group and therefore in blossom at the same time. Cross-pollination between an early-flowering and a late-flowering variety won't take place.

FAMILY TREES

A family tree is a single tree onto which two, three, or even four different apple varieties have been grafted. Why? The principal reason is that, if space is severely restricted and you have room for only one specimen, then a family tree solves the problem of how to ensure it is pollinated. Provided the different cultivars have been chosen so that they all flower simultaneously, then insects will transfer pollen from one variety to another, effectively fertilizing them all.

It's important that the varieties chosen for a family tree are not only compatible in terms of pollination but also have the same growing requirements and are of more-or-less equal vigour. If they are not, then one will tend to dominate and outgrow the others. Typical combinations include: 'Gala', 'Sunset', and 'Bountiful'; 'Charles Ross', 'Discovery', and 'James Grieve'; and 'Braeburn', 'Cox's Orange Pippin', and 'Worcester Pearmain'.

APPLE POLLINATION GROUPS

A

'Adams's Pearmain'
'Egremont Russet'
'George Cave'
'Gravenstein'
'Idared'
'Irish Peach'
'Lord Lambourne'
'Red Windsor'
'Ribston Pippin'
'Reverend W. Wilks'

(top to bottom) **'Egremont Russet'** an early-season eater, **'Idared'** an eater or a cooker, and **'Ribston Pippin'** a dessert apple that stores well. All flower early.

B

'Arthur Turner'
'Blenheim Orange'
'Bountiful'
'Bramley's Seedling'
'Broadholme Beauty'
'Charles Ross'
'Cobra'
'Cox'
'Cox's Orange Pippin'
'Discovery'
'Elstar'
'Emneth Early/Early Victoria'
'Falstaff'
'Fiesta/Red Pippin'
'Fortune'
'Granny Smith'
'Greensleeves'
'Grenadier'
'Herefordshire Russet'
'James Grieve'
'Jonagold'
'Jumbo'
'Katy'
'Kidd's Orange Red'
'Lane's Prince Albert'
'Limelight'
'Meridian'
'Queen Cox'
'Red Devil'
'Redsleeves'
'Saturn'
'Scrumptious'
'Spartan'
'Sunset'
'Tydeman's Early Worcester'
'Winter Gem'
'Worcester Pearmain'

Flowering times vary according to location and changing weather conditions from one year to the next. Trees are usually in blossom during April and early May.

C

'Ashmead's Kernel'
'Braeburn'
'Chivers Delight'
'Cornish Gilliflower'
'Crowngold'
'D'Arcy Spice'
'Ellison's Orange/Red Ellison'
'Gala'
'Golden Delicious'
'Golden Noble'
'Howgate Wonder'
'Laxton's Superb'
'Lord Derby'
'Orleans Reinette'
'Peasgood's Nonsuch'
'Pinova/Pinata/Sonata'
'Pitmaston Pine Apple'
'Pixie'
'Sandringham'
'Tydeman's Late Orange'
'Winston'

(top to bottom) **'Ellison's Orange'** is ready to pick and eat in early autumn. **'Golden Delicious'** ripens later and will keep. Both flower in late April to early May.

D

'Court Pendu Plat'
'Edward VII'
'Mother/American Mother'
'Newton Wonder'
'Suntan'

(top to bottom) **'Court Pendu Plat'** is a traditional dessert apple, **'Edward VII'** is a cooker, and **'Mother'** is a juicy dessert fruit. All flower late and store well.

Choosing a pollination group

Pollination groups indicate when in spring each apple variety flowers: early, middle, or late in the season. It's best to grow a collection of trees that come from the same pollination group. That way, their blossom will open at the same time and insects will be able to transfer pollen from one tree to another. Trees belonging to adjacent pollination groups should pollinate one another too, since their flowering periods are likely to overlap, at least to some extent.

However, there are a few apples with which you must take special care. Called triploids, they are not good at pollinating other varieties. They should therefore be grown with at least two different, compatible cultivars that are not triploids. The best know triploids include 'Blenheim Orange', 'Bramley's Seedling', 'Jonagold', and 'Ribston Pippin'.

RECOMMENDED APPLE COMBINATIONS

The combinations of apples given in this chart are from the same pollination groups, to ensure similar flowering times and, therefore, good fruit set. They will crop from early through to late season, providing apples for early picking and eating as well as winter storage.

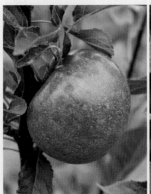  

	Eating apple for early picking	**Eating apple for winter storage**	**Cooking apple**
Early spring flowering (pollination group A)	'Lord Lambourne'	'Egremont Russet'	'Reverend W. Wilks'
Mid-spring flowering (pollination groups B and C)	'Discovery' 'Ellison's Orange' 'Greensleeves' 'James Grieve' (shown) 'Katy' 'Worcester Pearmain'	'Ashmead's Kernel' 'Cox's Orange Pippin' (shown) 'Fiesta' 'Pixie' 'Winter Gem'	'Arthur Turner' 'Bramley's Seedling' 'Golden Noble' (shown) 'Grenadier' 'Howgate Wonder' 'Lane's Prince Albert'
Late spring flowering (pollination group D)		'Court Pendu Plat' 'Mother'	'Edward VII' 'Newton Wonder'

Growing apples

Most apples are tough, tolerant, and long-lived. Only those grown on very dwarfing rootstocks are overly sensitive about the quality of the soil in which they are grown. That said, all apples are prey to a range of pests and diseases, and all need regular pruning, especially those trained as cordons, fans, and other espalier forms. A well-cared-for tree will repay your attention by producing larger quantities of better-quality fruit.

The year at a glance

	spring			summer			autumn			winter		
	M	A	M	J	J	A	S	O	N	D	J	F
plant bare-root	▬								▬	▬	▬	▬
plant container	▬	▬	▬	▬	▬	▬	▬	▬	▬			
summer-prune					▬	▬	▬					
winter-prune									▬	▬	▬	▬
harvest						▬	▬	▬	▬			

Choosing apple trees

Apples are sold as either bare-root or container-grown trees. Specialist nurseries offer a wider choice than garden centres but most of their trees will probably be bare-root and available only during autumn and winter, from about November onwards and possibly as late as March.

Newly purchased young trees are usually one, two, or three years old. One-year-olds will be either maiden whips or feathered maidens (see p.31). They are less expensive than older trees but they need training from scratch and will of course take longer to establish and to start cropping. Two- and three-year-olds will have had some training and pruning already done by the nursery. For a beginner they are probably the best choice.

When to plant

■ BARE-ROOT Plant November–March, when the trees are dormant, unless the soil is waterlogged or frozen. November is the ideal month.
■ CONTAINER-GROWN Plant at any time of year, although autumn is best. Avoid late spring and summer months if it is hot and dry.

(left) **Young, newly planted trees** need to be permanently staked if they are on dwarfing rootstocks. It's a good idea to position the stake on the side of the tree that faces into the prevailing wind.

(right) **Traditional orchard trees** are kept short, for ease of picking. Grass, on the other hand, may be allowed to grow fairly long except for an area immediately around the tree, which is kept clear to minimize competition for moisture and nutrients.

PLANTING AN APPLE TREE

Prepare the site in advance. Young apples on dwarfing rootstocks can't be grown successfully in grass, as they will struggle to compete with it for moisture and nutrients. So, if the planting site is already grassed, remove a square of turf, dig out any perennial weeds, work well-rotted compost or manure into the soil, and add some general, all-purpose fertilizer. Use a stake for freestanding trees and a system of wire supports for cordons and fans.

1 Use a sharp spade to slice out an area of turf about 1m (3ft) square.

2 Dig a hole deep enough and wide enough to accommodate the plant's roots. If you haven't already done so, work some well-rotted compost or manure into the soil.

3 For a bare-root tree, drive a stake into the ground to a depth of 60cm (2ft), about 8cm (3in) away from the centre of the hole. For a container-grown tree, use a shorter stake, driven in at an angle, to avoid damaging the rootball (see p.35).

4 Make a small mound of earth in the centre of the hole and gently spread the roots over it. Check the depth to ensure that the old nursery soil mark on the stem is level with the surface of your soil.

5 Carefully fill the hole with soil, ensuring there are no air pockets among the roots.

6 Gently firm down the soil – don't stamp or you will compact it.

7 Secure the tree to the stake with special tree ties. You may need one at the top and one at the bottom.

8 Water generously now and at regular intervals over the next few weeks.

9 Spread an organic mulch around the plant to help retain moisture and suppress weeds.

10 If the tree has not already been pruned by the nursery, you may need to do it immediately after planting (see p.68).

PLANTING DISTANCES

It's hard to be specific about planting distances. Everything depends on the vigour of the rootstock and the variety, on the soil and other growing conditions, and on the form into which the tree is to be trained. Use the distances given below as a general guide to spacing.

Standards and Half-standards

MM106	4–5.5m (12–17ft)
MM111	6.5–9m (21–28ft)
M25	7.5–10.5m (24–32ft)

Bushes

M27	1.2–2m (4–6ft)
M9	2–3m (6–10ft)
M26	3–4.5m (10–13ft)
MM106	4–5.5m (12–17ft)
MM111	5.5–8m (17–25ft)

Spindlebushes

M27	1.5–2m (5–6ft)
M9	2–2.5m (6-8ft)
M26	2–3.5m (6–11ft)
MM106	2.5–4.5m (8–13ft)

Pyramids

M27	1.2–1.5m (4–5ft)
M9	1.5–2m (5–6ft)
M26	2–2.2m (6–7ft)
MM106	2.2–2.5m (7–8ft)

Fans and Espaliers

M26	3–3.5m (10–11ft)
MM106	3.5–4.5m (11–13ft)
MM111	4.5–5.5m (13–17ft)

Cordons

75cm (30in)

Minarettes

60–75cm (24–30in)

Where to plant

Choose a warm, sheltered site where trees are protected from strong winds. Avoid frost pockets. Full sunshine is more important for dessert apples. Culinary apples will tolerate some shade.

Soil type

Most apples are easy-going, though they all prefer a deep, free-draining soil with a slightly acid pH of around 6.5. They dislike being waterlogged and will grow best if the soil has had plenty of well-rotted compost or manure added to it. Any apple will struggle on shallow soil over chalk, where it is prone to lime-induced chlorosis (see p.320). The smaller the tree and the more dwarfing the rootstock, the more important it is to give it a rich, fertile soil.

CRAB APPLES

Crab apples are certainly not grown for eating raw. Even when ripe they are so hard and so sour that it's hard to imagine they could ever be made edible. However, when cooked and sweetened they make a wonderful crab apple jelly.

Crab apples are widely grown as ornamental trees – for both their small, brightly coloured fruits and for their blossom. Many varieties remain in flower for some time and usually for longer than cultivated apples. For this reason, they are valuable in gardens, on allotments, and in orchards as sources of compatible pollen.

(below, left to right) **Most crab apples** are selected for the quality of their fruit or their attractive white, pink, or red spring blossom. There are numerous named varieties: 'Evereste', 'Golden Hornet', and 'John Downie' (shown here) are among the best known. **Flowering periods** for crab apples tend to be long, so grow them alongside culinary and dessert apples to ensure successful pollination.

Routine care

- WATERING Water young trees, cordons, minarettes, and espaliers regularly throughout the spring and summer, particularly in drought conditions and when the fruit is swelling. Older, established trees are less needy.

- FEEDING To ensure that trees produce as much fruit as possible, commercial growers boost the amounts of potassium, nitrogen, phosphorus, magnesium, and other elements in the soil with a complex regime of specialist fertilizers. However, unless your soil is very poor and your trees are not cropping well, an annual application of a general compound fertilizer each February or March before growth starts should be sufficient.

- MULCHING In March, after feeding, remove any weeds and spread an organic mulch around the base of young trees, wire-trained forms, and those grown on dwarfing rootstocks or in poor soils. It will help retain moisture and keep down the growth of new weeds.

- FROST PROTECTION Although apples usually flower later than pears, plums, cherries, and most other tree fruits they may still be vulnerable to damage from late spring frosts. Protecting large, mature trees is impractical but it may be possible to use an overnight covering of fleece on young trees, cordons, small espaliers, stepovers, and minarettes. Of course, late-flowering varieties are by definition less prone to frost damage.

(right, top to bottom) **The "June drop"** happens in early summer when most apple trees let a proportion of their young, acorn-sized fruitlets fall to the ground. It looks alarming but is quite normal; it's the tree's way of ensuring that it is not overloaded with fruit. **Further thinning** after the June drop is usually necessary to ensure that the best fruits grow to their optimum size. Thin out crowded clusters by selecting any small, diseased, or misshapen fruitlets and removing them. If they don't come away easily, cut their stalks cleanly using secateurs or scissors. Aim to leave 10–15cm (4–6in) between dessert apples and 15–23cm (6–9in) between larger, culinary ones.

GROWING APPLES IN CONTAINERS

Apples can be successfully grown in pots as long as you take care to choose the right variety and the right rootstock. Surprisingly perhaps, the most dwarfing M27 and M9 are not necessarily the best. They are very fussy about soil conditions and may or may not be happy in a container. A non-vigorous variety grown on an M26 rootstock might be a better bet. The best forms for containers are dwarf bushes, dwarf pyramids, and minarettes – although a small multiple cordon is possible, too.

Start with a young, one- or two-year-old tree and choose a container large enough to accommodate the rootball plus a little extra space all round. Fill it with multi-purpose, soil-based compost mixed with some sand or gravel to improve drainage. Feed with a high-potash fertilizer in spring, and keep the pot well-watered in spring and summer, less so in winter. Every year or two, re-pot the tree in a slightly larger container until it reaches the size at which you want to restrict it.

(left) **Container-grown apples** do best in a sheltered, sunny position. If late frosts are a threat after the blossom has opened, they can be protected with fleece or moved under cover. They can also be netted if birds pose a problem.

Harvesting and storing apples

How do you tell when an apple is ready to pick? The simplest test is to cup it lightly in your palm and twist gently. If it comes away easily with the stalk attached, it is ready. If it doesn't, leave it. Don't tug or tear it off or you may damage the spur. Early dessert varieties should be ready for picking in August, or even late July. They are best eaten immediately, before their pips have turned brown. Mid-season apples will keep for a little longer – for perhaps a month or two. And certain late-season apples can be stored for up to six months. Apples intended for storage should be picked and handled very carefully. If they are bruised they won't store well; nor will they if they are left on the tree for too long before picking. Only very few varieties can be left beyond the end of October.

Apples store best if they are kept somewhere dark, reasonably well-ventilated, and cool but frost-free. Most garages or sheds are fine. Cellars, basements, and attics may be too warm, dry, or stuffy. Spread out apples on slatted wooden or plastic trays, or in special moulded greengrocers' fruit liners, ensuring that they don't touch. Alternatively, wrap each apple in tissue paper or store them in polythene bags perforated with air

(left to right) **Start picking** the brightest, most colourful fruits. They are likely to be the ripest, and will probably be those nearest the top of the tree, on the side that gets most sun. **Keep harvesting** regularly, a few at a time, and handle the apples carefully. Don't bruise them. **Store apples** in well-ventilated conditions, keeping different varieties separate – they will ripen at different rates.

holes. Inspect stored fruit regularly and immediately remove any that show signs of rot. Varieties that store well right through the winter include 'Bramley's Seedling', 'Idared', 'Laxton's Superb', 'Jonagold', and 'Golden Delicious'.

Yield

Yields are hard to quantify as they vary widely according to variety, tree form, rootstock, growing conditions, and a host of other variables. However, average quantities you can expect are:

■ STANDARD or HALF-STANDARD 80–160kg (175–350lb).

■ BUSH 25–55kg (55–120lb).

■ DWARF BUSH 15–25kg (33–55lb).

■ SPINDLEBUSH or PYRAMID 15–25kg (33–55lb).

■ FAN 5.5–15kg (12–33lb).

■ ESPALIER 10–15kg (22–33lb).

■ CORDON 2.5–5kg (5$\frac{1}{2}$–11lb).

Month by month

January
■ If necessary, spray trees with a winter wash to protect against aphids, winter moths, and other pests.

February
■ Plant bare-root trees if the ground is not frozen.
■ Apply a general compound fertilizer around existing trees this month or next.

March
■ Weed and mulch around trees after feeding.
■ Last chance to plant bare-root trees.

April
■ Most apple varieties flower during this month or early next month. Protect blossom against frost if necessary.
■ Inspect trees and remove by hand any winter moth caterpillars.

May
■ If pollination is successful, fruitlets form now and begin to swell.
■ Water newly planted and wire-trained trees regularly if the weather is dry.
■ Codling moths mate this month, so hang pheromone traps to attract and catch males.
■ Check for powdery mildew and signs of scab on fruitlets.

June
■ Following the "June drop", further thin out young fruitlets.
■ Summer-prune young espaliers between now and September.
■ Check for greenfly and woolly aphid, and spray if necessary.

July
■ Summer-prune established espaliers and all types of cordon this month and next, cutting back new laterals and sideshoots.

(far left to right) **Buds swell** on bare branches in early spring as the days lengthen. **Leaves burst** and begin to unfurl in spring sunshine. **Blossom** appears on most apple varieties by mid-spring. In cold regions, it may need protecting from frosts. **Fruitlets** start to swell and will soon need thinning. **Ripe apples** – 'Falstaff' is the variety shown here – are ready for harvesting, depending on the variety, between late summer and mid-autumn. **Once harvested** eat early- and mid-season varieties; late-season varieties are best for storing.

August

■ Summer-prune young spindlebushes and pyramids.

■ Continue summer-pruning of cordons, cutting back new laterals.

■ Harvest early-season apples and eat them soon after picking.

■ Remove and destroy any fruit infected with scab or brown rot.

September

■ Harvest mid-season apples. Eat or store according to the variety.

October

■ Harvest late-season apples and store for the winter.

■ Tie sticky grease bands around trunks as a defence against winter moths.

November

■ New bare-root trees become available from specialist nurseries and can be planted between now and March. November is the optimum month for planting both bare-root and container-grown trees: the soil is still warm and trees have a chance to get established before growth starts next spring.

■ Start winter pruning this month. Aim to complete it before the dormant period ends next February.

■ Remove any rotten fruit still hanging on the tree. Rake up any diseased leaves.

■ Check stored fruit for signs of rot.

Pruning and training apples

Every apple tree needs pruning at least once a year. Without this, it will lose its shape, become congested and perhaps diseased, and gradually produce less and less fruit. The basic principles are simple. At the start of their lives, all young trees need training into shape. Thereafter, freestanding trees should be pruned in winter, when they are dormant, and wire-trained trees such as cordons and espaliers should be pruned twice a year, once in summer and once in winter. Beyond that, the only other key thing to know is whether your tree is a spur-bearer or a tip-bearer, because each is pruned slightly differently.

SPUR-BEARERS AND TIP-BEARERS

Most apples produce fruit on branches that are two years old, or older. Each year, fruit buds appear on short little stubs called "spurs". As the years go by, more and more spurs appear until knobbly clusters called spur systems are formed. Obviously, the more spurs you have the more you fruit you'll get – until you reach the point where they become so overcrowded that they require thinning.

A few apple varieties, however, are different. They produce fruit primarily on fresh, new wood that grew only last year. So most of their crop is borne on the ends of the branches instead of along their length. They are known as tip-bearers. When pruning them, the aim is to replace branches and sideshoots that have already borne fruit with new ones that will fruit in the next year or two. This technique is sometimes called renewal pruning.

To complicate things further, some apples produce fruit both on spurs and on the tips of branches and sideshoots. They are known as tip- and spur-bearers or partial tip-bearers.

(left, top to bottom) **Spur-bearing apple trees** have short, stubby sideshoots that carry flower buds, and later fruitlets. **Tip-bearing apple trees** bear flower clusters, and therefore fruit, mostly at the ends of branches. **Spur thinning** is carried out to reduce overcrowding and involves removing old spurs to improve air circulation, leaving a cluster of younger spurs, each with a flower bud.

General pruning tips

Pruning apple trees regularly with the help of sharp secateurs and a good-quality pruning saw will keep them healthy and productive. Get into the habit of removing any dead, damaged and diseased wood as well as thinning overcrowded growth.

(top to bottom) **Cut back** dead branches completely. **Remove** water shoots. **Prune out** any diseased shoots or stems.

(opposite) **Orchard pruning** is a big job, one that can last right through the winter from early November to the end of February. These trees are at least thirty years old and are pruned every year to maintain their open-centered bush form.

Pruning an apple bush or standard

The objective is to create an open-centred tree without a central leader but with a framework of well-spaced main branches spreading out from the trunk. A bush should have a clear trunk of at least 75cm (30in) in height; on a half-standard it should be 1.2m (4ft), and on a standard at least 2m (6ft).

1st winter pruning
NOVEMBER–FEBRUARY

- Your new tree may have been already pruned by the nursery. If not, prune immediately after planting, which is best done in winter when the tree is dormant (although not if the temperature is below freezing).
- If you have planted a one-year-old maiden whip, cut it off at a height of 60–75cm (24–30in), pruning just above a bud. Buds below the cut will shoot and form laterals next year.
- If you have planted a one- or two-year-old feathered maiden (as shown above), cut off the central leader or main stem to about the same height, leaving 3 or 4 healthy laterals below the cut.
- Prune back each of the laterals by two-thirds of its length. Cut to buds that face outwards or upwards.

2nd winter pruning
NOVEMBER–FEBRUARY

- Select the laterals and sub-laterals that you want to become main branches and cut them back by about a half.
- Cut back everything else to 4 or 5 buds.
- Remove any weak, crowded, or crossing stems and any new shoots growing from the main trunk.

3rd winter pruning
NOVEMBER–FEBRUARY

- Tip-prune the main branches by removing about one-quarter of the new growth they made last year.
- Prune strong sub-laterals or sideshoots to 4–6 buds and weaker ones to 2–3 buds. This should encourage growth next year.
- Remove any stems that are crossing or growing into the centre of the tree.

(right) **Light and air** are the two watchwords when pruning. Removing branches that grow into the centre of the tree opens it up and lets air circulate, which will help to reduce the risk of disease. It also allows sunlight to reach the ripening fruits.

Winter pruning an established spur-bearing bush
NOVEMBER–FEBRUARY

- By the 3rd or 4th summer after planting, the tree should be cropping, so winter pruning can be lighter.
- Concentrate on maintaining the overall shape, keeping the centre open, encouraging the growth of new spurs, and thinning old, overcrowded ones.
- Cut out any dead, damaged, or diseased wood.
- Thin any badly congested or tangled areas to let light and air into the centre of the tree.
- Tip-prune the leaders of strong sub-laterals or sideshoots and cut back any weaker ones by about a half of last year's new growth.
- Prune new sideshoots to 4–6 buds.
- Remove completely any new shoots growing from the main trunk.

(left to right) **Prune new sideshoots** to encourage the growth of new spurs. **Prune out** any branches or shoots that show signs of disease such as canker or powdery mildew. **Cut back** to buds facing the direction in which laterals should grow.

Winter pruning an established tip-bearing bush
NOVEMBER–FEBRUARY

(above) **Remove any new shoots** growing straight into the centre of the tree.

- Tip-bearers fruit on last year's new growth, so beware of removing too much.
- Concentrate on maintaining the overall shape, keeping the centre open, cutting back a few older sub-laterals and sideshoots that have been fruiting for some while, and encouraging the growth of new ones to replace them.
- Cut out any dead, damaged, or diseased wood, and thin the centre of the tree if it is congested.

- Lightly tip-prune the leaders of the main branches.
- Remove or cut back to a new shoot or strong bud some of the sub-laterals longer than 30cm (12in).
- Don't touch any sub-laterals shorter than 30cm (12in).

Pruning an apple spindlebush

A spindlebush is a tree with a central leader. The main, lower lateral branches spread out from the trunk almost horizontally, and the upper branches are pruned hard to keep them short. The tree therefore forms a roughly conical shape. It produces high yields and is popular with commercial growers. Spindlebushes need pruning twice a year, in winter and in summer. They reach a height of about 2–2.2m (6–7ft) and must be permanently staked.

(below) **Spindlebushes** are trees whose lower branches are encouraged to grow at a wide angle to the main trunk, almost parallel to the ground. This stimulates them to crop more heavily.

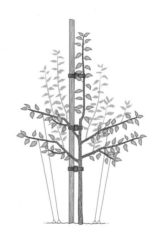

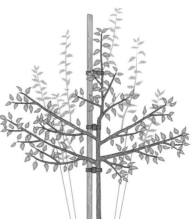

1st winter pruning
NOVEMBER–FEBRUARY

- Start with a one- or two-year-old feathered maiden, and prune immediately after planting.
- Select 4 well-angled laterals at a height of between 60–90cm (2–3ft) above ground level. These will become your main branches. Prune them back by a half, cutting to a downward-facing bud.
- Remove any laterals below your chosen 4.
- Cut off the central leader or main stem to about 3 buds above the highest lateral.

1st summer pruning
AUGUST

- By late summer, the topmost sideshoot will have grown to form a new central leader. Tie it in to the stake.
- Prune out all new shoots growing vertically upwards.
- If the 4 main branches are growing vigorously, tie them down to an angle of 20–30 degrees from the horizontal.
- If they are not growing vigorously, leave them as they are.

2nd winter pruning (not shown)
NOVEMBER–FEBRUARY

- Shorten the central leader by removing about one-third of last summer's new growth. Cut to a bud on the opposite side from the one you pruned to last winter.

2nd summer pruning
AUGUST

- Check and adjust ties on the 4 main branches. Release them when the branches no longer spring back. Horizontal growth encourages the production of more fruit.
- As a new, higher tier of laterals develops, tie them down too.
- Prune out all new shoots growing vertically upwards.

Winter pruning an established spindlebush
NOVEMBER–FEBRUARY

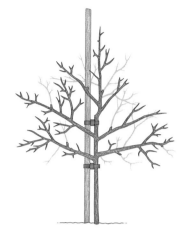

- Focus on maintaining the overall cone shape, cutting back a few older branches, and encouraging the growth of new shoots to replace them.
- Continue shortening the central leader by one-third or one-quarter of last year's growth.
- Thin overcrowded growth from lower branches, especially if it is growing vertically upwards.
- Make a selection of older sub-laterals and sideshoots that have already fruited for 3 years or more and remove them completely. New growth will take their place.
- Prune hard the laterals at the top of the trunk to maintain the tree's conical shape and ensure that fruit lower down receives maximum sunlight.

(top to bottom) **Older branches** should be cut back to the central leader. **Beneath the stub** will be a dormant bud that will start to grow.

(left) **"Festooning"** is the tying down of lateral branches so that they grow as horizontally as possible. They can be tied to stakes in the ground, to the main trunk, or to older, lower branches (as shown here). Its aim is to slow down growth and increase fruit production.

Pruning an apple pyramid

A pyramid is very like a spindlebush. It has the same cone shape with short branches radiating from the top of a central trunk and longer ones from the bottom. The branches themselves however, are not trained horizontally; they are left to grow upwards at a more natural angle. A dwarf pyramid is a compact tree grown on a dwarfing rootstock. Apple pyramids are pruned in exactly the same way as pear pyramids (see p.94).

(below) **Dwarf pyramids** are one of the best forms for a small garden. Their shape looks natural, and as long as they're lightly pruned in summer and again in winter they won't get too large.

Pruning an apple cordon

Cordons are single-stem trees. Any lateral branches are regularly pruned back to form short sideshoots or spurs on which the fruit is borne. For this reason, tip-bearers don't make good cordons; choose a spur-bearer instead. Prune them twice a year, in winter and in summer, and grow them against a wall or fence or supported by posts and wires. Cordons may be upright or oblique, and can also be trained into double ("U") or multiple (double-"U") forms. Low, horizontal cordons are called stepovers. And compact, upright cordons are called minarettes, columns, or ballerina trees.

(top to bottom) **Oblique cordons** are grown at a diagonal angle, usually in a closely planted row or line. The main trunks can then grow longer than those of upright cordons before they become so tall that the fruit is difficult to pick. **Stepovers** are small horizontal cordons, usually no more than knee-high. They are grown by bending over the central leader of a very young, flexible maiden whip and tying it into to a horizontal wire.

1st winter pruning
NOVEMBER–FEBRUARY

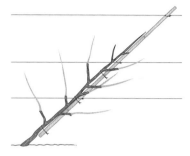

- Construct a support by tying a bamboo cane to three horizontal wires at angle of 45 degrees.
- Start with a one- or two-year-old feathered maiden. Plant it at an angle, tie it in to the cane, and prune immediately after planting.
- Cut back to 3 or 4 buds any laterals longer than 10cm (4in).
- Don't touch the central leader or any laterals shorter than 10cm (4in).

1st summer pruning
JULY–AUGUST

- New laterals and sideshoots will have started to emerge by summer.
- Cut back new laterals growing directly from the main trunk to 3 leaves, not counting the basal cluster.
- Cut back sub-laterals or sideshoots growing off existing laterals to just 1 leaf beyond the basal cluster.
- This should encourage the development of spurs on which fruit will be borne in coming years.

Winter pruning an established cordon
NOVEMBER–FEBRUARY

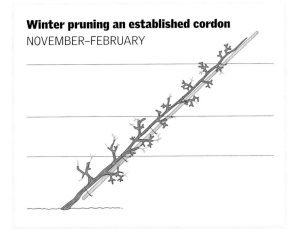

- ■ Established cordons should not need much winter pruning.
- ■ As trees age, the spur systems may become overcrowded. If so, thin them out by removing weak, overlapping, or congested spurs.
- ■ Cut out completely any very old spur systems that are no longer productive. New growth should replace them.

Summer pruning an established cordon
JULY–AUGUST

- ■ Continue cutting back new laterals growing directly from the main trunk to 3 leaves, not counting the basal cluster.
- ■ Cut back sub-laterals, or sideshoots growing off existing laterals or spurs, to just 1 leaf beyond the basal cluster.
- ■ When the tree reaches its full height, cut the central leader back to 1 leaf of new growth each spring.

(top to bottom) **By midsummer** new laterals may be growing alarmingly quickly. **Summer pruning** allows light and air to reach the ripening fruit.

Pruning an apple espalier

Espaliers are amongst the most dramatic of the trained forms. They're large, too – up to 6m (20ft) wide unless grown on dwarfing rootstocks – so they need a strong support system and plenty of space. Training them takes time. It will be several years before an espalier with multiple horizontal tiers becomes established.

1st winter pruning
NOVEMBER–FEBRUARY

- Construct a support system by securing horizontal wires 35–50cm (14–20in) apart to a wall, fence, or upright posts.
- Start with a one-year-old maiden whip, or a one- or two-year-old feathered maiden if it already has 1 or more pairs of appropriate laterals. Plant it, tie it in to a cane, and prune immediately after planting.
- Cut back the central leader to a strong bud just above the lowest wire, about 45cm (18in) from the ground. Make sure there are at least 3 healthy buds below your cut. The lower two should form the first laterals, and the top the new leader.

This mature espalier is in need of its winter prune to remove those long vertical shoots from the spurs on the upper arms. The fact that they have grown so long may be because they were pruned too early the previous summer, before growth had slowed down.

1st summer pruning
JUNE–SEPTEMBER

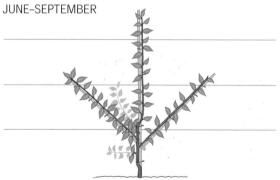

- Secure 2 canes to the horizontal wires at angles of 45 degrees.
- Tie in the new main laterals to the diagonal canes.
- Tie in the new central leader to the vertical cane.
- Cut back any other laterals or young shoots to 2 or 3 leaves.
- During the summer, gradually and carefully begin lowering the 2 diagonal canes.

2nd winter pruning
NOVEMBER

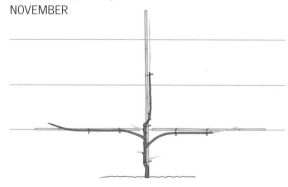

- Lower the 2 arms into a horizontal position and tie them to the bottom wire.
- Tip-prune the laterals by about one-quarter if they do not seem to be growing strongly. Cut to buds pointing downwards.
- Cut back the new central leader to just above the 2nd wire and to a bud facing in the opposite direction from last year's. Ensure you leave 3 strong buds – 1 for another new leader, and 2 for new left and right laterals.
- Remove completely any laterals below the first 2 arms in order to leave the main trunk clean.

2nd summer pruning
JUNE–SEPTEMBER

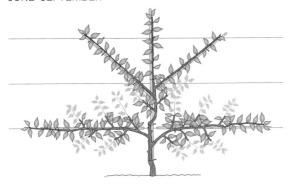

- Secure an additional 2 canes to the horizontal wires at angles of 45 degrees.
- Tie in the 2 main laterals that will form the new left and right arms to the diagonal canes, as you did last year.
- Tie in the new central leader to the vertical cane.
- Prune sub-laterals or sideshoots growing from the lower 2 arms to 3 leaves beyond the basal cluster.
- Cut back any other laterals or young shoots growing directly from the main trunk to 2 or 3 leaves.
- During the summer, slowly lower the 2 diagonal canes.

3rd winter and summer pruning
NOVEMBER and JUNE–SEPTEMBER

- Repeat the process of forming horizontal arms until you have as many tiers as you want.
- Then remove the vertical leading shoot.

Summer pruning an established espalier
JULY–AUGUST

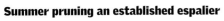

- Prune each arm of the espalier as if it was a cordon.
- Continue cutting back new laterals growing directly from the main left and right arms to 3 leaves, not counting the basal cluster – especially the vigorous growth that will probably shoot up from the top tier.
- Cut back all new sideshoots to just 1 leaf beyond the basal cluster.
- Keep the main trunk clean of all unwanted laterals and sideshoots.

Winter pruning an established espalier
NOVEMBER–MARCH

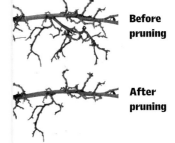

Before pruning

After pruning

- Established espaliers should need only light winter pruning.
- Thin out overcrowded spur systems by removing weak, overlapping, or congested spurs.
- Cut out completely any very old unproductive spur systems so that new growth can replace them.

PRUNING AN OLD, NEGLECTED TREE

The kind of pruning required to rescue a neglected apple tree and bring it back to healthy, productive shape is called renovation. You cannot, however, renovate a tree in in one go. It will take at least two years, perhaps more. If you attempt it in a single season by pruning the tree too hard, all you'll do is put it into shock and force it into producing a lot of new foliage and little or no new fruit.

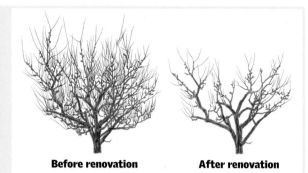

Before renovation   **After renovation**

1st winter pruning
NOVEMBER–FEBRUARY

- Start by cutting out all dead, damaged, and diseased branches and stems.
- Look for branches that are crossing and may be rubbing against one another. Remove them.
- Thin out some of the most densely crowded areas so that light and air can circulate.
- Don't remove more than about 25 per cent of the tree in any one year.

2nd winter pruning
NOVEMBER–FEBRUARY

- Continue pruning overlong branches and any that are hanging too low to the ground.
- Keep an eye on the overall shape, and try to open up the centre of the tree by cutting back to laterals facing in the appropriate direction.
- Cut off any water shoots that have sprouted around last year's pruning cuts.
- Start thinning out old, overcrowded spur systems.

Crossing branches are in danger of rubbing against each other. If they split or if the bark is rubbed away, infections can enter and may cause disease.

Diseased wood should be removed promptly, before the infection spreads. Cut back as far as clean, healthy wood that shows no sign of disease.

Tangled, congested areas should be thoroughly thinned out. If they're not, they keep out light and air, promoting the risk of disease.

What can go wrong

Buds and blossom

1 Blossom turns brown and wilts
First the flowers and then young leaves turn brown and wither. The cause is a fungus very closely related to the one responsible for brown rot.
■ See **Blossom wilt** (p.325) and **Brown rot** (p.326).

Blossom discolours and dies
Overnight frosts can damage young leaves and destroy blossom, especially in the case of apple varieties that flower early in the year. Less commonly, the cause may be insects called apple suckers.
■ See **Apple sucker** (p.334) and **Frost** (p.316).

Blossom remains closed and turns brown
If blossom fails to open and the petals are brown, suspect apple blossom weevil. Cut open the flower bud and you may find the white larva inside.
■ See **Apple blossom weevil** (p.334).

Leaves, stems, and branches

2 White, powdery coating on leaves
When young leaves and shoots are covered in a dry, powder-like, white mould the cause is the fungus, powdery mildew. New growth withers and dies, and affected fruit buds do not produce fruit.
■ See **Powdery mildew** (p.329).

3 Leaves curled and spun with silk
A number of different caterpillars spin a silk web, wrapping leaves around themselves as a protective cover. On apples, the fruit tree tortrix moth caterpillar is one of the most common.
■ See **Tortrix moth** (p.340).

4 Leaves eaten and tattered, with holes
Caterpillars feeding on leaves are the most likely cause of the damage. A severe infestation can strip leaves completely. Winter moths are the probable culprits – their caterpillars can often be found inside tightly curled new leaves.
■ See **Winter moth** (p.341).

5 Leaves curled and sticky
The undersides of tightly curled, distorted leaves will probably reveal aphids. The sticky upper surface is due to the honeydew that they excrete, and it may also develop a grey sooty mould. Several different species of aphid – varying in colour from green or blue to pink or brown – attack apples.
■ See **Aphids** (p.334), **Rosy apple aphid** (p.339), **Woolly aphid** (p.341).

6 Small, brown-edged holes in leaves
Red-brown spots on young leaves are caused by bright green capsid bugs feeding on new shoots. The spots develop into large, torn holes as the leaves grow and expand.
■ See **Capsid bugs** (p.335).

7 Looping, meandering lines on leaves
These yellow-brown, scribble-like markings are caused by tiny caterpillars feeding inside the leaves, tunnelling "mines" through the plant tissue as they eat.
■ See **Apple leaf miner** (p.334).

8 Brown patches on leaves
Irregular blotches or spots that may be dark green or brown, perhaps turning grey or black in the centre, can indicate scab. Infected leaves may yellow and fall. The fruits themselves may be affected too.
■ See **Scab** (p.330).

9 White woolly fluff on stems and branches
Waxy, cotton-wool-like tufts on branches, twigs, and shoots are signs of infestation by woolly aphids. They're more likely to build up around old pruning cuts and splits in the bark.
■ See **Woolly aphid** (p.341).

10 Cracked, flaky areas of bark
Discoloured, sunken, split, or flaky areas of bark can indicate apple canker. As it spreads, cracked rings form, the area around the site may become swollen, and growth ceases above and below it. Whole branches may die.
■ See **Apple and pear canker** (p.324).

Leaves mottled and bronzed
If upper surfaces of leaves are mottled and discoloured then become brittle, look underneath with a magnifying glass for tiny fruit tree red spider mites. In severe cases, you may also see fine silk webbing.
■ See **Red spider mite** (p.339).

Fruit

11 Pale brown, corky patches
Capsid bugs feeding on young fruitlets can cause them to become disfigured and to develop scars or cork-like patches.
■ See **Capsid bugs** (p.335).

12 Brown scabs and split skin
Scab-like patches appear on the fruits. As they spread, the skin dries out and is likely to split or crack, possibly allowing other infections to enter.
■ See **Scab** (p. 330).

13 Fruits develop patches of brown rot
Ripening fruits turn brown and may develop concentric rings of white fungal spores, sometimes around a central hole. They either fall to the ground or remain on the tree, gradually shrivelling to a mummified state.
■ See **Brown rot** (p.326).

14 Ragged holes in fruits
Birds, wasps, and flies feed on ripe fruits, often taking advantage of areas where the skin has already been holed or damaged.
■ See **Birds** (p.335) and **Wasps** (p.341).

15 Ribbon-like scars on skin
A meandering, slightly raised scar indicates where a young apple sawfly maggot has hatched and fed just below the skin. If the grub survives, it may continue tunnelling inside, causing the fruitlet to fall prematurely. If the grub doesn't survive, the apple may ripen normally – though it will still bear the scar.
■ See **Apple sawfly** (p.334).

16 Dark, sunken spots in skin
Small, round, concave spots appear on the skins, particularly in large cooking apples. They may spread down into the flesh and cause the fruit to taste bitter.
■ See **Bitter pit** (p.325).

17 Holes ringed with black-brown "frass"
The hole reveals where the larva of the codling moth ate its way out of the fruit after hatching and feeding. Inside, much of the apple may have been eaten and filled with frass (excrement). Apple sawfly grubs make similar holes.
■ See **Codling moth** (p.335) and **Apple sawfly** (p.334).

Leaf stuck to skin
A leaf attached to the skin of the fruit by a silk web may well be camouflage concealing a tortrix moth caterpillar.
■ See **Tortrix moth** (p.341).

Pears

For some reason, home-growers plant fewer pears than apples. Pears are certainly just as delicious – if not more so. Yet, whereas an apple tree is a common sight in even the most modest, small garden, a pear tree is more unusual. It's hard to know why. The reason may be to do with perception: pears are thought to be more troublesome and trickier to grow than apples. It's true that they're choosy about exactly where they will grow – they dislike being buffeted by wind and they need slightly more warmth and sunshine than apples. For this reason, they are commonly grown against a sheltered wall or fence as cordons, espaliers, or fans. But, if you can give them the sort of conditions they like, and if you can help them fend off the most common pests and diseases, they should thrive and produce a good crop every year. Moreover, pruning is easier than with apples, and, once established, the trees live longer. So, get the basics right, and you may well find that they're actually easier to grow.

Harvest pears while they are still slightly hard but come away easily in your hand. They will continue to ripen after you bring them indoors.

Which forms to grow

■ **Bushes** Open-centred trees and a good choice for pears. Be wary of trying standards or half-standards: they will almost certainly be too large.

■ **Spindlebush and pyramid** Freestanding trees with a central leader.

■ **Cordon** Wire-trained single or multiple stems that produce fruits on short sideshoots.

■ **Minarette** A short, single, vertical stem designed for close planting where space is restricted.

■ **Espalier and fan** Wire-trained forms with arms growing either side of a central stem or radiating from a short trunk.

Must-grow pears

1 'Buerré Superfin'
Pollination group B
A 19th-century French variety with an excellent, aromatic flavour. Needs to be grown in a warm, sheltered spot, so a good choice for wall-trained cordons or an espalier.
- **Harvest** September
- **Eat** September–October

2 'Doyenné du Comice'
Pollination group C
Regarded by many as the best-tasting pear of all. Fruits are a russet yellow-green when ripe, and the flesh is rich, sweet, and juicy. However, it is prone to scab, and it must be grown in a warm, sunny, sheltered site otherwise yields may be low and the fruits may not ripen to their fullest.
- **Harvest** October
- **Eat** October–December

3 'Conference'
Pollination group B
One of the most widely grown of all pears – both commercially and in gardens and on allotments. Hardy, dependable, and heavy-cropping. Fruits are long and narrow, and the flesh is sweet and juicy.
- **Harvest** September
- **Eat** October–November

4 'Catillac'
Pollination group C
A 17th-century French culinary pear that probably originated from the Bordeaux area. It requires long, slow cooking, but then its flesh turns pink and it has a wonderful, aromatic flavour. Stores well into the spring. Triploid.
- **Harvest** October
- **Eat** December–April

5 'Gorham'
Pollination group C
An old American variety with a sweet, musky flavour and a green-yellow skin. It is reliable and easy to grow, but doesn't always crop heavily.
■ **Harvest** September
■ **Eat** September–October

6 'Williams' Bon Chrétien'
Pollination group B
An early-cropping dessert pear, often claimed to be the world's most widely grown variety. Known in the USA as 'Bartlett', after the man who distributed it there in the early 19th century. Good flavour, but some susceptibility to scab. Does not keep.
■ **Harvest** September
■ **Eat** September

7 'Packham's Triumph'
Pollination group A
Originally bred in Australia at the end of the 19th century, with 'Williams' Bon Chrétien' one of its parents. The fine flavour makes it popular both as a grow-your-own fruit and commercially. However, it flowers early and may fall prey to frosts.
■ **Harvest** October
■ **Eat** November–December

8 'Pitmaston Duchess'
Pollination group C
An old-fashioned English pear, one of its parents is 'Glou Morceau' (see p.84). The large, green-yellow fruits have sweet, juicy, white flesh. Trees can grow large, so they need lots of space. Triploid.
■ **Harvest** September
■ **Eat** October–November

9 'Louise Bonne of Jersey'
Pollination group A

An old-fashioned French dessert pear with a lovely sweet, aromatic flavour. Flowers early in spring but seems able to survive all but the most severe frosts.
- **Harvest** September
- **Eat** October

10 'Beth'
Pollination group C

An excellent early dessert pear. Slightly small but with an outstanding, rich, sweet flavour. Trees crop when young and generally produce high yields.
- **Harvest** August–September
- **Eat** September

11 'Glou Morceau'
Pollination group C

A winter pear first bred in Belgium in the 18th century. Large fruits with a fine flavour and texture. Needs warmth and sun to develop fully. Stored carefully, they should keep until early January.
- **Harvest** October
- **Eat** December–January

12 'Onward'
Pollination group C

A cross between 'Doyenné du Comice' and 'Laxton's Superb', it shares the same excellent flavour. Easy to grow, reliable, and heavy cropping. Good for the average-sized garden. Keeps poorly so should be eaten soon after picking.
- **Harvest** September
- **Eat** September

13 'Buerré Hardy'
Pollination group B

Dates back to the early 19th century. Large, russeted fruits with smooth, white flesh and a fine flavour. Pick while slightly underripe and store until ready to eat.
- **Harvest** September
- **Eat** September–October

14 'Concorde'
Pollination group C

A cross between the English 'Conference' and French 'Doyenné du Comice'. It is as easy to grow and as heavy cropping as the former, and has the excellent flavour of the latter. A good choice for a small garden.
- **Harvest** September–October
- **Eat** October–December

9

11

12

13

'Invincible' (not illustrated)
Pollination group B
An unusual variety that flowers twice each spring, so if the first wave of blossom is damaged by frost a second wave follows on. Harvesting can last for more than 4 weeks in September and October, and fruits can be eaten soon after picking, or stored until late winter.
■ **Harvest** September–October
■ **Eat** September–February

'Red Williams' (not illustrated)
Pollination group C
A distinctive and unusual red-skinned variety of 'Williams' Bon Chrétien'. Texture and flavour are excellent, and it should be ready to pick and eat early in the season.
■ **Harvest** August–September
■ **Eat** September

'Moonglow' (not illustrated)
Pollination group C
An American pear that produces medium or large fruits with bright yellow skin that may become flushed with pink or red as they ripen. Smooth, juicy flesh with a mild, fragrant flavour.
■ **Harvest** August
■ **Eat** August–September

'Clapp's Favourite' (not illustrated)
Pollination group C
A 19th-century American pear first bred by Thaddeus Clapp of Massachusetts and still in cultivation. Fruits start off pale green then ripen to yellow with red markings. The fruit is best eaten soon after picking.
■ **Harvest** August-September
■ **Eat** August–September

'Durondeau' (not illustrated)
Pollination group B
A Belgian pear that dates back two hundred years to the early 19th century. Fruits are a slightly russet golden yellow–red, and leaves turn a lovely rich, dark red in autumn. Flesh is soft and sweet. Trees tolerate damp climates and are not over-vigorous, so they work well in small gardens.
■ **Harvest** September
■ **Eat** October–November

'Merton Pride' (not illustrated)
Pollination group B
A classic English dessert pear, bred from a cross between 'Glou Morceau' and 'Double Williams'. Not as widely grown these days as it once was, but still worth trying – though it is a triploid, and therefore needs two other pollinating partners. Fruits are a russet green-yellow and are sweet and juicy with an excellent flavour.
■ **Harvest** September
■ **Eat** September

'Robin' (not illustrated)
Pollination group C
Here's a traditional heritage pear that originates from Norfolk, where it was once widely grown. It is not so readily available nowadays, but the small fruits have an excellent flavour and trees are worth searching out from specialist nurseries. The name comes from the way ripening fruits turn red on the side where the sun strikes them, allegedly resembling the breast of a robin.
■ **Harvest** September
■ **Eat** September–October

Choosing and buying pear trees

As with apples, there are a number of things to bear in mind before buying a pear tree. First, the form: do you want it to be freestanding or wire-trained? Second, the rootstock, since that has a major effect on how large the tree will grow. Third, the pollination group to which it belongs, as that determines when it flowers. And, finally, the variety or cultivar.

Choosing a tree form
As a general rule, pears need a more sheltered and sunnier site than apples. If you can provide this, then consider a bush, spindlebush, or pyramid – as long as you have the space. If space is tight, then a row of cordons, an espalier, or a fan set against a warm, sunny wall might be a better option. Half-standards and standards grow too large for the average garden. They also take many years before they begin producing fruit, and they are extremely difficult to prune and to harvest.

Choosing a variety
The choice of varieties or cultivars is not as wide for pears as it is for apples. Nevertheless, there are still plenty to choose from – either one of the reliable, disease-resistant, heavy-cropping modern varieties or, if you search them out, traditional varieties whose ancestry may go back hundreds of years.

Like apples, pears are classified as either dessert or culinary. Culinary pears, which are less common, never ripen sufficiently to eat raw.

Very few pears are self-fertile. They need pollen from another tree for successful fertilization and fruit production. So, all pears should be planted with neighbouring trees from the same flowering or pollination group. However, if space is restricted, growing a family tree may be the solution: it is a single tree with more than one pear cultivar grafted onto the same rootstock (see p.53). The different varieties should cross-pollinate each other.

(opposite, clockwise from top left) **An arch** formed of cordons trained vertically then bent into curves overhead. **Container trees** are best grown on Quince C rootstocks. **Pyramid forms** look attractive trained on traditional metal frames. **Orchard pears** should all be from the same pollination group.

CHOOSING A ROOTSTOCK
Pears grown on their own roots tend to be very vigorous and grow very tall. They are also slow to crop, and prone to disease. Consequently, most fruit nurseries graft them onto quince rootstocks. Quince C and Quince A are most commonly used.

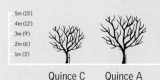

| 5m (15') |
| 4m (12') |
| 3m (9') |
| 2m (6') |
| 1m (3') |

Quince C　　Quince A

Quince C
- VIGOUR Semi-dwarfing.
- CHARACTERISTICS The least vigorous of the rootstocks, and therefore the one producing the best trees for small gardens. Quince C trees need richer, more fertile soil than those grown on Quince A, but they will begin cropping sooner after planting.
- SUPPORT Stake or support permanently.
- FORMS Bush, spindlebush, pyramid, cordon, minarette, espalier, fan.
- HEIGHT 2.5–5m (8–16ft).

Quince A
- VIGOUR Semi-vigorous.
- CHARACTERISTICS Stronger growing and a little less fussy about soil conditions. A better choice for poor soils and for slightly larger trees.
- SUPPORT Stake for first 2 years.
- FORMS Bush, spindlebush, pyramid, cordon, espalier, fan.
- HEIGHT 3–6m (10–20ft).

Winged insects transfer pollen betwen the blossoms of different pear trees and usually ensure cross-pollination. Always check that the trees you buy will be in blossom at the same time, as well as compatible with each other.

PEAR POLLINATION GROUPS

A	B	C
'Doyenné d'Eté'	'Beurré Hardy'	'Beth'
'Emile d'Heyst'	'Beurré Superfin'	'Bristol Cross'
'Louise Bonne of Jersey'	'Conference'	'Catillac'
'Packham's Triumph'	'Durondeau'	'Clapp's Favourite'
'Seckle'	'Fondante d'Automne'	'Concorde'
	'Garden Pearl'	'Doyenné du Comice'
	'Gieser Wildeman'	'Forelle'
	'Hessle'	'Glou Morceau'
	'Invincible'	'Gorham'
	'Jargonelle'	'Improved Fertility'
	'Joséphine de Malines'	'Moonglow'
	'Merton Pride'	'Onward'
	'Thompson's'	'Pitmaston Duchess'
	'Williams' Bon Chrétien'	'Red Williams'
		'Robin'
		'Sensation'
		'Winter Nelis'

'Packham's Triumph' blossoms in early spring so may need protection from frosts.

'Conference' is a popular, firm-fleshed pear that crops reliably in early autumn.

'Doyenné du Comice' flowers late in spring. Its large fruits have a superb flavour.

Choosing a pollination group

Pear blossom opens earlier than that of apples – usually in March and April. The pollination group the pear belongs to will give you an indication. It's important to grow at least two or three different trees from the same pollination group – or, at least, from an adjacent group – so that their flowers bloom simultaneously and insects can transfer pollen from one tree to another.

However, some pears are not good at pollinating other varieties. Called triploids, they should therefore be grown with at least two different, compatible cultivars that are not triploids. The best known triploids include 'Jargonelle', 'Merton Pride', and 'Catillac'.

Worse, there are a few pears that are virtually sterile and can't be relied upon to pollinate any neighbouring trees at all. 'Bristol Cross' is one. Other pears are very choosy and are incompatible with other specific varieties. For example, 'Louise Bonne of Jersey' will not pollinate 'Williams' Bon Chrétien', and vice-versa. Nor will 'Doyenné du Comice' and 'Onward' pollinate each other.

Growing pears

Growing apples and pears is very similar. In some ways pears are easier as they grow vigorously, tend to be more resistant to pests and diseases, and are less complicated to prune. But, in one respect, they are slightly more demanding: they need more warmth and sunshine than apples, and better protection from strong winds and frosts, so deciding where to plant them and which form to choose needs careful consideration.

The year at a glance

	spring			summer			autumn			winter		
	M	A	M	J	J	A	S	O	N	D	J	F
plant bare-root									▬	▬	▬	▬
plant container	▬	▬	▬	▬								
summer-prune				▬	▬	▬						
winter-prune									▬	▬	▬	▬
harvest					▬	▬	▬					

Planting pear trees

Pears are sold as either bare-root or container-grown trees. You'll have a much wider choice if you buy a bare-root tree from a specialist nursery than if you buy a container-grown tree from a garden centre. Bare-root trees, however, are available only during autumn and winter, between about October and March.

Newly purchased young trees are usually one, two, or three years old. Two- and three-year-olds are slightly more expensive to buy but, because the nursery will have already carried out a certain amount of training and pruning, they are probably the best choice for a beginner.

When to plant

■ BARE-ROOT Plant November–February, when the trees are dormant, unless the soil is waterlogged or frozen. November is the ideal month.
■ CONTAINER-GROWN Plant at any time of year, although autumn is best. Avoid late spring and summer months if it is hot and dry.

ASIAN PEARS

The Asian or Nashi pear is a different species from the familiar European pear. It is possible to grow these pears outside their native China, Japan, and Korea, but they need a sunny, sheltered site and protection from frosts because they flower very early. They lack the classic pear flavour.

Apple pear is another name for the Asian pear, owing to its round shape – more like an apple than European pears. 'Nijisseiki' (shown here) is just one of several cultivars that are commonly available.

Where to plant

Pears need a warm, sheltered site protected from strong winds. Avoid frost pockets. Grow cordons, espaliers, and fans against a sunny fence or wall.

Soil type

Pears grow best in deep, free-draining soil with a slightly acid pH of around 6.5. Although they dislike being waterlogged, they seem to tolerate heavy clay soils better than apples. They struggle on sandy soils, and also on alkaline, chalky soils, where they are prone to lime-induced chlorosis (see p.320).

Routine care

■ WATERING Take particular care to water young, recently planted trees and wire-trained forms such as fans and espaliers. Don't let them dry out.
■ FEEDING Use a general compound fertilizer each February, before growth starts. Pears may need more nitrogen than apples; an annual top dressing of ammonium sulphate will help boost levels.
■ MULCHING In March, after feeding, remove any weeds and spread an organic mulch around the base of young trees, wire-trained forms, and those growing in poor soils. It will help retain moisture and keep down the growth of new weeds.
■ FROST PROTECTION Pear blossom is vulnerable to frost damage. Protecting large, mature trees

PLANTING DISTANCES

Recommended spacings vary according to the vigour of the rootstock and the variety, the soil and other growing conditions, and the form into which the tree is to be trained.

Bushes
Quince C 3.5m (11ft)
Quince A 4.5m (13ft)

Spindlebushes
Quince C 2m (6ft)
Quince A 2.5m (8ft)

Dwarf pyramids
Quince C 1.2m (4ft)
Quince A 1.5m (5ft)

Fans and Espaliers
Quince C 3.5m (11ft)
Quince A 4.5m (13ft)

Cordons
75cm (30in)

Double cordons
1m (3ft)

Minarettes
60–75cm (24–30in)

PLANTING A ROW OF PEAR CORDONS

A south-facing wall provides a sunny, sheltered site that is ideal for cordons, espaliers, and fans. Prepare the site in advance by working some well-rotted compost or manure into the soil, and add some general, all-purpose fertilizer. Attach horizontal wires to the wall at intervals of 30–45cm (12–18in). For single cordons, start with a feathered maiden and immediately after planting prune as for an apple (see p.72). For double cordons, start with a maiden whip and cut back harder (as shown here).

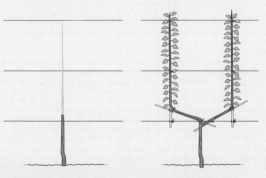

1 Plant the trees about 30cm (12in) away from the wall. Any closer and their roots will be at risk of drying out. Lean them in towards the wall slightly. Plant out the rest of the cordons in the row, allowing a space of about 1m (3ft) between each tree.

2 Tie the main stems securely to the lowest of the horizontal wires.

3 Cut off the central leader at a height of about 24cm (10in), just above the lowest wire, ensuring that there is one strong bud on each side of your cut.

TRAINING THE ARMS OF THE CORDON

The following summer, train the new laterals by tying them to bamboo canes, set first at an angle and then vertically. Cut back all new sideshoots to one leaf.

1st winter pruning
NOVEMBER–FEBRUARY

1st summer pruning
JULY–AUGUST

(left) **Double cordons** are perfect for a garden where space is limited. Not only do they look very decorative, they will also provide a reasonable crop, providing they are given support and a sunny, sheltered spot.

The "June drop" takes place in early summer when a proportion of young fruitlets fall to the ground. This is quite natural and is simply the tree's way of discarding diseased or damaged fruit and ensuring that its branches aren't crowded and overloaded.

(below) **Thinning pears** by removing more of the young fruitlets, shortly after the June drop, will encourage those that remain to grow to full size. If the crop is heavy, leave just one pear to each cluster, about 10–15cm (4–6in) apart, and if the crop is light, leave two pears per cluster.

is impractical, but it may be possible to use an overnight covering of fleece on young trees, minarettes, cordons, and small espaliers or fans.

Harvesting and storing pears

There's an art to picking pears at just the right moment. Unlike most fruit, they are best picked while they are still slightly unripe. The sure way to test whether or not early-season pears are ready to pick is simply to taste one. It will still be hard, of course, but if it tastes sweet it's ready, if it doesn't it's not. Once picked, bring them indoors and eat them when their flavour has developed and they have softened slightly. If you leave pears on the tree too long or let them over-ripen indoors, they go "sleepy" – unpleasantly soft, grainy, and perhaps even brown in the middle.

Late-season pears are for keeping. You can't tell by tasting them when they are ready to pick. The best test is to lift them in your hand and twist them gently. If they pull away easily they're ready. To store them, bring them indoors somewhere dark, reasonably well-ventilated, not too dry, and cool but frost-free. Spread them out on slatted trays or moulded greengrocers' fruit liners, ensuring that they don't touch. Don't wrap them in paper. Inspect them regularly and remove any that show signs of rot. Bring a few at a time into a warmer room so they can soften ready for eating. Varieties that store well include 'Doyenné du Comice', 'Glou Morceau', 'Invincible', and the culinary 'Catillac'.

Yield

Yields vary widely according to variety, tree form, rootstock, growing conditions, and other variables. However, average quantities are:
- BUSH 20–40kg (45–90lb).
- DWARF BUSH 15–20kg (33–45lb).
- SPINDLEBUSH 10–20kg (22–45lb).
- PYRAMID 10–20kg (22–45lb).
- FAN 5.5–11kg (11–25lb).
- ESPALIER 7–11kg (15–25lb).
- CORDON 2–3.5 kg (4.5–8lb).

Month by month

January
■ If necessary, spray trees with a winter wash to protect against aphids, winter moths, and other pests.

February
■ Plant bare-root trees if the ground is not frozen.
■ Apply a general compound fertilizer this month or next.

March
■ Weed and mulch around trees after feeding.
■ Blossom on early-flowering varieties opens this month. Protect against frost if possible.

April
■ Later varieties are in flower.
■ Inspect and remove by hand any winter moth caterpillars.

May
■ Water newly planted and wire-trained trees.
■ Hang pheromone traps to attract and catch male codling moths before they mate.
■ Check for powdery mildew and signs of scab.

June
■ Further thin out young fruitlets.
■ Summer-prune young espaliers and fans between now and September.

July
■ Summer-prune established espaliers and fans and all types of cordon this month and next, cutting back new laterals and sideshoots.

August
■ Continue summer-pruning wire-trained trees.
■ Remove and destroy any fruit infected with scab or brown rot.

September
■ Harvest early-season pears and, according to variety, eat as soon as ripe after picking.

October
■ Harvest late-season pears and store some for the winter.
■ New bare-root trees start to become available from specialist nurseries. Plant between now and February.
■ Tie sticky grease bands around trunks to deter winter moths.

November
■ Buy and plant new trees. November is the best month for planting both bare-root and container-grown trees.
■ Start winter pruning this month. Aim to complete it before the dormant period ends next February.
■ Remove any rotten fruit still hanging on the tree.
■ Rake up any diseased leaves.
■ Check stored fruit for signs of rot.

(top to bottom) **Buds** swell in late winter. **Blossom** opens as early as March. **Some fruitlets** will fall to the ground in the June drop. **'Louise Bonne' pears** ready for picking.

Pruning and training pears

Pears are pruned and trained in almost exactly the same way as apple trees. Both produce fruit on wood that is two years old or older, and need regular pruning to keep them in shape, to thin out or cut back over-vigorous growth, and to encourage healthy fruit production. Almost all pears are spur-bearers; there are very few tip-bearers (see p.67).

Pruning a pear bush

Both newly planted and established trees are pruned in the same way as apples, the aim being to create an open-centred tree without a central leader but with a framework of well-spaced main branches spreading out from the trunk (see p.68). Prune in winter, between November and February, when dormant.

Each year, check for any dead, damaged, or diseased wood and cut it out. Remove any crossing or congested branches, as well as any that are growing vertically upwards, crowding the centre of the tree. Cut to an outward-facing bud to encourage new growth.

On old, established trees, spur systems can get very crowded. Thin them out regularly to remove old, unproductive spurs and to give more room for the fruit.

Pruning a pear spindlebush

Spindlebushes are trees with a central leader and are roughly conical in shape, with long, spreading lateral branches at the base of the trunk and progressively shorter branches towards the top. Prune them twice a year, in winter and in summer, in the same way as for apples (see p.70).

Pruning a pear dwarf pyramid

Pyramids have a similar cone shape to that of spindlebushes. They, too, need careful pruning and training in the first few years in order to establish their basic shape. Thereafter, they are pruned twice a year: in summer to cut back new growth, and in winter to thin out crowded spur systems. Dwarf pyramids are compact trees usually no more than 2.2m (7ft) tall, and can be planted as closely as 1.2m (4ft) apart.

1st winter pruning
NOVEMBER–FEBRUARY

- Start with a feathered maiden. Stake and prune immediately after planting.
- Cut off the central leader or main stem to a bud 50–75cm (20–30in) above the ground.
- Prune each lateral or sideshoot to a length of about 15cm (6in), cutting to an outward-facing bud.
- Remove any laterals that are growing upright, are crossing, or are too close to the base.

1st summer pruning
JULY–AUGUST

- Very little pruning is required in the first summer.
- Cut back to a single leaf any new shoots growing vertically upwards, especially near the top of the tree.
- Tie in the central leader to the tree stake.

Pyramids and spindlebushes are often employed by commercial growers. They produce high yields, and the fruit can be picked without ladders.

2nd winter pruning
NOVEMBER–FEBRUARY

- Prune the central leader to leave about 25cm (10in) of last summer's new growth. Cut to a bud on the opposite side to the bud you cut back to last winter.
- Shorten the main laterals to leave 15–20cm (6–8in) of last summer's new growth. Cut to buds facing downwards and outwards.
- Shorten sub-laterals or sideshoots to just 2 or 3 buds. These will go on to form spurs.

Summer pruning an established dwarf pyramid
JULY–AUGUST

- Cut back the laterals that form the main branches to leave 5 or 6 leaves of this summer's new growth.
- Cut back sub-laterals growing off the main laterals to 3 leaves beyond the basal cluster.
- Cut back new sideshoots to 1 leaf beyond the basal cluster.
- Leave the central leader untouched.

Winter pruning an established dwarf pyramid
NOVEMBER–FEBRUARY

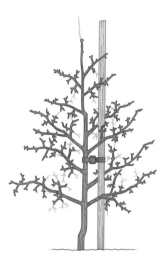

- When the tree has reached its full height, prune the central leader each winter to leave just 1 bud of last year's new growth.
- Thin out overcrowded or unproductive spurs.
- Reduce the number of fruit buds to 2 or 3 per spur.

Pruning a pear cordon

Pears make very good cordons – vertical, oblique, or multiple. They are pruned in the same way as apples (see p.72). Once established, prune them twice a year, in winter and in summer, regularly cutting back lateral branches to form short sideshoots or spurs on which the fruit is borne.

(opposite, clockwise from top) **A row** of oblique cordons with fruitlets in early summer. **Multiple cordon** – the four arms are clearly visible in winter. **A double cordon** is covered in spring blossom.

(right) **In summer,** new growth on this oblique cordon is very vigorous and must be pruned back to allow light and air to reach the young fruit.

Pruning a pear espalier

Train and prune a pear espalier just as you would an apple (see p.74), although you can perhaps start summer pruning a little earlier, in July rather than August. And in winter, be prepared to thin out spurs slightly more ruthlessly; most pears produce them more readily than apples and older spur systems can easily become overcrowded and unproductive.

(below) **In winter** it is easy to see the fruiting spurs on this expertly pruned mature espalier. Congested spurs have been thinned out to keep the tree as productive as possible.

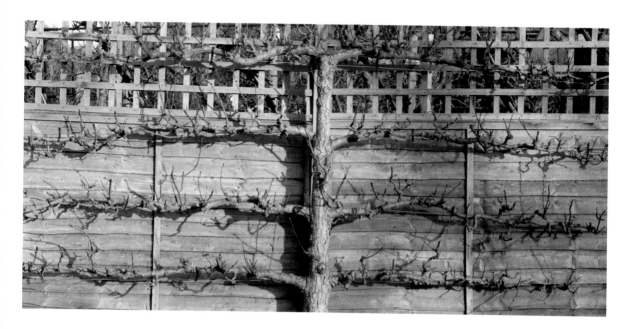

Pruning a pear fan

Like espaliers, pear fans are trained and pruned in the same way as apples. But, unlike espaliers, fans do not have a central leader. Instead, the laterals or ribs spread out either side of a short central trunk. Fans, espaliers, and all wire-trained trees need pruning twice a year, in summer and in winter. It's possible to buy pre-trained fans. They are expensive but may give you a year or two's head start on getting the tree established. Otherwise, begin with a maiden whip or a suitable feathered maiden.

1st winter pruning
NOVEMBER–FEBRUARY

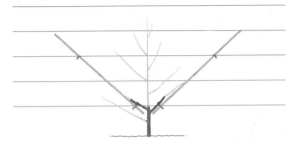

- Construct a support system by securing horizontal wires 30cm (12in) apart to a wall, fence, or upright posts. Attach 2 diagonal canes.
- Start with a feathered maiden. Plant it, and prune immediately after planting.
- Cut off the central leader and any top growth above 2 strong left- and right-facing laterals, at a height of about 45cm (18in) above the ground, just below the bottom wire.
- Cut back the 2 laterals to about 45cm (18in) and tie them in to the canes. They will become 2 of the main ribs.
- Remove any lower, unwanted laterals.

1st summer pruning
JUNE–SEPTEMBER

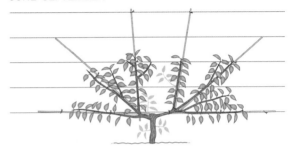

- As sub-laterals or sideshoots develop on the 2 main ribs, tie them in to additional canes and to the wires (right), ensuring that they are evenly spread.
- Remove completely any new shoots that are unwanted or growing inwards or outwards at right angles to the fan.

2nd winter pruning
NOVEMBER

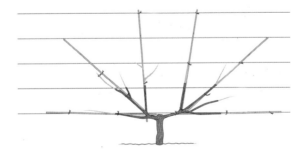

- Tip-prune the laterals by one-quarter or one-third of last summer's new growth.
- Now that leaves have fallen, ensure that the laterals are all tied in securely.
- Remove any unwanted shoots growing directly from the main trunk.

2nd summer pruning
JUNE–SEPTEMBER

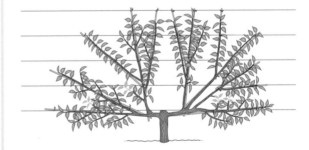

- Attach more canes as required and tie in new sub-laterals destined to form additional ribs of the fan.
- Aim for a balanced, even shape, and keep the centre uncluttered.
- Where growth becomes crowded, prune sub-laterals or sideshoots growing from the main ribs to 3 leaves beyond the basal cluster.

Winter pruning an established fan
NOVEMBER–MARCH

- Established fans should need only light winter pruning.
- Thin out overcrowded spur systems by removing weak, overlapping, or congested spurs.
- Cut out completely any very old spur systems that are no longer productive so that new growth can replace them.
- Remove any dead, diseased, or damaged wood.

(clockwise from top left) **Cut back long shoots** to a healthy spur that is outward-facing. **Prune crowded spurs** to reduce the number of branches they produce. **Remove wood** showing any signs of disease. **A mature pear fan** will remain productive and keep its shape if routine pruning is carried out each winter.

Summer pruning an established fan
JULY–AUGUST

- Prune each main rib of the fan as if it was a cordon.
- Continue cutting back new laterals growing directly from the main ribs to 3 leaves, not counting the basal cluster – especially prune any vigorous vertical growth.
- Cut back all new sideshoots growing from existing laterals and spurs to just 1 leaf beyond the basal cluster.

(clockwise from top left) **Cut back sideshoots** growing from laterals to 1 leaf. **Prune to** 3 leaves any laterals growing from the main branches or ribs. **An established** pear fan in full leaf will need pruning in summer so that new growth doesn't shade the fruit, and to let in light and air.

What can go wrong

Buds and Blossom

Blossom discolours and dies

Pears flower early in spring, and frosts often damage young leaves and blossom. Less commonly, the cause may be insects called pear suckers.

■ See **Frost** (p.316) and **Pear sucker** (p.337).

Leaves, stems, and branches

1 Leaves curled and tattered with holes

The most likely cause of the damage is moth caterpillars feeding on leaves and curling the edges around themselves. A severe infestation can strip leaves completely.

■ See **Tortrix moth** (p.340) and **Winter moth** (p. 341).

2 Orange spots on leaves

The spots or patches may be yellow in colour with an orange or dark brown centre. The cause is European pear rust.

■ See **Rust** (p.330).

3 Yellow-black blisters on leaves

A rash of raised blisters or blotches appears on young leaves, starting off yellow or pink then becoming black as the summer progresses. Pear leaf blister mites feeding on the leaves are responsible.

■ See **Pear leaf blister mite** (p.337).

4 Brown blotches on leaves

Irregular, dark-brown blotches or spots usually indicate scab, a disease that commonly affects pears. The fruits themselves may be affected, too.

■ See **Scab** (p.330).

5 Leaves tightly curled and coloured red or black

If young leaves curl upwards into tight rolls, and turn red then black, suspect pear leaf midge.

■ See **Pear leaf midge** (p.337).

6 Leaves wither and die back

Leaves and shoots appear scorched and die. Peel back a small area of bark and you may see orange-red markings.

■ See **Fireblight** (p.327).

7 Leaves curled and sticky

Infestations of aphids or pear suckers cause leaves to curl tightly and become distorted. Their upper surfaces are sticky with the honeydew that the insects excrete, and may develop a grey sooty mould.
■ See Aphids (p.334) and Pear sucker (p.337).

Cracked areas of bark and dieback

Discoloured, sunken, split, or flaky areas of bark can indicate canker. As it spreads, cracked rings form, the area around the site may become swollen, and growth ceases above and below it. Whole branches may die.
■ See Apple and pear canker (p.324).

Fruit

8 Brown scabs and split skin

Scab-like patches appear on the fruits. As they spread, the skin dries out and is likely to split or crack, possibly allowing other infections to enter. Fruitlets are shrunken and misshapen.
■ See Scab (p.330).

9 Fruits develop patches of brown rot

Ripening fruits turn brown, and may develop concentric rings of white fungal spores, sometimes around a central hole. They either fall to the ground or remain on the tree, gradually drying out and shrivelling.
■ See Brown rot (p.326).

10 Ragged holes in fruits

Birds, wasps, and flies feed on ripe fruits, particularly if the skin has already been holed or damaged.
■ See Birds (p.335) and Wasps (p.341).

Holes ringed with black-brown "frass"

Larvae of the codling moth hatch and feed inside the fruit, then eat their way out leaving an exit hole. Inside, much of the pear may have been eaten and filled with frass (excrement).
■ See Codling moth (p.335).

Misshapen, blackened fruits fall while still young

Small, young fruitlets swell and their skins turn black. They're likely to drop prematurely. Inside, you may still find well-fed pear midge larvae that are responsible for the damage.
■ See Pear midge (p.337).

Pale brown, corky patches

Capsid bugs feeding on young fruitlets can cause them to become disfigured and to develop scars or cork-like patches.
■ See Capsid bugs (p.335).

Fruits dimpled and misshapen

Infected pears are lumpy or knobbly, and may be hard, woody, or unpleasant-tasting. The cause is a virus which, though it is unlikely to affect all the fruits on a tree, can spread.
■ See Pear stony pit virus (p.328).

Plums

The term "plum" covers a wide variety of related fruits. European plums, along with gages, their green- or yellow-skinned relatives, originated in the Caucasus and southern central Asia, probably as a cross between cherry plums and wild blackthorns or sloes. Damsons, bullaces, and mirabelles are usually smaller, more acidic, and better for cooking, preserving, and making jams. Then there are Japanese plums. They are extremely sweet and juicy and, because they come into flower very early, are best grown in warm climates. In the USA, Japanese plums have long been cross-bred with native species as well as with imported European cultivars to produce modern North American varieties, some of which have since found their way to Britain and the rest of Europe.

Plums are not hard to grow, especially now that modern dwarfing rootstocks have helped restrict the size of the trees. They need a lot less pruning than apples and pears. Your biggest challenge is likely to be harvesting the ripe fruit before birds, wasps, and other insects beat you to it.

Plums ripen from July onwards, though the best time to pick them depends on the variety – and the weather. Late varieties, including many damsons and bullaces, may last on the tree until early October.

Which forms to grow

■ **Bushes** Best grown only on semi-dwarfing rootstocks.
■ **Pyramid** A neat, manageable form and therefore a good choice for most gardens and allotments.
■ **Cordon** Plant either single minarettes or columns, or perhaps a row of oblique cordons.
■ **Fan** Ideal for a sheltered, sunny fence or wall.

Must-grow plums

1 'Early Laxton'
Pollination group B
One of the very first plums to ripen. Attractive, juicy, medium-sized, yellow-red fruits with an acceptable if unexciting flavour.
■ **Fertility** partly self-fertile
■ **Harvest** late July–early August

2 'Victoria'
Pollination group B
Still widely regarded as the best all-round plum of them all. Heavy cropping with fruits of excellent flavour for both eating and cooking.
■ **Fertility** self-fertile
■ **Harvest** late August–early September

3 'Opal'
Pollination group B
A relatively modern culinary variety from Scandinavia now acknowledged as perhaps the best of the early ripening plums. Heavy cropping, its fruits ripen to red and have a good flavour.
■ **Fertility** self-fertile
■ **Harvest** late July–early August

4 'Warwickshire Drooper'
Pollination group A
An old-fashioned variety with large, yellow plums so heavy that they earn their wonderful name by weighing down the branches of the tree.
■ **Fertility** self-fertile
■ **Harvest** mid–late September

5 'Jubilee'
Pollination group B
A new variety from Sweden, claimed to be superior to 'Victoria'. The fruits are larger and equally well-flavoured. It is also hardy, heavy cropping, and disease-resistant. Search it out now.
■ **Fertility** self-fertile
■ **Harvest** mid–late August

6 'Marjorie's Seedling'
Pollination group C
Large, oval, well-flavoured fruits are perfect for cooking but can also be

eaten fresh if left to ripen fully.
Purple skin with yellow flesh.
■ **Fertility** self-fertile
■ **Harvest** late September–early
October

7 **'Shiro'**
Pollination group A
A Japanese plum with medium to large,
round, yellow-skinned fruits. The flesh is
translucent, sweet, and extremely juicy.
■ **Fertility** partly self-fertile
■ **Harvest** August

8 **'Giant Prune'**
Pollination group C
An American plum, also known as
'Burbank's Giant'. It produces heavy
crops of large, oval, red-purple fruits
that taste and keep well. Frost- and
disease-resistant.
■ **Fertility** self-fertile
■ **Harvest** mid–late September

'Blue Tit' (not illustrated)
Pollination group C
Reliable, dual-purpose plum for eating
or cooking. Juicy, medium-sized, and
deep blue in colour. Blossom opens late,
so a good variety for frost-prone areas.
■ **Fertility** self-fertile
■ **Harvest** early–mid August

'Czar' (not illustrated)
Pollination group B
Traditional cooking plum dating back to
the 19th century and still widely grown.
Fruits have dark purple skins and
yellow-green flesh with a good flavour.
■ **Fertility** self-fertile
■ **Harvest** early August

'Guinevere' (not illustrated)
Pollination group C
A recently introduced modern variety.
The large, sweet, dark purple fruits
will keep well in the fridge.
■ **Fertility** self-fertile
■ **Harvest** September

'Methley' (not illustrated)
Pollination group A
A Japanese plum with red-purple skin
and blood-red, very sweet, very juicy
flesh. It flowers early and so may need
frost protection.
■ **Fertility** self-fertile
■ **Harvest** July

Gages

1 'Oullins Golden Gage'
Pollination group C
Green-yellow fruits with pale yellow flesh.
Reliable, reasonably sweet, with a good
flavour for both cooking and eating raw.
- **Fertility** self-fertile
- **Harvest** mid-August

2 'Old Green Gage'
Pollination group C
Also referred to as 'Reine Claude-Vraie'
(the "true" greengage) in recognition of
its 16th-century French ancestry. Small
yellow-green fruits with the archetypal,
rich greengage flavour.
- **Fertility** self-infertile
- **Harvest** late August–early September

Damsons & bullaces

1 'Shropshire Damson'
Pollination group C
Sometimes called 'Prune Damson', this old
variety can be harvested as late as October.
Trees are hardy and compact.
- **Fertility** self-fertile
- **Harvest** late September–early October

2 'Langley Bullace'
Pollination group B
The small, almost black fruits are far too tart
to eat raw, but make superb jams. Crops are
generous and reliable, but trees can be large.
- **Fertility** self-fertile
- **Harvest** late September–early October

3 'Merryweather Damson'
Pollination group B
An old variety, its classic blue-black fruits
have juicy, yellow flesh. Use them for cooking.
- **Fertility** self-fertile
- **Harvest** late September

3 'Cambridge Gage'
Pollination group C
Bred from the original 'Old Green Gage', this variety is more vigorous and produces more fruit. It retains the same excellent flavour.
■ **Fertility** partly self-fertile
■ **Harvest** late August–early September

'Denniston's Superb' (not illustrated)
Pollination group B
Strictly speaking a plum with green–yellow skin, it is nevertheless usually listed as gage – and indeed sometimes called the 'Imperial Gage'. North American in origin, it is said to date back to the late 18th century.
■ **Fertility** self-fertile
■ **Harvest** late August

Cherry plums (mirabelles)

1 'Golden Sphere'
Pollination group A
Large, apricot-sized, golden-yellow fruits. A recent variety crossbred from plums and cherry plums in the Ukraine. It is very hardy.
■ **Fertility** partly self-fertile
■ **Harvest** August

2 'Gypsy'
Pollination group A
Bright red fruits with a strong cherry-plum flavour are ideal for bottling and for making jam. Also from the Ukraine.
■ **Fertility** partly self-fertile
■ **Harvest** August

Growing plums

Traditionally, plums were grown as stand-alone bushes or standard trees, but fruits of mature trees were hard to pick and difficult to protect from birds. Thankfully, modern rootstocks restrict growth to about 2–2.2m (6–7ft) high on semi-dwarfing Pixy, and to about 2.2–2.7m (7–9ft) high on semi-vigorous St Julien A. In small gardens, a pyramid is the best freestanding form of plum to grow. If you have a warm, sheltered wall or fence that gets the sun, take advantage of it by opting for a fan shape, or perhaps a row of oblique cordons.

Plums flower from March through to April, depending on the variety you've chosen. For successful pollination to take place, trees that are planted together for compatibility must also be in blossom at the same time.

The year at a glance

	spring			summer			autumn			winter		
	M	A	M	J	J	A	S	O	N	D	J	F
plant bare-root												
plant container												
summer-prune												
harvest												

Flowering and pollination

When choosing plums you need to know the following. First, is the variety self-fertile? And, second, when does it flower? Plums that are self-fertile (or self-compatible) will set fruit from their own pollen. If you intend to plant just a single tree, choose one of these. Others are either partially self-fertile or completely self-infertile, and need cross-pollinating from another suitable variety. In practice, this means you'll need to plant two or more compatible trees near to one another. Even self-fertile plums, however, are more likely to produce better crops if they are in a position to be cross-pollinated from other trees.

Not all plums flower at the same time. Cross-pollination won't take place between an early-flowering and a late-flowering variety, since insects can only transfer pollen from flower to flower when the blossom is open. You should, therefore, always make sure you choose varieties from the same flowering or pollination group, or at worst, adjacent groups. Plums in, say, group B should pollinate each other because they will all be in flower at the same

PLUM POLLINATION GROUPS

A

Plums
'Avalon'
'Blue Rock'
'Coe's Golden Drop'
'Mallard'
'Valor'
'Warwickshire Drooper'

Gages
'Jefferson'

Cherry plums
'Golden Sphere'
'Gypsy'

B

Plums
'Cox's Emperor'
'Czar'
'Early Laxton'
'Edwards'
'Herman'
'Jubilee'
'Opal'
'Pershore'
'Rivers' Early Prolific'
'Sanctus Hubertus'
'Seneca'
'Victoria'

Gages
'Denniston's Superb'
'Golden Transparent'

Damsons & Bullaces
'Langley Bullace'
'Merryweather Damson'

C

Plums
'Belle de Louvain'
'Blue Tit'
'Giant Prune'
'Guinevere'
'Kirke's Blue'
'Marjorie's Seedling'

Gages
'Cambridge Gage'
'Early Transparent'
'Old Green Gage'
'Oullins Golden Gage'

Damsons
'Bradley's King'
'Farleigh'
'Shropshire'

(top to bottom)
'Jefferson' and
'Golden Sphere'.

(top to bottom)
'Opal' and
'Merryweather'.

(top to bottom)
'Giant Prune' and
'Shropshire Damson'.

'Early Laxton' belongs to pollination group B. It will cross-pollinate successfully with other plums from the same group.

time. However, provided that the blossom is open for long enough, there may be some overlap with trees from group A and group B, in which case they may cross-pollinate, too. It's unlikely that trees from groups A and C will.

If this were not complex enough, there's a further complication. Some plums are so choosy that they won't cross-pollinate certain other specific varieties – or even if they do, the crop will be very disappointing. To all intents and purposes, they are incompatible. For that reason, it's best to avoid the following combinations: 'Blue Rock' and 'Rivers' Early Prolific'; 'Coe's Golden Drop' and 'Jefferson'; 'Cambridge Gage' and 'Old Green Gage' or other gages in the 'Reine-Claude' group.

If you are unsure about which plums to plant with which, ask at the fruit tree nursery or choose self-compatible varieties such as 'Victoria'.

Growing in containers

Plums can be grown in large pots or tubs, but only those on the semi-dwarfing Pixy rootstock. Compact, single-column minarettes are probably the best choice. Start off young, one- or two-year-old trees in a container with a minimum diameter and depth of 45cm (18in) and fill it with multi-purpose, soil-based compost with added sand or gravel to improve drainage. Feed with a high-potash fertilizer in spring, and keep the pot well-watered. After two years, repot in a 60cm (24in) container.

Choosing trees

Plums are sold as either bare-root or container-grown trees. Specialist nurseries offer a wider choice than garden centres, but the trees will probably be bare-root and available only in autumn and winter, between October and March.

When to plant

■ BARE-ROOT Plant November–March, when the trees are dormant, unless the soil is waterlogged or frozen. November is the ideal month.

Gages belong to the same family as plums but are green or golden-yellow in colour. They are thought to be named after Sir William Gage, who imported them from France in the 18th century.

PLANTING A PLUM TREE

Prepare the site in advance by removing any perennial weeds, working well-rotted compost or manure into the soil, and adding some general, all-purpose fertilizer. Use a stake for freestanding trees and a system of wire supports for cordons and fans.

1 Dig a hole deep enough and wide enough to accommodate the plant's roots comfortably. If you haven't already done so, add some well-rotted compost or manure and work it into the soil.

2 For a bare-root tree, drive a stake into the ground to a depth of 60cm (2ft), about 8cm (3in) away from the centre of the hole. For a container-grown tree, use a shorter stake, driven in at an angle, to avoid damaging the rootball (see p.35).

3 Make a small mound of earth in the centre of the hole and gently spread the roots over it. Check the depth to ensure that the old nursery soil mark on the stem is level with the surface of your soil. Carefully fill the hole with soil, ensuring there are no air pockets among the roots.

4 Gently firm down the soil – don't stamp and compact it. Water generously now and at regular intervals over the next few weeks.

5 Secure the tree to the stake with a belt tie. You may need one at the top and one at the bottom.

6 Spread an organic mulch around the plant to help retain moisture and suppress weeds.

■ CONTAINER-GROWN In theory, you may plant at any time of year, providing that trees are available, but autumn is best. Avoid late spring and summer months if the weather is hot and dry.

Where to plant

Choose a warm, sunny, sheltered site, away from strong winds and not in a frost pocket. A south- or west-facing wall is ideal for fans or cordons.

Soil type

Plums are tolerant, but prefer a deep, free-draining soil with a slightly acid pH of around 6.5. Like most fruit trees, they dislike being waterlogged and prefer soil with plenty of well-rotted organic matter added.

Planting distances

■ STANDARDS 5.5–6.5m (17–21ft) apart.
■ BUSHES Pixy 2.5–3.5m (8–11ft), St Julien A 3.5–4.5m (11–13ft) apart.
■ PYRAMIDS Pixy 2.5–3m (8–10ft), St Julien A 3–3.5m (10–11ft) apart.
■ FANS Pixy 3.5–4.5m (11–13ft), St Julien A 4.5–5.5m (13–17ft) apart.
■ CORDONS Pixy 75cm–1m (30in–3ft) apart.

(left and right) **From June onwards,** begin thinning out young fruitlets. Aim to leave 5–8cm (2–3in) between small fruits, and 8–10cm (3–4in) between larger ones.

Routine care

■ WATERING Water regularly throughout the spring and summer, particularly for wall-trained cordons and fans. Irregular watering when the weather is hot and dry may cause the skins of the fruits to split as they swell.

■ FEEDING Each February, just before growth starts, apply a general compound fertilizer to maintain nutrient levels.

■ MULCHING In March, after feeding, remove any weeds and spread an organic mulch around the base of your trees. This will help retain moisture and restrict the growth of new weeds.

■ NETTING Birds can be a problem both in winter, when they eat new fruit buds, and in summer as fruit ripens. Netting large trees may not be practical, but it's easier in the case of cordons and fans.

■ FROST PROTECTION Plums are among the first fruit trees to flower – especially Japanese and cherry plums. They may need covering with fleece overnight if there is a danger of hard frosts.

Harvesting and storing plums

In a year when the fruit set has been good, most plums produce a bigger crop than the trees can physically support. Some fruitlets will fall naturally as part of the "June drop", but you should thin them out further in order to avoid branches breaking under the weight. Heavily laden trees may still need supporting with ropes or forked stakes.

Early varieties should be ready for picking in late July. Others, such as damsons and bullaces, may last until October. Even on the same tree, plums do not all ripen at the same time. You'll need to go over each tree more than once testing the fruit. It will taste at its best when just slightly soft, though plums for cooking, preserving, and freezing can be picked a little earlier. Leave a short length of stalk attached to prevent the skins from tearing and to avoid damaging next year's fruit buds. Eat ripe plums straight away; those picked while still slightly underripe should keep for a couple of weeks.

Yield

Yields are hard to quantify as they vary from variety to variety and from year to year. However, average quantities you can expect are:

■ BUSH 14–27kg (30–60lb).
■ PYRAMID 14–23kg (30–50lb).
■ FAN 7–11kg (15–25lb).
■ CORDON 3.5–7kg (8–15lb).

PLUM/APRICOT HYBRIDS

Plums and apricots have been crossbred to produce hybrid fruits. The first was the Californian "plumcot", half plum and half apricot. Next came the "pluot", about 75 per cent plum and 25 per cent apricot, and the "aprium", roughly 75 per cent apricot and 25 per cent plum.

Month by month

January
■ If necessary, spray trees with a winter wash to protect against aphids.

February
■ New buds will be visibly swelling.
■ Plant bare-root trees if the ground is not frozen.
■ Apply a general compound fertilizer around existing trees.

March
■ Buds start to burst, and blossom opens on earliest flowering varieties. Protect against frost if necessary.
■ Weed and mulch around trees.
■ Spring-prune young trees whose overall shape you are still establishing.
■ Last chance to plant bare-root trees.

April
■ Blossom appears on mid-season and late-flowering varieties. Continue to protect against frost if necessary.
■ Spring-prune young trees this month if you didn't do so in March.
■ Pinch out unwanted new buds and shoots on wire-trained trees.
■ Watch out for winter moth caterpillars and mealy plum aphids.

May
■ Fruitlets form and begin to swell.
■ Weed and water regularly.

June
■ Start thinning out young fruitlets.

■ If necessary, lightly summer-prune established bush, standard, and pyramid trees this month or next. Cut out dead, damaged, or diseased wood, and thin badly congested areas. Tie in new growth and prune back sideshoots.
■ Hang pheromone traps to attract and trap male plum fruit moths.

July
■ Harvest the first early-season plums.
■ Continue light summer-pruning of established trees.
■ Summer-prune young pyramid and wire-trained trees, cutting back laterals and sideshoots.

August
■ Harvest early and mid-season fruit.

September
■ Harvest mid- and late-season fruit.
■ Prune wire-trained plums after harvesting.

October
■ Harvest late-season fruit, such as damsons and bullaces.
■ New bare-root trees start to become available from specialist nurseries. Plant between now and March.
■ Tie sticky grease bands around trunks as a defence against winter moths.

November
■ Buy and plant bare-root trees. November is the optimum month: the soil is still warm and trees can get established before growth starts next spring.

Pruning and training plums

The most important thing to remember is not to prune in winter. Plums, cherries, and other stone fruit are unlike apples and pears; instead of being pruned when the trees are dormant, they are pruned after new growth has begun, making it harder for silver leaf (see p.331) and bacterial canker (see p.324) to enter and infect the tree via pruning wounds. After the first couple of years, freestanding plums need very little pruning – much less than apples and pears. Trained forms, such as cordons and fans, do need regular summer pruning to maintain their shape and productivity.

Pruning a plum bush or standard

Aim for an open-centred tree with a framework of well-spaced main branches. A bush should have a clear trunk of at least 75cm (30in) between the lowest branch and the ground; a half-standard or standard will be taller.

Summer pruning an established tree
JUNE–JULY

- Prune only if necessary.
- Cut out any dead, damaged, or diseased wood.
- Thin any badly congested or tangled areas to let light and air into the centre of the tree.
- Remove any overly vigorous, vertical new shoots.

1st spring pruning
MARCH

- Whatever time of year you plant, don't prune until the buds begin to open.
- Select 3 or 4 well-spaced main laterals and prune back each by a half or two-thirds of its length – unless the job has already been done by the nursery. Cut to buds that face outwards.
- Cut off the central leader to just above the topmost lateral.

2nd spring pruning
MARCH

- The laterals you left last year will by now have produced new growth in the form of sub-laterals. Choose 3 or 4 of each and cut them back by about a half.
- Remove all other growth, including any weak, crowded or overlapping stems, and any new shoots growing from the main trunk.
- The tree now has a basic framework.

Pruning a plum pyramid

The key to a successful pyramid is its conical, Christmas-tree-like shape, formed from lateral branches radiating out from a central trunk. Pyramids should be kept to a maximum height of about 2–2.5m (6–8ft).

1st spring pruning
MARCH

- Start with a feathered maiden and do not prune before March.
- Cut off the central leader with an angled cut just above a bud at a height of about 1.5m (5ft).
- Remove all laterals lower than 45cm (18in) from the ground.
- Prune back the remaining laterals by a half. Cut to buds that face outwards.

1st summer pruning
JULY

- Cut back main laterals to about 20cm (8in) from the start of this year's new growth. Cut to buds that face downwards.
- Cut back new sideshoots or sub-laterals to about 15cm (6in).
- Leave the central leader untouched.

2nd spring pruning
MARCH

- Cut back the central leader to about one-third of last year's growth.
- Thereafter, in March each year, continue to prune the central leader by removing two-thirds of last summer's growth until it reaches its maximum height.

Summer pruning an established tree
JUNE–JULY

- Cut out any dead, damaged, or diseased wood.
- Remove old, unproductive growth from congested areas.
- Tip-prune the central leader, cutting it back to about 2.5cm (1in) of last summer's growth.
- Remove any vigorous growth from the upper branches in order to preserve the tree's conical shape.

(top to bottom) **Pinch out** the tips of new plum shoots by hand before growth ripens and requires pruning with secateurs. **Prune plums** in summer to reduce the risk of infection by silver leaf disease. **Plums fruit** along the length of laterals that are two or more years old, rather than on spur systems, like apples and pears.

Pruning a plum fan

Grow a plum fan against a sheltered, sunny wall, fence, or a series of wooden posts strung with horizontal wires 30cm (12in) apart. Allow a space 4m (12ft) wide and 2.5m (8ft) high for a fan on St Julien A rootstock, and 3m (10ft) wide and 2m (6ft) high for one on Pixy rootstock. Established fans put on a lot of new growth each year and need regular pruning to keep them under control and to avoid areas of the fan becoming overcrowded.

(left and right) **Cut back laterals** growing out at right angles, away from the wall, and tie in those that will form the main arms.

1st spring pruning
MARCH

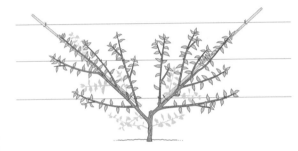

- Start with a feathered maiden planted 25cm (10in) from a wall or fence. Do not prune before March.
- Remove all laterals except 2 strong, equal-sized ones on either side of the central leader, about 25cm (10in) above ground.
- Prune back them back to about 40cm (16in), cutting to a downward-facing bud and tie them in to canes.
- Prune lower laterals to 1 bud as reserves for the main laterals.
- Cut off the central leader with an angled cut just above the higher of the 2 laterals.

1st summer pruning
JULY

- The 2 main laterals will have lengthened. Tie in their new growth to the bamboo canes.
- New sideshoots or sub-laterals will have been produced, too. Select the ones you want to keep, fan them out, and tie them in to the horizontal wires.
- Cut back unwanted sideshoots to just 1 leaf.
- Remove any new shoots growing from the trunk beneath the 2 main arms of the fan.
- For 2nd and 3rd year pruning, see Peaches (p.153).

Spring pruning an established tree
MARCH–APRIL

Spring prune only when trees have started into new growth, not when they are still dormant.

- Remove any new buds or shoots growing into or directly out from the wall or fence.
- Pinch out new shoots growing in the "V" between laterals and sideshoots (as you would with tomatoes).
- To avoid congestion, thin remaining sideshoots to at least 10cm (4in) apart.

Summer pruning an established tree
JUNE–JULY then again in SEPTEMBER

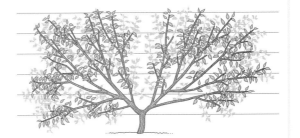

- In early summer, select new laterals to fill out any gaps in the framework of the fan and tie them in.
- Prune new growth on sideshoots back to 5–6 leaves.
- Remove old, crowded, unproductive growth, and any dead or diseased wood.
- After harvesting, cut back to just 3 leaves all the sideshoots you pruned in midsummer.

(below, far left to right) **Newly planted fans** need careful training to stimulate growth and ensure an even spread of equally spaced laterals. **After a few years** the main structure should be in place. **Established fans** can quickly get out of control if not pruned regularly. The naturally vigorous vertical growth seen here urgently needs taming.

What can go wrong

Buds and Blossom

New buds eaten by birds

Birds – in particular, bullfinches – may attack the buds during winter and early in spring, damaging them or eating them entirely. They may also peck ripe fruit in summer.
■ See **Birds** (p.335).

Blossom discolours and dies

Because plums flower early in the year, there is always a danger of frost scorching young leaves and damaging or destroying flowers.
■ See **Frost** (p.316).

Blossom turns brown and wilts

First the flowers and then young leaves turn brown and wither. The cause is the same fungus responsible for brown rot.
■ See **Blossom wilt** (p.325) and **Brown rot** (p.326).

Leaves, stems, and branches

1 Sticky leaves and stems covered with greenfly

A covering of sticky honeydew and the grey sooty mould that grows on it are signs of aphids. In early summer, they are likely to be mealy plum aphids. They are green, and may or may not be covered in a white, powdery, wax-like coating.
■ See **Mealy plum aphid** (p.337).

2 New leaves curled and distorted

On the undersides of the tightly curled leaves you will see tiny yellow-green aphids. They hatch early in spring from eggs that have overwintered on the trees. The insects feed on sap in the leaf tissue.
■ See **Plum leaf-curling aphid** (p.338).

3 Leaves with holes eaten out of them

The most likely culprits are the caterpillars of winter moths. A severe infestation can strip leaves completely. The caterpillars have pale green bodies with stripes along their sides, are up to 2.5cm (1in) long, and have black heads. When not feeding, they are often found inside tightly curled new leaves.
■ See **Winter moth** (p.341).

4 Leaves appear silvery

A silvery sheen develops on leaves, and shoots and branches may start to die back. If the problem is initially restricted to just one or two branches and if the wood is stained dark brown in the centre when you cut into it, suspect silver leaf. If the whole tree turns silver, then so-called false silver leaf, usually caused by lack of water, is more likely.
■ See **False silver leaf** (p.327) and **Silver leaf** (p.331).

5 Leaves wither and bark oozes gum

The symptoms of bacterial canker show in both leaves and bark. Leaves develop small brown spots with pale edges that turn into round holes. They may turn yellow and wither. Infected bark dies, and orange gum oozes from flat, sunken patches.
■ See **Bacterial canker** (p.324).

Leaves mottled and bronzed

If upper surfaces of leaves become mottled and discoloured, then begin to dry up and die, look underneath with a magnifying glass for tiny fruit tree red spider mites. In severe cases, you may also see fine silk webbing.
■ See **Red spider mite** (p.339).

Fruit

6 Ragged holes or splits in fruits

Birds, wasps, and flies find plums irresistible. The holes they create when feeding not only make the fruits unappetizing but also accelerate decay.
■ See **Birds** (p.335) and **Wasps** (p.341).

7 Small holes ringed with black "frass"

In the case of young fruits, a small hole surrounded by sticky black excrement called "frass" is a sure sign that the plum contains a plum sawfly grub. Cut the fruit open and you'll probably find a small white maggot with a brown head. Later in the summer, when the plums are more mature, the culprit may be the caterpillar of the plum fruit moth.
■ See **Plum sawfly** (p.338) and **Plum fruit moth** (p.338).

8 Fruits develop patches of brown rot

Brown rot is a fungus that commonly infects plums, usually via holes in the skins. The fruits turn brown and may develop concentric rings of white fungal spores. Plums either fall to the ground or remain on the tree in a shrivelled, mummified state.
■ See **Brown rot** (p.326).

Plums ripen unnaturally early

The pink caterpillars of the plum fruit moth hatch in midsummer, tunnel into the fruits, and eat the flesh around the stone. When full-grown, they burrow their way out leaving the centre of the plum full of excrement and an exit hole in the skin. The fruits ripen early and may rot.
■ See **Plum fruit moth** (p.338).

Shrivelled, hollow fruits

Deformed, hollow, green fruits without any stones may be the product of a fungal disease known as pocket plum. As the plums shrivel and dry out, they may be covered with white spots.
■ See **Pocket plum** (p.329).

Leathery patches on skin

Dark green or brown, dry, leathery patches or spots on the fruits, and sometimes on the leaves too, are a form of scab. The skin may split and gum may ooze out.
■ See **Scab** (p.330).

Cherries

It's only relatively recently that cherries have become easy to grow. A generation or so ago, they were a real challenge for home growers. The trees grew so large that picking the fruit required ladders. Pollination was hit-and-miss: even if spring frosts spared the fragile blossom, most varieties were not self-fertile and had to be planted alongside other, carefully selected, compatible trees. And, unless crops were protected with huge, unwieldy nets, birds would invariably strip the trees of all their fruit. Nowadays, most modern varieties are self-fertile, so a single tree can be grown on its own. And new dwarfing rootstocks mean that trees are much smaller – making them more practical for an average garden, easier to net against birds, and less difficult to harvest.

Cherries fall into two main categories: sweet varieties, which can be eaten raw; and acid varieties, which are too sour to be eaten without cooking. 'Morello' is the best known of the latter. In addition, there are duke cherries, which are a sour-sweet cross between the two.

The colour of cherries can vary. They're certainly not all red. Some are bright pink, others almost black. In addition, there are so-called white cherries, which are actually a pale yellow, sometimes flecked with orange.

Which forms to grow

■ **Bush** Stand-alone trees with an open centre. Beware: unless grown on dwarfing rootstocks, they are very large.
■ **Pyramid** Freestanding trees with a central leader.
■ **Minarette** A short, single, vertical stem, designed for close planting where space is restricted.
■ **Fan** A wire-trained form usually grown against a wall or fence.

Must-grow cherries

1 'Sweetheart'
Pollination group D
This is the one to choose for late-season cherries. Unlike most varieties, the dark red fruits ripen gradually, usually lasting until the end of August.
- **Fertility** self-fertile
- **Harvest** mid–late August

2 'Nabella'
Pollination group C
A recently introduced rival to the acid cherry 'Morello'. Bred in Germany, it is more compact but heavier cropping.
- **Fertility** self-fertile
- **Harvest** August

3 'Morello'
Pollination group D
The best-known and most commonly grown of the acid cherries. Ideal for cooking and preserving. It will tolerate cooler growing conditions and a shadier site than sweet varieties.
- **Fertility** self-fertile
- **Harvest** August–September

4 'Vega'
Pollination group B
An unusual, new variety with large, juicy, pale-yellow fruits. Birds don't seem to find these as appealing as red cherries.
- **Fertility** not self-fertile
- **Harvest** mid–late July

5 'Napoleon Bigarreau'
Pollination group C
Large, pale yellow fruits flushed or mottled with red. Other 'Bigarreau' varieties are similarly sweet-tasting.
- **Fertility** not self-fertile
- **Harvest** late July–early August

6 'Stella'
Pollination group C
A breakthrough variety when introduced in Canada in the 1960s – one of the first modern, self-fertile, sweet cherries that could be successfully grown on it own, without another pollinator. It produces large, dark-red, delicious fruits.
- **Fertility** self-fertile
- **Harvest** mid–late July

7 'May Duke'
Pollination group B
This is the one to choose if you want to grow a duke cherry. Its dark red fruits have more of a tang than sweet cherries.
■ **Fertility** partly self-fertile
■ **Harvest** mid-July

8 'Lapins'
Pollination group C
Also known as 'Cherokee', this late-season sweet cherry has large fruits that are almost black when ripe.
■ **Fertility** self-fertile
■ **Harvest** late July-early August

'Celeste' (not illustrated)
Pollination group C
A relatively modern sweet cherry, it has dark red, well-flavoured fruit. Trees tend to stay small, so work well in containers.
■ **Fertility** self-fertile
■ **Harvest** mid-July

'Merton Glory' (not illustrated)
Pollination group B
An early cropper bearing large, pale yellow-white fruits with a red flush and an excellent sweet flavour.
■ **Fertility** not self-fertile
■ **Harvest** late June–early July

'Penny' (not illustrated)
Pollination group C
A new variety that produces heavy crops of late-season fruits. Almost black when ripe, the cherries are particularly large.
■ **Fertility** not self-fertile
■ **Harvest** late July–early August

'Regina' (not illustrated)
Pollination group C
A hardy cherry with tasty fruits. It crops long after most other varieties are over.
■ **Fertility** not self-fertile
■ **Harvest** mid-August

'Summer Sun' (not illustrated)
Pollination group C
A modern, self-pollinating variety that is reliable and easy to grow, particularly in cooler regions. A heavy cropper.
■ **Fertility** self-fertile
■ **Harvest** mid-late July

'Sunburst' (not illustrated)
Pollination group C
The first black, self-fertile, sweet cherry, perfect for an average-sized garden.
■ **Fertility** self-fertile
■ **Harvest** early–mid July

Choosing and buying cherry trees

These days, most of the widely available cherries are self-pollinating. They are by far the easiest varieties to grow. By all means try one of the older, traditional varieties but bear in mind that they are unlikely to be self-fertile and must be planted with a compatible neighbour to ensure successful pollination. Cherries are naturally vigorous, so unless you have a sheltered site with plenty of space, you'll definitely need a tree that has been grafted onto a modern dwarfing rootstock.

CHOOSING A ROOTSTOCK

Most cherries sold today are grafted onto Colt or Gisela 5 rootstocks. Both have enabled the cultivation of small, manageable trees well suited to gardens and allotments

5m (15')
4m (12')
3m (10')
2m (6')
1m (3')

Colt   Gisela 5

Colt

- VIGOUR Semi-dwarfing.
- CHARACTERISTICS More vigorous than the recently introduced Gisela 5 but trees are still less than half the height they once were. A good choice for allotments and larger gardens.
- SUPPORT Stake or support permanently.
- FORMS Bush, pyramid, large fan.
- HEIGHT 4–5m (12–15ft).

Gisela 5

- VIGOUR Dwarfing.
- CHARACTERISTICS First developed in Germany, and now used widely around the world. Trees grown on Gisela 5 are small, fully hardy, heavy cropping, and easier to protect against frost, rain, and birds. They do, however, require good growing conditions.
- SUPPORT Stake or support permanently.
- FORMS Dwarf bush, dwarf pyramid, small fan, minarette.
- HEIGHT 2–3m (6–10ft).

Choosing a tree form

All sweet cherries need a sheltered, sunny site. If you can provide this, then consider a bush or a pyramid. If not, then you're likely to have more success with a fan trained against a sheltered wall or fence, or with dwarf varieties grown as minarettes or in containers. Acid cherries are less particular: they can even be grown as fans against north-facing walls or fences.

Choosing a variety

There is a wider choice of sweet cherry varieties than of acid. However, bear in mind that many sweet cherries are demanding: not only do they

Bees and other insects transfer pollen from tree to tree to ensure that fertilization takes place and fruits can form. They can only pollinate flowers, however, when those on neighbouring trees are also open. Cross-pollination won't take place between trees that flower early in the season and those that flower late.

CHERRY POLLINATION GROUPS

A

'Early Rivers'
'Mermat'
'Noir de Guben'

B

'Elton Heart'
'Governor Wood'
'Inga'
'May Duke'
'Merchant'
'Merton Favourite'
'Merton Glory'
'Roundel Heart'
'Starkrimson'
'Van'
'Vega'

C

'Amber Heart'
'Celeste'
'Hertford'
'Lapins/Cherokee'
'Merton Bigarreau'
'Merton Crane'
'Nabella'
'Bigarreau Napoléon'
'Penny'
'Regina'
'Roundel'
'Stella'
'Summer Sun'
'Sunburst'

D

'Bradbourne Black'
'Florence'
'Gaucher Bigarreau'
'Morello'
'Sweetheart'

Flowering time is the factor that determines which pollination group a particular cherry variety belongs to. Cherries in group A flower first in spring, and group D cherries flower last. Unless they are actually incompatible, all the cherries in one group should fertilize each other, since they are in flower at the same time, allowing insects to carry pollen from one to another. Because flowering times can overlap, they may even pollinate varieties in an adjacent pollination group.

'Van' is not self-fertile and needs another early-flowering partner from group B, but it is a good pollenizer for other varieties.

'Lapins' is self-fertile and doesn't need a partner itself but it is often used as a pollenizer for other cherries.

'Morello' like all acid cherries, is both self-fertile and a good late-flowering pollenizer for cherries that need a partner.

need a warmer site and better growing conditions, many are not self-fertile and need a compatible partner for successful pollination, particularly if they are heritage varieties. Almost all acid cherries are self-fertile and most can therefore be grown on their own if necessary. Sweet cherries will not pollinate acid cherries, and although acid cherries should in theory be able to pollinate sweet cherries, their blossom is unlikely to be open at the same time.

Choosing a pollination group

Although all cherries flower early in the spring, not all come into blossom at the same time. If you are growing trees that are not self-fertile and that need pollinating by one or more compatible neighbours, it's important to choose varieties from the same pollination group. If you do so, their flowers should open simultaneously, and insects will be able transfer pollen from one tree to another.

A few cherries, however, are incompatible and will not cross-fertilize. 'Merton Favourite' and 'Van,' for example, will simply not pollinate one another. Fortunately, incompatibility is less of an issue with modern, self-fertile cultivars, but if you plan to grow traditional varieties it is worth taking advice from a specialist nursery.

Growing cherries

Modern hardy, self-fertile varieties have made growing cherries easier than it has ever been. However, to fruit successfully, trees still require a sunny, sheltered site, and they still need protecting from frost, from birds, and even from rain when the cherries are ripening. There's a lot to be said, therefore, for growing a fan against a sheltered wall or fence, where it can be covered if necessary. Buying a pre-trained fan is worth the extra expense.

The year at a glance

	spring			summer			autumn			winter		
	M	A	M	J	J	A	S	O	N	D	J	F
plant bare-root	▬							▬	▬	▬	▬	▬
plant container	▬	▬	▬	▬	▬	▬	▬	▬	▬	▬	▬	▬
spring-prune	▬	▬	▬									
summer-prune				▬	▬	▬						
harvest				▬	▬	▬						

Choosing trees

Cherries are sold as either bare-root or container-grown trees. Buying a bare-root tree from a specialist nursery will give you a wider choice than buying a container-grown tree from a garden centre, but bare-root trees are available only in autumn and winter, between about October and March.

Fan-trained cherries grow particularly well against warm, sunny walls, which show off their decorative shape and form. You will get the best crops from trees in such protected spots.

PLANTING A CHERRY TREE

Prepare the site in advance, in early autumn if possible. Remove all perennial weeds, and work plenty of well-rotted compost or manure into the soil, adding some general, all-purpose fertilizer. Use stakes for stand-alone trees and a system of wire supports for fans.

1 Dig a hole deep and wide enough to accommodate the plant's roots. Check and ensure that the old nursery soil mark on the stem is level with the surface of your soil.

2 For a bare-root tree, drive a stake into the ground to a depth of 60cm (2ft), about 8cm (3in) away from the centre of the hole. For a container-grown tree, use a shorter stake, driven in at an angle, to avoid damaging the rootball (see p.35).

3 Set the tree in the hole, carefully spreading out the roots, and replace the soil around them.

4 Gently firm down the soil, ensuring there are no air pockets amongst the roots. Tread firmly, but don't stamp. Water generously.

5 Spread an organic mulch around the tree to help retain moisture and suppress weeds.

6 Secure the tree to its stake with special tree ties. You may need one at the top and one at the bottom.

7 Your tree now has everything it needs to develop a strong root system and healthy top growth.

Cherry blossom opens early in the year and is vulnerable to frosts. If cold nights are forecast, make sure you protect the fllowers with a covering of fine netting or fleece so you get a reasonable crop.

PLANTING DISTANCES

Recommended spacings vary according to the vigour of the rootstock and the variety, the soil and other growing conditions, and the form into which the tree is to be trained.

SWEET CHERRIES

Bushes
Gisela 5   3m (10ft)
Colt   5m (15ft)

Pyramids
Gisela 5   2.5m (8ft)
Colt   4–5m (12–15ft)

Fans
Gisela 5   5m (15ft)
Colt   5.5m (17ft)

Minarettes
60–75cm (24–30in)

ACID CHERRIES

Bushes
Gisela 5   3–4m (10–12ft)
Colt   4–5m (12–15ft)

Pyramids
Gisela 5   2.5–3m (8–10ft)
Colt   3–4m (10–12ft)

Fans
Gisela 5   4m (12ft)
Colt   5m (15ft)

Minarettes
60–75cm (24–30in)

When to plant
■ BARE-ROOT Plant November–March, when the trees are dormant, unless the soil is waterlogged or frozen. November is the ideal month.
■ CONTAINER-GROWN Plant at any time of year, although autumn is best. Avoid late spring and summer months if it is hot and dry.

Where to plant
Choose a warm, sunny, sheltered site where trees are protected from strong winds. Avoid frost pockets. A south- or west-facing wall is ideal for a sweet cherry fan. Acid varieties are less demanding; an acid fan should crop successfully even if grown against a north-facing wall.

Soil type
All cherries grow best in a deep, free-draining but moisture-retentive soil with a slightly acid pH of around 6.5. They dislike being waterlogged, and will struggle on shallow or sandy soils.

Growing in containers
Cherries can be grown in large pots or tubs, but bear in mind that they are naturally vigorous trees. Choose a self-fertile, compact variety on a dwarfing rootstock – and perhaps grow it as a single-column minarette. Start with a container that has a minimum diameter and depth of 45cm (18in) and fill it with multi-purpose, soil-based compost mixed with some sand or gravel to improve drainage. Cherries are hungrier than most container-grown trees, so feed with a high-potash fertilizer in spring, and keep the pot well-watered. After two years, repot the tree in a 60cm (24in) container.

Routine care

■ WATERING Water young, recently planted trees and wall-trained fans regularly, particularly in drought conditions. If you let them dry out then suddenly give them a soaking, the cherry skins are likely to split.

■ FEEDING Use a general compound fertilizer each February, before growth starts.

■ MULCHING In March, after feeding, remove any weeds, and spread an organic mulch around the base of young trees and fans.

■ THINNING Cherries do not need thinning.

■ NETTING Birds are a major problem, both in winter when they eat the new fruit buds and in summer as fruit ripens. Netting dwarf trees and fans is an absolute must.

■ FROST PROTECTION When in blossom, cover young trees, minarettes, and small fans overnight with fleece or fine netting.

Harvesting and storing

Leave cherries on the tree to ripen fully before picking – unless the skins start to split, in which case they should be harvested and eaten immediately. Cut them off with scissors or secateurs, leaving the stalks attached to the fruits.

Eat or cook cherries as soon as possible after picking, though they will keep for a day or two if washed, dried, and stored in the fridge. Red and black cherries can be frozen successfully, but white and yellow varieties may not keep their colour.

Yield

Yields are hard to quantify as they vary widely according to a host of variables, including how successful you are at preventing birds from taking the fruit. However, average quantities you can expect from mature, manageable-sized trees are:

■ BUSH sweet 15–40kg (33–90lb), acid 15–20kg (33–45lb).

■ PYRAMID sweet 15–25kg (33–55lb), acid 15–20kg (33–45lb).

■ FAN 5–15kg (11–33lb).

■ MINARETTE 2.5–7 kg (5.5–15lb).

(below left to right) **Netting** is the only way to stop hungry birds from decimating your crop. **Pick ripe cherries** by cutting them from the tree with their stalks intact. Leaving the stalks behind can cause disease.

Month by month

January
■ If necessary, spray trees with a winter wash to protect against aphids, winter moths, and other pests.

February
■ Apply a general compound fertilizer around existing trees this month or next.

March
■ Last chance to plant bare-root trees.
■ Weed and then mulch around trees after feeding.
■ Start spring pruning once trees are no longer dormant.

April
■ Most cherries flower this month. Protect blossom against frost if possible.

May
■ Keep newly planted and wire-trained trees regularly watered.

June
■ Summer-prune cherry fans this month or next, tying in new replacement shoots and cutting back unwanted growth.
■ Net trees against birds.
■ Harvest early-season cherries towards the end of the month.

July
■ The prime month for harvesting sweet cherries.

August
■ Most acid cherries will be ready for picking this month or next.
■ After harvesting, summer-prune a second time to reduce congestion, remove some of the wood that has just fruited, and cut back shoots that have regrown over the summer.
■ Remove and destroy any remaining fruit infected with brown rot.

September
■ Last chance for pruning before trees enter their dormant period and the risk of disease returns.

October
■ New bare-root trees start to become available from specialist nurseries. Plant between now and February.
■ Tie sticky grease bands around trunks as a defence against winter moths.

November
■ Buy and plant new trees. November is the best month for planting both bare-root and container-grown trees.
■ Rake up and destroy any diseased leaves.

Pruning and training cherries

Sweet and acid cherries produce fruit quite differently so need different pruning regimes. Sweet cherries fruit at the base of last year's new growth, and mostly on stems and branches that are two or more years old, whereas acid cherries fruit only on shoots and stems that grew the previous year. Don't prune either sweet or acid cherries in winter or you'll risk infection from silver leaf disease (see p.331) and bacterial canker (see p.324). Wait until spring or summer, when the trees are in growth and their sap is flowing.

(left to right)
Acid cherries bear fruit along much of the length of one-year-old stems. **Sweet cherries** fruit in clusters at the base of one-year-old stems as well as on older wood.

Pruning a sweet cherry bush or pyramid

Training and pruning is the same as for a plum (see pp.114–15). Aim for an open-centred bush with a balanced framework of main branches, or a well-formed conical pyramid. Once the tree is established, very little pruning should be necessary. In April or May, cut out any dead, damaged, or diseased wood, and thin out any overly congested areas.

Pruning an acid cherry bush or pyramid

Initial training and pruning of a young tree is the same as for a plum (see pp.114–15). However, after three or four years, when the basic shape has been established, it can be treated more like a peach (see p.156). Both acid cherries and peaches fruit solely on new growth from the previous year, so aim to remove old wood that will no longer fruit. This will encourage new shoots on which cherries will be borne the year after. Prune twice a year: once in March, to reduce congestion and to cut longer, older branches back to young sideshoots or growth buds, and again in summer, after picking your crop.

Summer pruning an established acid cherry tree
AUGUST

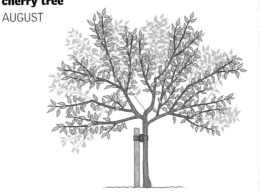

■ After harvesting, prune up to one-quarter of the shoots that have just fruited this year. Cut each right back to a new, lower sideshoot so that next year's fruit is borne closer to the centre of the tree.

■ Cut out any dead, damaged, or diseased wood.

■ Thin out a few old laterals and sub-laterals that no longer bear fruit, especially if the tree is overcrowded.

Pruning a sweet cherry fan

Grow against a south- or southwest-facing wall or fence. Allow a space 4m (12ft) wide and 2m (6ft) high for a small fan, more for a vigorous variety grown on Colt rootstock. Start with a suitable feathered maiden or a two- or three-year-old pre-trained fan, and train and prune the tree as you would a plum fan (see pp.116–17).

Once the fan is about four years old and its basic framework is established, carry out regular pruning, perhaps as often as three times a year: once in March or April to remove unwanted new growth, again in June or early July to shorten new shoots, and finally in September to prune back additional growth it has put on during the summer.

- Remove any new growth that is projecting directly out from or back into the wall.
- Cut out any dead, damaged, or diseased wood.
- Prune back to new sideshoots any older branches that are growing too tall or that are getting overcrowded.

Spring pruning an established sweet cherry fan
MARCH–APRIL

(right, top to bottom) **In spring,** as soon as new growth starts, it is inevitable that a number of vigorous new shoots will start to grow directly out from the wall or fence, seeking the light. Prune them back immediately. If you don't, they will give the fan a shaggy, unkempt look and cast shade over the fruit developing beneath them.

(far left to right) **Dead or damaged** stems are not only unsightly but also pose a potential risk. They are prone to disease, which may then spread and infect otherwise healthy wood. Cut them out completely.

Summer pruning an established sweet cherry fan
JUNE–JULY then again in SEPTEMBER

- Select new laterals to fill out any gaps in the framework of the fan and tie them in.
- Prune other sideshoots back to 5–6 leaves beyond the basal cluster.
- Cut back to sideshoots any vigorous vertical growth, or bend and tie them down horizontally.
- In September, after harvesting, cut back to just 3 leaves all the sideshoots you pruned to 5–6 leaves in midsummer. This should help produce fruit buds next year.

(right, top to bottom) **Tie in** the new shoots on the fan that you want to keep, and prune back those you don't.

Pruning an acid cherry fan

Plant, train, and prune an acid cherry fan in almost exactly the same way as a peach fan (see p.153). Once it has become established, prune it twice a year. In late March or April remove old wood to stimulate new growth, and cut back any awkward, outward- or inward-pointing shoots. The second pruning is carried out in August or September, after the fruit has been picked: to tidy things up and to prune back this year's stems – they have now fruited and will not do so again.

In the early years, concentrate on developing strong laterals that will form the main ribs of the fan. Don't worry if there is an empty space in the middle: the tree will naturally fill that in later on.

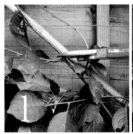

Summer pruning an established acid cherry fan
AUGUST–SEPTEMBER

1 Cut back stems that have fruited this year to a lower replacement sideshoot. It will form the stem that fruits next year.

2 Spread out replacement shoots so that they fill any gaps in the framework of the fan and tie them in to the canes or wires.

3 Remove any new growth that is congested, crossing or growing directly outwards. This will help keep the fan flat against the wall.

What can go wrong

Buds and blossom

Blossom discolours and dies
Cherries flower early in spring and frosts often damage young leaves and blossom.
■ See **Frost** (p.316).

Blossom turns brown and wilts
First the flowers and then young leaves turn brown, wither, and die. The cause is most likely to be the same fungus responsible for brown rot.
■ See **Blossom wilt** (p.325) and **Brown rot** (p.326).

New buds eaten by birds
Birds damage or strip new buds in winter and early spring, returning in summer to take the fruit.
■ See **Birds** (p.335).

Leaves, stems, and branches

1 **Young leaves curled, distorted, and sticky**
A species of aphid called cherry blackfly causes new leaves to curl tightly and become distorted. Their upper surfaces are sticky with the honeydew that the insects excrete and may develop a grey sooty mould. Heavy infestations damage new shoots.
■ See **Aphids** (p.334).

2 **Small brown spots or holes appear on leaves**
Leaves develop small brown spots with pale edges that can turn into round, so-called "shot-holes". Foliage may turn yellow and wither. Various fungal infections may be responsible, or possibly bacterial canker if bark also dies and orange gum oozes from flat, sunken patches.
■ See **Bacterial canker** (p.324), **Fungal leaf spot** (p.327), **Shot-hole disease** (p.330).

3 **Irregular holes eaten in leaves**
The most likely cause of the damage is moth caterpillars feeding on the foliage. Some species spin silk webs and curl the leaves around themselves.
■ See **Winter moth** (p.341).

4 **Yellow leaves with green veins**
Yellowing of leaves between the veins may indicate lack of the nutrients iron or manganese ("lime-induced chlorosis"), or magnesium.
■ See **Iron deficiency** (p.320), **Manganese deficiency** (p.321), **Magnesium deficiency** (p.321).

5 **Looping, meandering lines on leaves**
These yellow-brown, scribble-like markings are caused

1

2

3

4

5

by tiny caterpillars feeding inside the leaves, tunnelling "mines" through the plant tissue as they eat.
■ See **Apple leaf miner** (p.334).

6 Bark or stems ooze gum
Orange resin or gum oozing from twigs or branches is not unusual in cherries. It can be a symptom of injury to the tree or of poor growing conditions. More seriously, it may be an indication of bacterial canker.
■ See **Bacterial canker** (p.324).

Leaves appear silvery
A silvery sheen develops on leaves, and shoots and branches may then start to die back. If the problem is localized it could be silver leaf. If it affects the whole tree, then it may be so-called false silver leaf.
■ See **False silver leaf** (p.327) and **Silver leaf** (p.331).

Leaves wither and die but do not fall
Leaf scorch is a fungus that causes leaves to turn brown and die. In winter, they hang on the tree without falling.
■ See **Cherry leaf scorch** (p.326).

Small black slugs on leaves
Actually, these are not black slugs at all, but yellow sawfly larvae that cover themselves in slimy black mucus. They are unsightly but rarely very harmful.
■ See **Slugworm** (p.340).

Fruit

7 Ragged holes eaten in fruits
Wasps and flies feed on ripe fruits, particularly if the skin has already been holed or damaged. Birds are even more voracious and can strip a tree of the whole crop.
■ See **Birds** (p.335) and **Wasps** (p.341).

8 Fruits develop patches of brown rot
Ripening fruits turn brown and may develop concentric rings of white or cream fungal spots, sometimes around a central hole. They either fall to the ground or remain on the tree, gradually withering and becoming mummified.
■ See **Brown rot** (p.326).

Splits in skins of fruits
A common problem but not one that can be blamed on a pest or disease. Rather, it is caused by sudden heavy rainfall or irregular watering, which causes the flesh of ripening cherries to swell after their skins have stopped growing.
■ See **Routine care** (p.129).

Apricots

Apricots have much in common with peaches and nectarines: they are equally succulent, juicy, and wonderful to eat, but also equally difficult to grow successfully in cool temperate climates. Apricots are, on the whole, very hardy and happily survive cold winters, but they flower very early in spring – so early that frost damage is almost inevitable, unless you can offer them protection. That's why they are so often grown as wall-trained fans, in containers, or in glasshouses or polytunnels. However, in recent years, a number of new cool-climate varieties have come onto the market, increasing the chances of success. Bred in North America and in France, they flower later and more abundantly than traditional varieties, thus reducing the risk of frost damage and increasing the likelihood of fruit forming and setting. If you plant one, you'll still need to choose your site carefully and you'll still be dependent on a long, hot summer for the fruit to ripen fully, but it's certainly worth a try.

Apricots are tough plants but will only produce a decent crop in cool regions if you grow them against a warm wall. They don't keep particularly well, so eat them fresh or preserve them soon after picking. 'Flavorcot' (shown here) is a reliable late-summer variety.

Which forms to grow

■ **Bushes and pyramids** Suitable only for warm climates unless you grow a dwarf variety in a container.
■ **Fan** Grow against a sheltered, sunny wall – the best choice for temperate climates.

Must-grow apricots

1 'Alfred'
A reliable, well-established variety with lovely orange flesh. Fruits are sweet, juicy, and medium-sized. Thin them out or the tree may bear fruit only every other year.
■ **Harvest** late July–early August

2 'Tomcot'
This is a French-bred variety that grows well in cooler climates. It, too, flowers later and produces more blossom than most other apricots. Fruits have an excellent flavour, a lovely colour, and can grow very large indeed.
■ **Harvest** late July–early August

3 'Petit Muscat'
As its name suggests, a variety that produces clusters or bunches of small but intensely flavoured fruits with very small stones.
■ **Harvest** August

4 'Moorpark'
This old, long-established variety is still popular and widely grown. Its large, juicy, orange-red fruits ripen later than many. The closely related 'Early Moorpark' is similar, but crops earlier.
■ **Harvest** late August

5 'Flavorcot'
Like 'Tomcot', this is another modern variety bred for cooler climates. It flowers quite late and produces a lot of blossom, thus increasing the likelihood of a good crop. The large fruits have an excellent flavour.
■ **Harvest** late July–early August

'Gold Cott' (not illustrated)
A North American variety, this golden yellow apricot is also suited to cool temperate regions. The fruits store very well in the fridge.
■ **Harvest** August

'New Large Early' (not illustrated)
This 19th-century variety is an early apricot with a good flavour. The large, oval fruits have thin, pale-yellow skin.
■ **Harvest** July

Growing apricots

Apricots are not hard to grow. In many ways they are easier than peaches and nectarines, as they seem less prone to pests and diseases – peach leaf curl, for example, rarely affects them. Probably, the two key requirements are these: first, a sunny, sheltered site; and, second, protection from frost in the spring. Neither is difficult to provide if apricots are grown as small, wall-trained fans or in containers, but may be less practical in the case of large, freestanding trees.

The year at a glance

	spring			summer			autumn			winter		
	M	A	M	J	J	A	S	O	N	D	J	F
plant bare-root								▬	▬	▬		
plant container	▬	▬	▬					▬	▬	▬	▬	▬
spring-prune	▬	▬	▬							▬	▬	▬
summer-prune				▬	▬	▬						
harvest					▬	▬						

When to plant
■ BARE-ROOT Plant November–February, when the trees are dormant, unless the soil is waterlogged or frozen. November is the ideal month.
■ CONTAINER-GROWN In theory, you may plant at any time of year, although autumn is best. Avoid late spring and summer months if it is hot and dry.

Flowering and pollination
Apricots flower very early in the year – usually even earlier than peaches and nectarines – so protection against frost is essential, and hand pollination is advisable (see p.148). However, the trees are self-fertile, so a single tree can be planted on its own and will bear fruit.

Protecting early-spring blossom
Vulnerable flowers must be protected from frost by covering them overnight with fleece, hessian, or a plastic sheet. Remove it during the day, or leave it open at the sides to give access to any pollinating insects that may be about early in the season.

Choosing trees
Young trees are sold either bare-root or container-grown. Bare-root trees are generally available only in autumn and winter, but container-grown trees can be bought virtually all year round. Most trees on sale have been grafted onto the semi-vigorous St Julien A or Torinel rootstocks, or onto the semi-dwarfing Pixy.

Protect delicate apricot blossom from frost and rain with some kind of covering. This purpose-built frame around wall-trained apricots is draped with waterproof sheeting. The sides have been left open to allow pollinating insects to fly in.

Leave apricots to ripen on the tree for as long as possible. Pick them when they are slightly soft and at their sweetest, and if possible eat them immediately.

Where to plant

Freestanding bushes and pyramids need a sunny, sheltered site. A sloping hillside may be suitable as long as it is well above a low-lying frost pocket. Otherwise, in cool temperate climates, train a fan against a south- or southwest-facing fence or wall, plant in containers, or grow under glass.

Soil type

Apricots like a deep, fertile, free-draining soil with a neutral or slightly alkaline pH of 6.7–7.5. Sandy or chalky soils are not suitable unless they have been enriched with organic matter.

How to plant

A month or two in advance of planting, dig in plenty of well-rotted compost or manure. Before planting a fan, attach horizontal wires to your wall or fence about 30cm (12in) apart. Plant new trees so that the old nursery soil mark is level with the surface of your soil.

Planting distances

- BUSHES 3–5.5m (10–17ft) apart.
- FANS 4–5m (12–16ft) apart.

Growing in containers

A number of different dwarf varieties are available as compact, patio trees for growing in containers. Use a loam-based compost mixed with some sand or gravel to improve drainage. Feed with a general liquid fertilizer in spring and summer, and keep the pot well-watered. Once a year, top-dress with fresh soil, and every two years pot on into a larger container. In late winter and spring, bring the trees under cover to protect them against frost, and in summer, move them to a warm, sunny spot so that the fruit will ripen fully.

Routine care

- FROST PROTECTION Outdoor trees need covering overnight to protect blossom from frost damage.
WATERING Water regularly during spring and summer, particularly newly planted young trees and wall-trained fans.
- FEEDING Each February feed with a general compound fertilizer.
- MULCHING In March, after feeding, weed thoroughly and mulch around the base of the tree.
- THINNING FRUIT In a good year, when the crop is heavy, thin fruits to leave about 8–10cm (3–4in) between each one. Remove any diseased or damaged fruits first.
- NETTING Birds can be a problem in summer as fruits ripen. If necessary, net fans and trees grown in containers. In the case of large trees, where all-over netting may not be practical, it may be possible to net individual fruit clusters.

Harvesting and storing

In most places, apricots are harvested in July or August. When they start to soften, test to see if they are ready. Cup one in your hand and give it a gentle twist. If it pulls away easily, leaving the stalk behind, it is ripe. Apricots will keep for a day or two if kept somewhere cool, but they are best eaten soon after picking. If you want to store them for longer you must remove the stones and bottle or freeze them.

Yield

Yields are hard to quantify as they vary from tree to tree and from year to year. However, average quantities you can expect are:
- BUSH 10–25kg (22–55lb).
- FAN 7–15kg (15–33lb).

Month by month

February
- Last chance to plant bare-root trees.
- In a warm spring, buds may start to burst by the end of the month.
- Bring container-grown trees indoors under cover.
- Prune newly planted and young fan-trained trees this month or next.
- Apply a general compound fertilizer around existing trees.

March
- Blossom opens. Protect against frost and hand pollinate if necessary.
- Weed and mulch around trees.

April
- Spring-prune established fans this month and next.
- As fruitlets form, begin thinning them out.

May
- Weed and water regularly.
- Give trees a liquid feed while fruits are developing between now and August.

June
- Finish thinning out young fruitlets.
- On young, fan-trained trees, start tying in new sideshoots and cutting back unwanted growth.
- On established bush trees, cut out old, unproductive branches and remove some of the shoots that fruited last year.

July
- Early-season varieties are ready to harvest.

August
- Harvest mid- and late-season varieties.
- After harvesting, summer-prune established fan-trained trees.

September
- Complete all pruning before the dormant period begins.

November
- This is the best month to buy and plant bare-root trees: the soil is still warm and trees have a chance to get established before they start into growth next February.

(top to bottom) **Flower buds** may break in late winter. **Foliage** begins to unfurl as the blossom fades. **Fruits** need plenty of warmth and sunshine in order to ripen fully.

Pruning and training apricots

Apricots are like peaches, plums, cherries, and all other stone fruit: they should be pruned in spring or summer, not in winter when they are dormant. In winter they are most at risk of infection from silver-leaf disease (see p.331) and bacterial canker (see p.324), which enter through pruning cuts. When their sap is flowing, they are more resistant. Rather like plums, apricots bear fruit both on shoots and stems that grew last year, and on clusters of older fruiting spurs.

Pruning an apricot bush or pyramid
Prune and train bushes and pyramids in the same way as a plum (see p.114). With a bush form, aim for an open centre with a balanced framework of well-spaced, uncrowded branches. With a pyramid, aim for a tapering, conical shape that allows light to reach all the branches of the tree. Once trees are established, prune them once a year in early summer.

Pruning an apricot fan
A newly planted fan is trained and pruned in the same way as a peach fan (see pp.152–53). Slightly shorten the leaders of the main ribs in February or March, and then either thin out, cut back, or tie in new growth between June and September. Once the fan is established, prune it as you would a plum (see p.117).

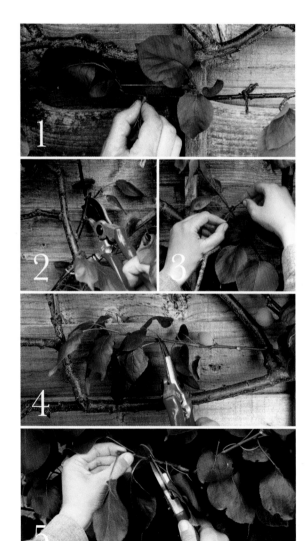

1 In spring, pinch out overcrowded new shoots. There should be a minimum of 10cm (4in) between them.

2 Prune out completely any new shoots growing downwards, directly into the wall, or straight out towards you from the fan.

3 Select new shoots that you want to keep for future growth, and tie them in so that they fill in any gaps.

4 In early summer, shorten shoots that you don't want to grow on. Cut them back so that just 5 or 6 leaves remain beyond the basal cluster.

5 After harvesting, cut back to 3 leaves the shoots you pruned to 5 or 6 leaves earlier in the summer. Cut back to just 1 leaf any new sideshoots that have grown from them.

What can go wrong

Buds and blossom

Blossom discolours and dies
Apricots flower earlier in the year than almost any other fruit tree, and are therefore extremely prone to frost damage.
■ See **Frost** (p.316).

Blossom turns brown and wilts
First the flowers and then young leaves turn brown and wither. Blossom wilt is caused by a fungus very closely related to the one responsible for brown rot.
■ See **Blossom wilt** (p.325) and **Brown rot** (p.326).

Leaves, stems, and branches

1 Leaves and stems wither, then turn brown
Dieback is quite common on apricots. Young shoots, leaves, and stems wilt, turn brown, and die. The cause is usually a fungus, though it can be made worse if the tree is already under stress – due to frost damage or lack of water or nutrients, for example.
■ See **Dieback** (p.326).

2 Small spots and holes appear in leaves
Leaves develop small brown spots with pale edges that turn into round, so-called "shot-holes". Foliage may turn yellow and wither. Various fungal infections may be responsible, or possibly bacterial canker if bark also dies and orange gum oozes from flat, sunken patches.
■ See **Bacterial canker** (p.324) and **Shot-hole disease** (p.330).

Leaves are curled and yellow-green
Aphids feeding on sap on the undersides of leaves cause them to curl up and become misshapen. Foliage may be sticky with honeydew, too.
■ See **Aphids** (p.334).

Leaves mottled and bronzed
Upper surfaces of leaves becoming speckled or mottled with pale yellow-bronze spots, then beginning to dry up and die, may indicate attack by red spider mites. In severe cases, you may also see fine silk webbing.
■ See **Red spider mite** (p.339).

Leaves appear silvery
A silvery sheen develops on leaves, and shoots and branches may start to die back. If the problem is localized it could be silver leaf. If it affects the whole tree, then it may be so-called false silver leaf.
■ See **False silver leaf** (p.327) and **Silver leaf** (p.331).

Small, brown, shell-like insects on stems
Scale insects – sometimes called brown scale – may be found on stems and branches, especially on plants grown under glass. They are elliptical in shape and covered with a domed shell.
■ See **Scale insects** (p.339).

Fruit

3 Red-brown spots on fruits
A measles-like rash of spots, especially when coupled with leaves that are tattered with holes, may indicate shot-hole disease.
■ See **Shot-hole disease** (p.330).

4 Ragged holes in fruits
Birds, wasps, flies, and other insects feed on ripening fruits. They either make holes in the skin or aggravate existing ones. The damage they cause will accelerate rot and decay.
■ See **Birds** (p.335) and **Wasps** (p.341).

Fruits develop patches of brown rot
Brown rot is a fungus that may infect fruits via a hole in the skin. The fruits turn brown and may develop concentric rings of white fungal spores.
■ See **Brown rot** (p.326).

Peaches and nectarines

Peaches are thought to originate from ancient China. Confucius wrote about them in the 1st century BC, and they appear in drawings hundreds of years before that. The Greeks and Roman grew and ate them. However, it wasn't until the 16th century that they spread to northwest Europe, and cultivation was even later in North America, during the 17th century. Smooth-skinned nectarines, which have a similar flavour, are thought to be an accidental mutation or "sport" of the peach.

In cool temperate climates, growing peaches and nectarines can be a challenge. Surprisingly, it's not the cold winters that are the problem, though. The trees are fairly hardy, and do, in fact, need a cold spell during the months when they are dormant in order to spur them into fruiting successfully. Spring frosts are the principal cause of much trouble, damaging the fragile, early blossom. Also, the lack of sufficient heat and sunshine in summer can often result in the fruits not ripening fully. In warm, sunny areas with reliably hot summers you should have no trouble. Elsewhere, be prepared to grow them against a sheltered, south-facing wall, in containers, or under glass.

Growing perfectly ripe peaches
outdoors relies on good summers and a very sheltered site. Nectarines require similar conditions. If you can't provide them, try growing compact varieties of both in pots, moving them into the warmest, sunniest position when they are most in need of heat and sunshine.

Which forms to grow

■ **Bushes and pyramids** Attempt only in warm climates unless growing a dwarf variety in a container.

■ **Fan** A fan-trained tree grown against a sheltered, sunny wall is the best choice for temperate climates.

Must-grow peaches and nectarines

1 'Fantasia'
Nectarine
Easy to grow, resistant to frost and canker. The large, yellow-fleshed fruits have a good flavour.
■ **Harvest** August

2 'Garden Lady'
Peach
A specially bred dwarf variety that produces a compact tree ideal for growing in containers.
■ **Harvest** July–August

3 'Bonanza'
Peach
A dwarf variety originally bred in California, specifically for growing in containers. Good choice for a sunny patio, terrace, or balcony.
■ **Harvest** August

4 'Duke of York'
Peach
An early-cropping variety that is reliable and widely grown. Large, delicious, yellow-fleshed fruit.
■ **Harvest** July

5 'Red Haven'
Peach
A vigorous, heavy-cropping variety that is well-suited to fan-training. Fruits have firm yellow flesh with a fine flavour. Some resistance to peach leaf curl.
■ **Harvest** August

6 'Lord Napier'
Nectarine
Perhaps the best-known and most widely grown nectarine in temperate regions. Given the right conditions, it bears large, juicy, white-fleshed fruits.
■ **Harvest** August

7 'Peregrine'
Peach
One of the best peaches for temperate climates. Reliable, heavy cropping, white-fleshed fruits with excellent flavour.
■ **Harvest** August

8 'Hale's Early'
Peach

An early variety that may be ready for picking as soon as mid-July. Fruits are a very pale yellow, with red markings when ripe. In a good year, crops can be so heavy that thinning the fruit is vital.
■ **Harvest** July

'Avalon Pride' (not illustrated)
Peach

A modern variety with resistance to peach leaf curl. Discovered by chance as a seedling in Washington State, USA. Sweet, juicy, yellow flesh.
■ **Harvest** August

'Early Rivers' (not illustrated)
Nectarine

Worth searching out from specialist suppliers as this is one of the first nectarines to ripen: fruit may be ready to harvest by mid- or late July. Generally produces good crops with pale yellow-red skin and juicy, yellow flesh.
■ **Harvest** July

'Nectarella' (not illustrated)
Nectarine

A dwarf variety that is easy to grow and unlikely to grow taller than about 1.5m (5ft). For planting outdoors or in a container. Produces heavy crops of large, tasty fruits.
■ **Harvest** August

'Pineapple' (not illustrated)
Nectarine

Outstanding flavour, but because it doesn't ripen until late in the season it needs a very good summer. Alternatively, grow it under glass.
■ **Harvest** early September

'Redwing' (not illustrated)
Peach

Large fruits turn a deep red as they ripen and develop a sweet, juicy flavour. 'Redwing' comes into blossom late and is therefore less prone to frost damage. A good choice for northern regions.
■ **Harvest** August

'Rochester' (not illustrated)
Peach

One of the best and least troublesome peaches for growing outdoors in temperate climates. What it lacks in flavour it makes up for in dependability.
■ **Harvest** August

'Saturne' (not illustrated)
Peach

An unusual flat peach that originates from China. Excellent, sweet, honeyed flavour. Resistant to frost but needs a warm, sunny site to ripen fully.
■ **Harvest** August

Growing peaches and nectarines

Of the two, peaches are slightly easier to grow, and crop more heavily than nectarines – in cool temperate regions, at least. However, they both need warmth, sunshine, and protection from wind. If you can't provide this, don't attempt a freestanding tree. Instead opt for a wall-trained fan or grow in containers or under cover.

The year at a glance

	spring			summer			autumn			winter		
	M	A	M	J	J	A	S	O	N	D	J	F
plant bare-root									▬	▬	▬	▬
plant container	▬	▬	▬	▬				▬	▬	▬	▬	▬
spring-prune	▬	▬	▬									▬
summer-prune					▬	▬	▬					
harvest					▬	▬	▬	▬				

Flowering and pollination

Peaches and nectarines are self-fertile, which means that a single tree planted on its own should pollinate itself and not require pollen from neighbours. However, the blossom opens early in the year when it may still be too cold for many insects to be active. Hand pollination may be necessary.

Choosing trees

Young trees are sold as either bare-root or container-grown. Bare-root trees are generally available only in autumn and winter, whereas container-grown trees can be bought all year round. Most trees are sold grafted onto semi-vigorous St Julien A rootstocks, as are many plums.

When to plant

■ BARE-ROOT Plant November–February, when the trees are dormant, unless the soil is waterlogged or frozen. November is the ideal month.
■ CONTAINER-GROWN In theory, you may plant at any time of year, although autumn is best. Avoid late spring and summer months if it is hot and dry.

Where to plant

Choose a warm, sunny, sheltered site where trees are protected from strong winds. In cool temperate climates, grow a fan against a south- or southwest-facing fence or wall. Avoid frost pockets. Otherwise, grow in containers or under glass.

Soil type

Peaches and nectarines need a deep, fertile, free-draining soil with a slightly acid pH of 6.5–7.0. Like most fruit trees, they dislike being waterlogged.

How to plant

Prepare the site a month or two in advance by digging in plenty of well-rotted compost or manure.

Hand pollinate peaches if there are no insects around in the garden. Use a small, soft brush to transfer pollen carefully from one flower to another.

(left to right) **Spring blossom opens** very early – sometimes at the end of February or the beginning of March. Grown outdoors, both peaches and nectarines are likely to need protection against frost damage at flowering time. **A plastic rain cover** over a peach fan may be unattractive, but without it there is a high chance of infection from rain-borne peach leaf curl (see p.328).

Before planting a fan, attach horizontal wires to your wall or fence about 30cm (12in) apart. Plant new trees so that the old nursery soil mark on the stem is level with the surface of your soil.

Planting distances
■ BUSHES and PYRAMIDS 5–6m (16–20ft) apart.
■ FANS 4–5m (12–16ft) apart.

Growing in containers
Compact dwarf varieties are available that are ideal for container growing, and there are distinct advantages to growing peaches and nectarines in pots. Most importantly, containers are mobile so you can bring them indoors under cover to protect against frost and against peach leaf curl. You can also move them into the warmest, sunniest part of your garden or patio when the fruit is ripening.

Start off young trees in small containers with a diameter of 38–45cm (15–18in), filled with loam-based compost mixed with a little sand or gravel to improve drainage. Feed with a high-potash fertilizer in spring and summer, and keep the pot well-watered. Once a year, top-dress with fresh soil, and every two years pot on to a larger container.

Growing under glass
In cool, temperate climates, summers may not be warm enough to guarantee that peaches and nectarines ripen properly when grown outdoors. Instead, there is a long tradition of growing them under glass – admittedly, most often in the large glasshouses of kitchen gardens that were once attached to grand country houses. If you plan to grow peaches or nectarines in a greenhouse, it should be unheated – the trees require a cold spell during their dormant period. They need rich, fertile soil, plentiful watering, and high humidity, both before and after the period when they are in flower. Blossom may need hand pollinating.

Routine care
■ WATERING Water regularly throughout the spring and summer, particularly wall-trained fans, which are prone to drying out.

■ FEEDING Each February, just before growth starts, apply a general compound fertilizer to maintain nutrient levels. Between May and August, while fruits are developing, water trees with a diluted, high-potassium tomato fertilizer or similar liquid feed.

■ MULCHING In March, after feeding, remove any weeds and mulch around the base of your trees.

■ NETTING Birds can be a problem in summer as fruit ripens. Netting large trees may not be practical, but it's easier in the case of fans.

■ FROST PROTECTION Outdoor trees need covering with fleece overnight in spring to protect blossom from frost damage.

■ RAIN PROTECTION A plastic cover to keep rain

(left to right) **Thinning peaches** and nectarines to give them space to grow is done in two stages: usually in April and June. At the first stage, thin each fruit cluster to a single peach. At the second, remove remaining fruits that are still too close together.

off buds and flowers between December and May helps reduce the risk of peach leaf curl (see p.328).

Thinning peaches

Both peaches and nectarines must be thinned, or the tree will be overburdened and fruit won't grow to its full size. Thin once, to one fruit per cluster, when they are very small, and space them out again when they are larger. Peaches should be 20–25cm (8–10in) apart, and nectarines 15cm (6in) apart.

Harvesting and storing

Fruits are ready for picking when they become slightly soft at the top, around the stalk. Cup them in your hand and give them a gentle twist. If they don't come away easily, leave them a little longer. Kept somewhere cool, peaches and nectarines will last for a few days, but if you want to store them for longer you must remove the stones and bottle or freeze them.

Yield

Yields are hard to quantify as they vary from tree to tree and from year to year. However, average quantities you can expect are:

■ BUSH 14–27kg (30–60lb).
■ FAN 4.5–11kg (10–25lb).

Give peaches plenty of room by thinning them out when they are still small, as early as April if fruitlets have already formed. The fewer there are the larger they will grow.

Month by month

January
■ Spray trees with copper fungicide to reduce the risk of peach leaf curl.

February
■ Last chance to plant bare-root trees, as they are now coming out of their dormant period.
■ In a warm spring, buds may start to burst by the end of the month.
■ Bring container-grown trees indoors under cover.
■ Prune newly planted and young fan-trained trees this month or next.
■ Apply a general compound fertilizer around existing trees.

March
■ Blossom opens. Protect against frost and hand pollinate if necessary.
■ Weed and mulch around trees.

April
■ Spring-prune established fans this month and next.
■ As fruitlets form and begin to swell, start thinning them out.

May
■ Weed and water regularly.
■ Give trees a liquid feed while fruits are developing, between now and August.

June
■ Finish thinning out young fruitlets.
■ On young, fan-trained trees, start tying in new sideshoots and cutting back unwanted growth.
■ On established bush trees, cut out old, unproductive branches and remove some of the shoots that fruited last year.

July
■ Early-season varieties are ready to harvest.

August
■ Harvest mid- and late-season varieties.
■ After harvesting, summer-prune established fan-trained trees.

September
■ Complete all pruning before the dormant period begins.

November
■ This is the best month to buy and plant bare-root trees: the soil is still warm and trees have a chance to get established before growth starts next February.

December
■ Put up plastic rain covers to protect against peach leaf curl.

(top to bottom) **In warm springs,** buds are ready to burst in late February. **Blossom** may need hand-pollinating. **Fruitlets** on a nectarine fan have been thinned to one per cluster. **Nectarines** should be ripe enough for picking by mid- or late summer.

Pruning and training peaches and nectarines

Don't prune in winter or you'll risk infection from silver leaf (see p.331) and bacterial canker (see p.324). As with plums, cherries, and other stone fruit, wait until spring when new growth has begun. Peaches and nectarines both fruit only on shoots and stems that grew last year, so the aim of all pruning is to remove some of the old growth on which fruit has already been borne and encourage the tree to produce new growth that will fruit the following year.

For successful cropping, give peaches plenty of room by thinning them out when they are still small – as early as April if fruitlets have already formed. The fewer there are on the stem, the larger they will grow.

Pruning a fan

Grow against a south- or southwest-facing wall or fence. Allow a space 4m (12ft) wide and 2m (6ft) high. Either start with a suitable feathered maiden or pay a little more and buy a two- or three-year-old pre-trained fan. The latter will give you a head start in getting the tree established.

1st spring pruning

FEBRUARY–MARCH

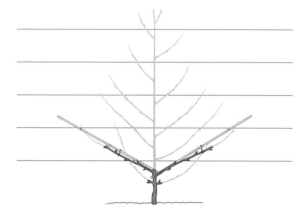

- Construct a support system by securing horizontal wires 30cm (12in) apart to a wall or fence. Attach 2 diagonal canes.
- If you are starting with a feathered maiden, cut off the central leader and any top growth above 2 strong left- and right-facing laterals, at a height of 25–30cm (10–12in) above the ground, just below the bottom wire.
- Cut back the 2 laterals to about 35cm (14in) and tie them in to the canes. They will become the 2 main arms.
- Remove any lower, unwanted laterals.

1st summer pruning
JUNE–SEPTEMBER

- As sideshoots grow from the main laterals, select 2 above and 1 below to form the ribs of the fan. Tie them in to additional canes.
- Cut back all other shoots to 1 leaf.

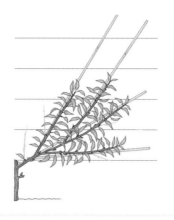

2nd spring pruning
FEBRUARY–MARCH

- Cut back the leader of each lateral and sub-lateral by one-quarter of the growth it made last year.
- Cut to buds facing in the direction you want the branch to grow.

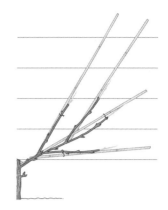

2nd summer pruning
JUNE–SEPTEMBER

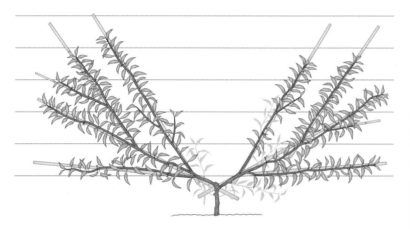

- Continue adding canes and tying in new sideshoots.
- Remove completely any new buds or shoots growing into or out from the wall or fence.
- Prune out new shoots growing vertically into the centre or below the main arms.

3rd spring pruning
FEBRUARY–MARCH

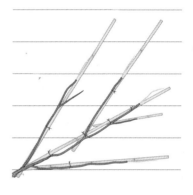

- Again, cut back the leaders of the main branches by one-quarter of the growth they made last year.

3rd summer pruning
JUNE–SEPTEMBER

- In early summer, thin out new sideshoots growing off the main ribs of the fan. Leave just 1 every 10–15cm (4–6in).
- Later, prune back crowded, crossing, or outward-growing sideshoots to 2–4 leaves, not counting the basal cluster.
- Continue adding canes and tying in new sideshoots.

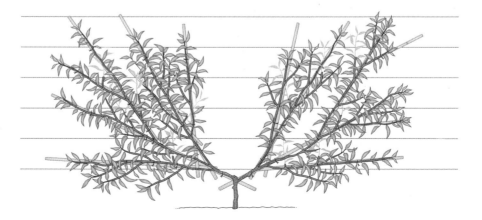

Spring pruning an established fan
APRIL–MAY

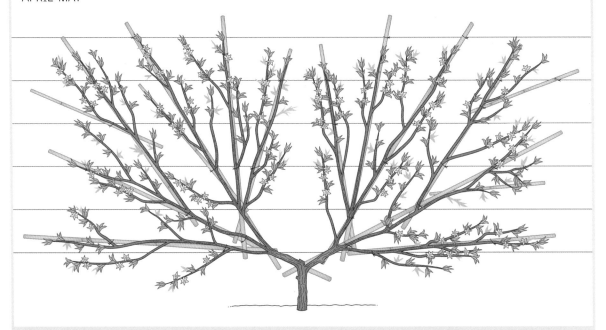

- On each of the main laterals and sub-laterals select 2 new sideshoots to grow on and bear fruit next year, choosing the first just below the lowest flower and the second to keep in reserve. Cut back all others to 1 leaf.
- Remove completely any new buds or shoots growing directly into or out from the wall or fence, as well as any that are closer than 10–15cm (4–6in) apart.
- Cut out any dead, damaged, or diseased wood.

(opposite) **A fan-trained nectarine** can put on an impressive amount of growth, as can be seen from this half-pruned mature fan growing in a large glasshouse. Spring pruning keeps new growth in check as well as reducing shading and ensuring good air circulation around the fruitlets.

(below, left and centre) **Cut back new shoots** that are growing outwards. They produce unnecessary growth that will spoil the shape of the fan and create too much shade. (right) **Start thinning** fruits and tie in any vigorous new sideshoots.

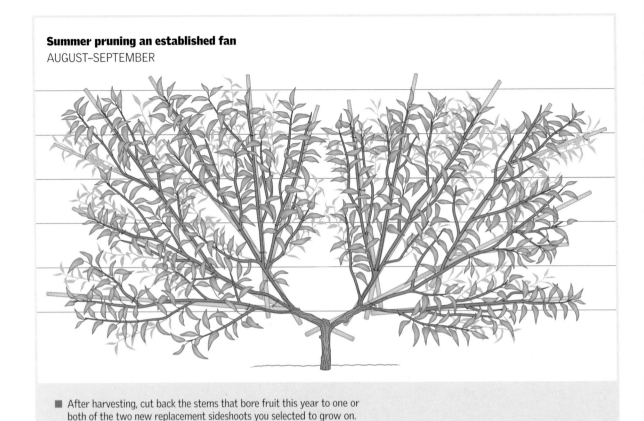

Summer pruning an established fan
AUGUST–SEPTEMBER

- After harvesting, cut back the stems that bore fruit this year to one or both of the two new replacement sideshoots you selected to grow on.
- Tie in the new shoots to the canes so that they fill in the gaps.

Pruning a bush or pyramid

Initial training and pruning of a young, newly planted tree is the same as for a plum (see pp.114–15). Aim for an open-centred bush with a balanced framework of main branches, or a well-formed conical pyramid. Thereafter, prune established trees once a year in early summer, in the same way as you would an acid cherry.

Summer pruning an established tree
JUNE–JULY

- Remove up to one-quarter of the shoots that fruited last year.
- Cut back to a pointed growth bud rather than a fat fruit bud (see p.43) in order to stimulate new shoots.
- Cut out any dead, damaged, or diseased wood.
- Thin out a few old laterals and sub-laterals that no longer bear fruit.

What can go wrong

Buds and blossom

Blossom discolours and dies
Peaches and nectarines flower so early in the year that they are highly prone to frost damage.
- See **Frost** (p.316).

Blossom turns brown and wilts
First the flowers and then young leaves turn brown and wither. Blossom wilt is caused by a fungus very closely related to the one responsible for brown rot.
- See **Blossom wilt** (p.325) and **Brown rot** (p.326).

Leaves, stems, and branches

1 New leaves are distorted, blister, and turn red
Almost as soon as they appear, new young leaves pucker, turning bright red or purple. The cause is peach leaf curl, a notoriously common fungal disease.
- See **Peach leaf curl** (p.328).

2 Leaves are curled and yellow-green
Green or black aphids feeding on sap on the undersides of leaves cause them to curl up and become misshapen. Foliage may be sticky with honeydew, too.
- See **Aphids** (p.334).

3 Leaves mottled and bronzed
If upper surfaces of leaves become speckled or mottled with pale yellow-bronze spots, then begin to dry up and die, look underneath with a magnifying glass for tiny red spider mites. In severe cases, you may also see fine silk webbing.
- See **Red spider mite** (p.339).

4 Yellow leaves with green veins
Yellowing of new leaves between the veins may indicate lack of the nutrients iron or manganese. Called "lime-induced chlorosis", it's common in alkaline soils with a high pH.
- See **Iron deficiency** (p.320), **Manganese deficiency** (p.321).

Leaves appear silvery
A silvery sheen develops on leaves, and shoots and branches may start to die back. If the problem is localized it could be silver leaf. If it affects the whole tree, then it may be so-called false silver leaf.
- See **False silver leaf** (p.327) and **Silver leaf** (p.331).

Holes appear in leaves and bark oozes gum
The symptoms of bacterial canker show in both leaves and bark. Leaves develop small brown spots with pale edges that turn into round holes. They may turn yellow and wither. Infected bark dies, and orange gum oozes from flat, sunken patches.
- See **Bacterial canker** (p.324).

Small, brown, shell-like insects on stems
Scale insects – sometimes called brown scale – may be found on stems and branches, especially under glass. They are elliptical in shape and covered with a domed shell.
- See **Scale insects** (p.339).

Fruit

5 Fruits develop patches of brown rot
Brown rot is a fungus that may infect fruits via a hole in the skin. The fruit turns brown and may develop concentric rings of white fungal spores. It either falls to the ground or remains on the tree, slowly shrivelling.
- See **Brown rot** (p.326).

Ragged holes in fruits
Birds, wasps, flies, and other insects feed on ripening fruits. They either make holes in the skin or aggravate existing ones. The damage they cause accelerates rot and decay.
- See **Birds** (p.335) and **Wasps** (p.341).

Quinces

Quinces are small- to medium-sized trees best grown as bushes, like apples or pears. It's possible, but not easy, to grow them as wall-trained fans. They are originally from the central and southwest regions of Asia, where hot summers mean they ripen fully and become soft and sweet enough to eat raw. In northern, temperate regions they remain rock hard and sour, and they need cooking. However, they make excellent jellies, jams, and pastes, and when stewed with apples, or baked in the oven with roast meats, their flesh turns pink and releases a wonderful, aromatic flavour.

(above and left) **Quinces** are ready to pick in early to mid-autumn, but leave them on the tree for as long as you can. Harvest before they drop, and well before the first frosts. Ripe fruits will keep until mid- or even late winter. Store them separately, in a cool place or their strong perfume will taint other fruits, such as apples and pears.

Growing quinces

Quinces grow on their own rootstocks – usually Quince A and Quince C, the same as those most commonly used for pears (see p.86). Trees grown on Quince A tend to reach 3.5–4.5m (11–15ft) in height, and those on Quince C 3–3.5m (10–11ft).

The year at a glance

	spring			summer			autumn			winter		
	M	A	M	J	J	A	S	O	N	D	J	F
plant bare-root	▬							▬	▬	▬	▬	▬
plant container	▬	▬	▬	▬	▬	▬			▬	▬	▬	▬
winter-prune									▬	▬	▬	▬
harvest							▬	▬				

Choosing a variety

Unsurprisingly, the choice of varieties or cultivars is much more limited than for apples or pears. The most commonly grown include 'Meech's Prolific', 'Champion', 'Vranja', 'Portugal' (sometimes called 'Lusitanica'), and 'Serbian Gold'.

Quinces are self-fertile and will pollinate themselves. A single tree can therefore be grown on its own.

When to plant

■ BARE-ROOT Plant November–March, when the trees are dormant, unless the soil is waterlogged or frozen. November is the ideal month.
■ CONTAINER-GROWN Plant at any time of year, although autumn is best. Avoid late spring and summer months if it is hot and dry.

Where to plant

Quinces grow best in a warm, sheltered corner, or close to a wall, away from any danger of frost pockets. They need sun if the fruit is to ripen successfully.

Plant quince trees in the same way as apples (see pp.58–59), making sure to stake them for the first few years.

Quince blossom is spectacular. It's almost worth planting a tree solely for the flowers. Either pure white or flushed with pink, they resemble wild dog roses, appearing after the new, bright-green foliage has opened.

Soil type

Quinces are fairly tolerant, although they grow best in a deep, fertile, moisture-retaining soil with a slightly acid pH of around 6.5.

Routine care

■ WATERING Take care to water young, recently planted trees.

■ FEEDING and MULCHING In the early years, and especially on light soils, use a general compound fertilizer each February, before growth starts. Follow it in March with an organic mulch around the base of the trees.

■ FROST PROTECTION Quinces flower later in spring than most other tree fruit and, except in northern regions, they are less vulnerable to damage from frost.

Harvesting and storing

It's best to leave quinces on the tree for as long as possible – until late October or even early November, provided there are no air frosts. After picking, store them somewhere cool and dark. Don't wrap them, don't let them touch each other, and keep them separate from other fruits. They should last for a month or two.

Pruning

Established trees shouldn't need much pruning. They fruit primarily on the tips of growth from the previous summer, so treat them like tip-bearing apples (see p.69). Prune in winter when the trees are dormant.

(right) **Young fruits** are often covered in a soft, fuzzy, white or grey-brown down, although as they ripen this disappears and the skins deepen to a lovely, almost luminous golden yellow.

WHAT CAN GO WRONG

Many of the pests and diseases that afflict apples (see pp.78–79) and pears (see pp.100–101) may also affect quinces. The most common include: brown rot (see p.326), powdery mildew (see p.329), and a particular fungal disease called quince leaf blight (see p.329). Fruits are also prone to splitting if watering is irregular.

(below, left to right) **Quince leaf blight** is a form of fungal leaf spot. Red-brown spots appear on leaves, which turn yellow, wither, and die. **Brown rot** seems to afflict quinces particularly badly, both while the fruit is ripening and also when it is in storage. **Fruits may split** if a period of drought is suddenly followed by a spell of wet weather. Rot is then likely to develop.

Mulberries

Mulberries seem strangely out of place here amongst the tree fruit. Instead, they look as if they should be found growing on canes or bushes, like blackberries or loganberries, rather than on trees. But tree fruit they are – and large, handsome trees, too. Mulberries are not commonly grown these days. They should be. First, the fruit is wonderful: a ripe, black mulberry bursts in your mouth with an intense, sweet-sharp flavour that is quite unique. Second, you're unlikely ever to taste fresh mulberries unless you grow them yourself; the fruits don't travel well and so are extremely unlikely ever to make it into supermarkets.

(above and left) **Black mulberries** are the ones to grow and eat, though their dark purple juice can make them a nightmare to harvest. The white mulberry is related – but not generally eaten. It is the type on which silk worms feed, not humans.

Growing mulberries

Mulberries are not hard to grow, although they are slow to establish. It could be as many as ten years before you get your first crop. They are grown on their own rootstocks, usually as bushes, half-standards or standards, or as wall-trained espaliers. Stand-alone trees are not suitable for small gardens: a full-grown, mature mulberry can reach 10m (30ft) in height.

The year at a glance

	spring			summer			autumn			winter		
	M	A	M	J	J	A	S	O	N	D	J	F
plant bare-root	▬							▬	▬	▬	▬	▬
plant container	▬	▬	▬				▬	▬	▬	▬	▬	▬
summer-prune				▬	▬							
winter-prune									▬	▬	▬	▬
harvest					▬	▬	▬					

Choosing a variety

Only one or two different varieties or cultivars are commonly available. They include 'Large Black' and 'King James' or 'Chelsea', reputed to have been bred from an original 17th-century tree that grew in what is now the Chelsea Physic Garden in London.

Mulberries are self-fertile and will pollinate themselves. A single tree can therefore be grown on its own.

When to plant

■ BARE-ROOT Plant November–March, when the trees are dormant, unless the soil is waterlogged or frozen.

■ CONTAINER-GROWN Plant at any time of year, although autumn or early spring are best. Avoid late spring and summer months if it is hot and dry.

Where to plant

Mulberries grow best in a warm, sunny, sheltered position. Plant them in the same way as apples (see pp.58–59), and stake them for the first few years.

Soil type

Mulberries will grow happily in most soils but prefer a fertile, free-draining one with a pH of 5.5–7.0. They may struggle in very heavy, wet ground.

Routine care

■ WATERING Take care to water young, recently planted trees.

■ FEEDING and MULCHING In the first few years after planting, use a general compound fertilizer each February or March, before growth starts. Two or three weeks later, spread an organic mulch around the base of the trunk.

■ FROST PROTECTION Mulberries flower late in spring and, except in northern regions, tend not suffer frost damage.

Harvesting and storing

As they ripen, mulberries turn from light red, through dark red, to black. For eating raw, leave them on the tree for as long as possible before picking – until early September, if you can – although by that stage they will have begun to drop naturally, staining the ground with their dark purple juice. For cooking and for making jams and jellies, pick them in August when still slightly underripe.

Pruning

Prune mulberries in the same way as you would an apple tree – freestanding trees in winter when they are dormant (see pp.68–69), and established espaliers in summer (see pp.74–75).

What can go wrong

Mulberries are relatively pest- and disease-free. Birds are likely to be the biggest nuisance, and, if you're unlucky, mulberry canker (see p.328).

Medlars

Medlars are one of the oddest-looking fruits in this chapter. When ripe, they are rather like giant, brown rosehips, about the size of crab apples. Even more odd is the manner in which they are eaten. They are deliberately left until almost rotten, then the flesh is squeezed or spooned out once it has turned into a soft, sweet, brown paste. Related to the quince and hawthorn, medlar trees are undoubtedly handsome, with a decorative, drooping form. However, the fruit is an acquired taste.

(above) **After harvesting,** fruits are stored until the flesh "blets" or starts to decompose, when it develops a soft, caramel-tasting quality. If that sounds too unappetizing, medlars can also be used for making jams or jellies, in much the same way as quinces.

(below) **Pretty, pink-tinged spring flowers** and wonderful autumn colour make medlars attractive, as well as productive, garden trees. For reliable flowering, cropping, and good leaf colour, plant trees in a sunny site.

Growing medlars

Medlars are rarely grown on their own roots. Instead, they are usually sold grafted onto a Quince A rootstock. Grown as bushes or half-standards, they are likely to reach 4–6m (12–20ft) in height.

The year at a glance

	spring			summer			autumn			winter		
	M	A	M	J	J	A	S	O	N	D	J	F
plant bare-root												
plant container												
winter-prune												
harvest												

Choosing a variety

Only a handful of different varieties or cultivars are available. The most common are 'Nottingham', 'Dutch', 'Royal', and 'Breda Giant'.

Medlars are self-fertile and will pollinate themselves. A single tree can be grown on its own.

When to plant

■ BARE-ROOT Plant November–March, when the trees are dormant, unless the soil is waterlogged or frozen. November is the ideal month.
■ CONTAINER-GROWN Plant at any time of year, although autumn is best. Avoid late spring and summer months if it is hot and dry.

Where to plant

Medlars grow best in a warm, sunny, sheltered position. They will tolerate some shade.

Plant medlar trees in the same way as apples (see pp.58–59), making sure to stake them for the first few years.

Soil type

Medlars are unfussy, although they prefer a deep, fertile, free-draining soil with a pH of 6.5–7.5.

Routine care

■ WATERING Take care to water young, recently planted trees.

■ FEEDING and MULCHING In the early years, and especially on poor soils, use a general compound fertilizer each February or March, before growth starts. Follow it with an organic mulch around the base of the trees.
■ FROST PROTECTION Medlars flower later in spring than most other tree fruit and, except in northern regions, are less vulnerable to damage from frost.

Harvesting and storing

As they ripen, medlars turn from green to brown, fatten up, and develop a russet-like covering. Leave them on the tree for as long as possible before picking – until late October or early November if there is no danger of frost. When they are ready, they will pull away easily with their stalks attached. Don't eat them straight away. Instead, dip the stalks in a concentrated salt solution, then store them somewhere cool and dark, upside-down, stalks in the air. After a few weeks they will have "bletted": that is, the flesh inside should be soft and sweet, and on the point of decomposing without actually having begun to rot.

Pruning

Prune medlars as you would an apple (see pp.68–69), in winter when they are dormant. Established trees shouldn't need much pruning at all.

What can go wrong

Medlars are generally trouble-free. They sometimes become infected with a form of fungal leaf spot (see p.327), and you may find that moth caterpillars feed on the leaves at certain times of year. The effects can be unsightly but are rarely serious.

Figs

Lots of claims are made about the ancestry of figs. They are routinely declared to be one of the oldest of all cultivated plants, dating back to the Neolithic period, more than 11,000 years ago. Certainly, they pre-date the farming of wheat and other cereals, and there are records of their popularity amongst the ancient Egyptians, Greeks and Romans, both for their flavour and as a reputed aphrodisiac. The foliage also played a key part in preserving the modesty of many classical sculptures. Figs are by nature best suited to warm climates. Growing them outdoors in cool temperate regions is perfectly feasible, but getting them to fruit reliably can be a challenge. Summers are simply not long and hot enough for fruits to be borne and ripen in the same year. Instead, embryonic fruits that have formed one year must be protected over winter in the hope that they will develop and ripen the following year. Under glass, fruiting becomes more reliable, and in a heated greenhouse figs may crop twice or even three times a year.

Figs with pale green, yellowish-green, or even green- and yellow-striped skins tend to have pale-coloured flesh, while that of the classic, dark purple-skinned varieties tends to be a rich, deep red.

Which forms to grow

■ **Bushes and half-standards** Attempt only in warm, sheltered sites, unless growing in a container.
■ **Fan** A fan-trained tree grown against a sheltered, sunny wall is the best choice for cool temperate climates.

Must-grow figs

1 'Brunswick'
A hardy variety that can usually be grown outdoors in all but the coldest regions. Large, pear-shaped fruits with pale green skins, flushed with brown or purple. Inside, the flesh is sweet and yellow-red in colour.
- **Colour** green
- **Harvest** mid August

2 'Rouge de Bordeaux'
This one is for only the sunniest, most sheltered of sites or for growing under glass. Often claimed to be the best-tasting fig of them all, the small to medium-sized fruits have purple skins, red flesh, and a wonderfully rich, aromatic flavour.
- **Colour** purple
- **Harvest** August–September

3 'Panachee'
Dating back to the 17th century, 'Panachee' is almost worth growing for its looks alone. The fruits are striped yellow and green, and the flesh is bright red and sweet-tasting. Best grown as a fan against a warm, sheltered wall or in a container.
- **Colour** yellow and green stripes
- **Harvest** late July–August

4 'Brown Turkey'
The tried-and-tested favourite for growing outdoors in cool temperate climates. It is hardy and reliable, producing good crops of sweet, purple-brown figs with red flesh. You may also come across it referred to as 'Brown Naples' or 'Fleur de Rouge'.
- **Colour** purple-brown
- **Harvest** August–September

5 'White Marseille'
Sometimes sold as 'White Genoa', 'White Naples', or even 'Figue Blanche', this variety produces large, pale green fruits with sweet-tasting white flesh that is almost transparent. It needs a warm, sheltered position if it is to be grown outdoors. Otherwise, grow it in a container or under glass.
- **Colour** pale green
- **Harvest** August–September

'Violetta' (not illustrated)
Originally from Bavaria, and sometimes referred to as the 'Bavarian Fig' or in full as 'Bayernfeige Violetta', this is an extremely hardy variety that will tolerate low temperatures and is easy to grow. In favourable conditions – even in cool temperate regions – it may produce two crops a year. The large, red-fleshed fruits have a good flavour.
- **Colour** green-purple
- **Harvest** late July–September

Growing figs

Except in very cold regions, growing figs is fairly easy. The hard part, in cool temperate zones at least, is getting them to produce a worthwhile crop of ripe fruit. Sun and warmth are crucial. So, too, is an understanding of how their annual fruiting cycle works. In hot, subtropical climates, or when grown in a heated greenhouse, figs can produce fruits two or three times a year, but outdoors in temperate climates you can expect only one crop – from fruits that form in late summer, overwinter as pea-sized embryonic figs, then ripen the following summer.

The year at a glance

	spring			summer			autumn			winter		
	M	A	M	J	J	A	S	O	N	D	J	F
plant	▬	▬	▬				▬	▬	▬	▬		
spring-prune		▬										
summer-prune				▬	▬							
harvest indoors			▬	▬			▬	▬	▬			
harvest outdoors				▬	▬	▬						

Flowering and pollination

Figs grown in temperate regions are what is termed "parthenocarpic". This means that they don't need pollinating or fertilizing in order to produce fruit. In fact, they don't appear to have flowers at all – at least, not visible ones. Actually, the flowers are hidden, contained within the embryo fruits. Figs do not produce seeds either, so propagation is done from cuttings.

Choosing trees

Young figs are usually supplied container-grown and can be bought all year round. The trees grow on their own roots and are not grafted onto other rootstocks.

When to plant

The best time to plant a fig is November to March, when the tree is dormant – although not if the soil is waterlogged or frozen. Avoid late spring and summer months if it is hot and dry.

Figs crop better if pot-bound, so don't be tempted to pot them on into over-large containers. Keep them well-watered during the spring and summer, and feed with high-potash tomato fertilizer when the fruits are ripening.

GROWING FIGS UNDER GLASS

In cool, temperate climates it may be better to grow figs under glass. Planting them directly into the ground in a greenhouse means they will be under cover all year round, and you'll have the opportunity of growing tender varieties that will struggle outdoors – 'Rouge de Bordeaux', for example. You'll also get a much heavier crop, especially if the greenhouse is heated.

Figs are large trees and a wire-trained fan is likely to take up a large area of wall or roof space. In small greenhouses, it's probably much more practical to grow figs in containers. In summer, when the trees are in full leaf, they can be moved to a warm, sunny spot outside.

In autumn, figs that won't ripen this year may drop from the tree. This is a natural shedding process and not an indication that the tree is in poor health.

Where to plant
Choose a warm, sunny, sheltered site, protected from strong winds. In cool temperate climates, grow a fan against a south- or southwest-facing fence or wall. Avoid frost pockets. Otherwise, grow in containers or under glass.

Soil type
Figs will grow in almost any well-drained ground, even shallow, sandy soils and slightly alkaline, chalky soils. In fact, in rich, very fertile, moisture-retentive ones, they tend to grow too vigorously, with too much foliage and too few fruits.

How to plant
Because figs are naturally vigorous, there is a tradition of planting them in sunken containers or specially constructed "fig pits", in order to restrict their roots deliberately. This curbs the growth of the tree, keeping it to a manageable size, and encourages it to produce fruit rather than foliage. Freestanding figs need staking for the first few years after planting.

Planting distances

■ BUSHES and HALF-STANDARDS restricted 4–6m (12–20ft), unrestricted 6–8m (20–25ft) apart.

■ FANS restricted 2.5–4m (8–12ft), unrestricted 4–5m (12–15ft) apart.

Growing in containers

Figs are ideal for growing in pots. In fact, they thrive in them. The container restricts root growth so that the tree does not grow over-large. And, provided it is not too big and heavy, the pot can be brought indoors to a cold conservatory or unheated greenhouse during winter, or covered with fleece to protect it against frost. The tree can then be moved into the warmest, sunniest part of your garden or patio in summer, when the figs are ripening.

Trees in containers are best grown as dwarf half-standards, with a clear stem or leg of about 40–75cm (16–30in) before the lateral branches spread out to form a bushy, open-centred head. A multi-stemmed dwarf bush is suitable, too. Plant young trees in containers with a diameter of 25–35cm (10–14in), filled with loam-based compost mixed with some sand or gravel to improve drainage and plenty of stones or crocks at the bottom. Keep the pot well-watered, and each spring top-dress with fresh soil mixed with some slow-release general fertilizer. Every two or three years repot or pot on into a slightly larger container.

Routine care

■ WATERING Regular watering throughout the spring and summer is very important, particularly for young trees, wall-trained fans, and figs planted in containers or grown in pits to restrict their roots. They will all drop their fruit if allowed to dry out.

■ FEEDING Each March, at the beginning of

BUILDING A FIG PIT

A fig pit is basically a concrete-lined box sunk into the ground, with a layer of rubble at the bottom. It is designed to restrict the spread of the tree's roots, and is suitable for both freestanding trees and wall-trained fans.

1 Dig a hole and line it with 60 x 60cm (24 x 24in) paving slabs, each set on edge and protruding above the surface of the soil by about 5cm (2in). Put a 20cm (8in) layer of tightly packed broken bricks or rubble in the bottom to restrict roots but also to provide drainage.

2 Plant the young tree in the centre of the pit, filling the hole with good-quality soil or loam-based compost, mixed with well-rotted organic matter and a slow-release general fertilizer.

3 Ensure the old nursery mark on the stem is level with the surface of the soil, firm it down, and water well. If you are planting in winter, prune the stem to a healthy bud about 45cm (18in) above soil level.

the growing season, apply a general compound fertilizer. Between May and August, while fruits are developing, water weekly with a diluted, high-potash tomato fertilizer or similar liquid feed.

■ MULCHING In March, after feeding, remove any weeds and spread a mulch of well-rotted compost or manure around the base of freestanding and wall-trained trees.

■ NETTING Birds can be a problem in summer as fruit ripens. Netting large trees may not be practical, but it's easier in the case of fans and trees in pots.

■ THINNING UNRIPE FRUIT In November remove and discard any green fruits that have failed to ripen. It is too late for them to do so now, and outdoors they will not survive the winter. But don't touch the recently formed, tiny, embryo figs; they will grow, ripen, and crop next year.

■ FROST PROTECTION Figs do not flower so there is no blossom to worry about, but embryo fruits remain on the tree over winter and, along with young shoots, are at risk of frost damage. Bring container-grown trees under cover, and protect wall-trained fans with fleece, or with a warm, insulating blanket of dry bracken or straw. Pack the dried material in snugly and secure it in place with netting. Remove it in May.

Harvesting and storing

Fruits are ready for picking when they are fully coloured, become slightly soft, and the stalks begin to bend so that the fruits tip downwards. A tell-tale sign is when the skin around the eye splits and a bead of nectar appears. Figs will keep for a while after harvesting, but if they are really ripe they're best eaten straight from the tree. Resist the temptation to pick them before they are ready: they won't ripen any further once they are off the tree.

Yield

Yields vary too widely to quantify.

(below, left to right) **Remove any unripe figs** larger than a pea in November. Even the biggest will no longer ripen this year, and in any case they will be killed off during the winter. **Full-grown, ripe figs** as well as smaller, embryo fruitlets are commonly seen on the same tree simultaneously.

Month by month

March
■ Last chance to plant trees before they come out of their winter dormancy.
■ Apply a general compound fertilizer, then weed and mulch around trees.

April
■ A first wave of new fruitlets starts to form. In hot climates and under glass, they should ripen by late summer. Outdoors in cool climates, they are unlikely to ripen at all.
■ Spring-prune established trees and fans this month or next, cutting back unwanted growth and encouraging new fruiting shoots.

May
■ Remove straw or bracken used to protect wall-trained fans over the winter.
■ Begin regular watering.
■ Give trees a liquid feed while fruits are developing, between now and August

June
■ In hot climates and under glass, trees may produce a small, early crop from fruit borne on last year's new growth.
■ Summer-prune established trees and fans this month and next. Pinch out growing shoots to encourage the formation of new fruitlets, and tie in new growth on fans.

July
■ Early-season varieties may be ready to harvest late this month.

August
■ Harvest mid-season varieties.
■ A second wave of new fruitlets appears. They

(above, left to right) **New buds** break and fruitlets start to form almost as soon as the tree emerges from its winter dormancy. **Spring foliage** unfurls dramatically. **Fruits** that have overwintered as tiny embryos swell and ripen. (below) **Ripe figs** don't store well so eat them as soon as possible after picking.

should overwinter as tiny embryo fruits. In hot climates and under glass, they may produce a small crop in early summer the following year. Outdoors in cool climates, they should ripen and form a main crop in mid- to late summer the following year.

September
■ Harvest late-season varieties.

October
■ Bring container-grown figs under cover before the onset of frosts.
■ Insulate wall-trained fans with a protective blanket of straw or dry bracken.

November
■ Remove any figs as large or larger than a pea if they have not ripened this year.
■ A good month to buy and plant bare-root trees: the soil is still warm and trees have a chance to get established before growth starts next spring.

Pruning and training figs

Most figs produce new young fruits twice a year. The first wave appears on new shoots in spring, gradually fattening up during the summer. In hot climates and in heated greenhouses, these ripen and can be harvested in early autumn. However, outdoors in cool, temperate climates, they never ripen and should be removed. The second wave of fruits starts to appear in August and September, forming tiny, embryonic figs, each no larger than a pea, at the tips of the year's new growth. Left on the tree, they should overwinter and provide a crop next year – for harvesting in spring in hot climates or under glass, and in late summer in cool temperate regions.

Whether grown as freestanding trees or wall-trained fans, established figs should be lightly pruned twice a year: once in spring to thin out old or damaged wood and to maintain the overall shape; and again in early summer to stimulate the production of the embryo fruits that will develop and ripen next year.

Fig sap can be an irritant. If you react adversely to it, wear gloves when pruning and take care not to get any on your skin.

Pruning a fig bush or half-standard
Initial training and pruning of a young, newly planted tree is similar to that for an apple (see p.68). Aim for an open-centered bush with a balanced framework of main branches. Thereafter, prune established trees in spring and early summer.

Spring pruning an established tree
APRIL

- Select a few lengthy laterals that are now fruiting only at their tips and prune them back hard to a bud 5–8cm (2–3in) from the trunk or main branch. This will promote new growth closer to the heart of the tree.
- Cut back to undamaged wood any shoots that have been attacked by frost during the winter.
- Remove congested growth from the centre of the tree.
- Cut out any dead, damaged, or diseased wood.

Summer pruning an established tree
JUNE or JULY

- Pinch out the growing tip of each new shoot as soon as 5–6 leaves have appeared. This will stimulate the formation of the second wave of embryo fruits. It also allows sunlight to reach existing fruits that are now in the process of ripening.

Pruning a fan

Grow against a south- or southwest-facing wall or fence. Allow a space
4m (12ft) wide and 2.2m (7ft) high. Start with a two- or three-year-old tree.
Initial training and pruning is similar to that for a peach (see pp.152–53),
although the ribs may need spacing farther apart as fig leaves are larger.

(below, left to right) **In spring**, the stucture of the budding fan is clearly visible. **By early summer**, the fig has put on an impressive amount of foliage.

Spring pruning an established fan
APRIL–MAY

- Select a couple of the oldest, least productive main laterals and cut them right back to a single bud. This should help open up congested areas.
- Prune to 1 bud or leaf about half of the sideshoots growing from the main ribs or arms of the fan. This will encourage new fruiting growth.
- Remove completely any new buds or shoots growing directly into or out from the wall or fence.
- Cut out any dead, damaged, or diseased wood, including any shoots attacked by frost during the winter.
- Tie in new shoots that will help form the framework of the fan as it grows.

(left to right) **Cut out old stems** at the base to encourage new, more vigorous growth. **Prune sideshoots** on either side of the fan in spring, cutting back to one bud.

Summer pruning an established fan
JUNE or JULY

- Pinch out the growing tips of new shoots once they have 5–6 leaves. This encourages the formation of embryo fruits and lets sunlight ripen existing fruits.
- If you can, identify figs that will not ripen this year, and cut off the shoots bearing them. New growth should break from the stumps, producing further embryo fruits. If you can't, don't worry. Pick off unripe fruit later in the year, in autumn.
- Continue tying in new shoots.

(right) **Remove shoots** with small, unripe figs by making a clean cut with a pair of sharp secateurs.

In a greenhouse, a fig can be trained vertically upwards then fanned out across a series of overhead horizontal wires stretched beneath the roof.

Carefully bend the current year's new lateral shoots into position and tie them in to the wires using string or flexible plant ties. Don't secure them too tightly.

Aim for a framework of well spaced ribs with plenty of room for air to circulate and for sunlight to reach the ripening fruits.

What can go wrong

Leaves, stems, and branches

1 Leaves mottled and bronzed
If upper surfaces of leaves become speckled or mottled with pale yellow-bronze spots, then begin to dry up and die, look underneath with a magnifying glass for tiny red spider mites. In severe cases, you may also see fine silk webbing. Spider mites are much more likely to be a problem on figs grown under glass.
■ See **Red spider mite** (p.339).

2 Small, white, wax-covered insects on stems
Mealybugs feed on sap that they suck from stems and branches. They are recognizable by the fluffy, white wax with which they are coated.
■ See **Mealybugs** (p.337).

3 Small, brown, shell-like insects on stems
Scale insects – sometimes called brown scale – may be found on stems and branches, especially on figs grown under glass. They are elliptical in shape and covered with a domed shell. If leaves are also covered with sticky honeydew, then the cause may be the type known as soft scale.
■ See **Scale insects** (p.339).

Pink spots on stems and branches
Small, pink or orange pustules appearing on stems and branches that have died back indicate coral spot, a fungal disease. The problem is likely to be worse in damp conditions.
■ See **Coral spot** (p.326).

Fruit

4 Unripe figs drop from the tree prematurely
In summer, this is probably due to a shortage of water. In autumn or winter, figs that have not ripened are likely to fall naturally or be killed off by frosts.
■ See **Routine care** (pp. 171–72).

5 Fruit partially or wholly eaten
Sadly, the closer figs are to being perfectly ripe the more irresistible they are to birds, wasps, flies, and other insects. They feed on the ripening fruit, making holes in the skin or aggravating existing ones.
■ See **Birds** (p.335) and **Wasps** (p.341).

Soft fruit

The term "soft fruit" is something of a catch all, meaning – in essence – any fruit that doesn't grow on trees. The main categories are bush fruit (currants, gooseberries, blueberries, and cranberries), cane fruit (raspberries, blackberries, and hybrid berries), and in a group of their own, strawberries. Strictly speaking, grapes are a type of soft fruit, too, although in this book they are treated separately. Many of the fruits termed "tender and exotic" (melons, cape gooseberries, kiwifruit, and more) are soft fruits as well but they have been grouped together owing to their particular climatic growing requirements.

Soft fruits have a special appeal as grow-your-own crops. They almost all taste at their absolute best when left to ripen on the plant, then picked and eaten immediately. But at that point they are fragile, and unlikely to survive the long journey to a supermarket shelf. Consequently, commercially grown fruit is usually picked before it is ripe, when it is firmer and more resilient. The result? It will never have the sweetness, juiciness, aroma, and flavour of fruit you have grown and picked yourself.

Blackberries might seem an odd choice of fruit to grow in your garden or allotment. After all, they're easy to find growing wild. However, cultivated varieties crop more heavily, and some are mercifully thornless.

Growing soft fruit

Planting a selection of soft fruit is a fairly long-term commitment. It's certainly longer term than growing annual vegetables, which are there one year and gone the next, though it's obviously not such an investment in the future as planting a fruit tree. Apart from strawberries, you can expect most soft fruit bushes or canes to live and to continue producing fruit for several years. Choosing the appropriate site and providing your soft fruit crops with the right growing conditions are, therefore, crucial.

Vertical cordons are a great way of growing redcurrants. They are economical on space, the fruit is easy to pick, and if trained against a sheltered wall they enjoy a perfect microclimate.

Buying soft fruit

Like fruit trees, new soft-fruit plants can be bought either bare-root or potted up in containers. Specialist nurseries usually sell bare-root plants, only between about November and March, when they are dormant. Garden centres tend to sell container-grown plants, which are available all year round – though the choice may be more limited.

Always buy plants from a source that can guarantee they are officially certified disease-free.

Planting soft fruit

Most soft fruits are cool-climate plants, and are tolerant about where they are planted. However, they all prefer somewhere sheltered, out of strong winds, and will all ripen better in sunshine. Soil requirements vary but fertile, free-draining soil is always a good thing, and no plants will grow well in heavy, waterlogged ground. Prepare your site by digging in plenty of well-rotted manure or garden compost. Add some general fertilizer, and balance the pH of the soil if necessary.

The best time to plant is November or thereabouts, when the soil is still warm enough for the roots to establish themselves. Or March, when it is beginning to warm up again. The worst times are in the depths of winter when the ground is so waterlogged or frozen that it's difficult even to dig a planting hole, and July and August, when the weather is at its hottest and driest.

Pruning and training soft fruit

Gooseberry, currant, and blueberry bushes usually grow satisfactorily without support, but raspberries, blackberries, and hybrid berries, as well as any soft fruit grown as cordons or fans, will need training and tying in to fences, walls, or post-and-wire structures. Standard gooseberries and redcurrants require staking.

Regular pruning helps to keep plants tidy, healthy, and productive. Specific pruning techniques vary from fruit to fruit, but here are a few general guidelines:

■ IMMEDIATELY REMOVE any growth that is **dead, damaged,** or **diseased** – sometimes known as **"the three Ds".**

■ THIN OUT CROWDED and congested areas so that light can get in and air can circulate.

■ TIE UP OR CUT BACK any growth that is hanging too low or touching the ground.

■ AFTER HARVESTING raspberries, blackberries, and hybrid berries, cut out the canes that have fruited, as they won't fruit again.

■ EACH WINTER, remove a few of the older stems from established gooseberry, currant, and blueberry bushes. This will make way for new growth.

■ PRUNE SIDESHOOTS on gooseberries, redcurrants, and whitecurrants in both winter and summer to encourage them to produce lots of fruiting spurs. But don't do this with blackcurrants: they fruit differently.

■ ROUTINELY REMOVE strawberry runners, using them to propagate new plants if required.

Protecting soft fruit

Apart from the usual range of diseases, disorders, and infestations, birds are by far the most serious threat to soft fruit crops. Scarers may work for a while, but birds are smart and learn to ignore them very quickly. Nets are the only guaranteed protection, and a purpose-built, walk-in fruit cage is the ultimate defence.

(right, top to bottom) **A double system** of protection ensures a perfect crop of strawberries: below, a thick layer of straw lifts the fruits off the earth and keeps them clean; above, a cover of netting protects them from birds. **Gooseberries** put on a lot of new growth in summer, so cut back sideshoots to let in light and air.

Strawberries

Strawberries are irresistibly seductive. Few things rival the luscious aroma and flavour of ripe, sweet, freshly picked fruit. In the past, however, that pleasure was fleeting. The season for traditional summer-fruiting strawberries came and went over the course of just a few short weeks in June or July. Commercial growers and breeders, therefore, have long been in search of the Holy Grail: the year-round strawberry. They have made some progress. As well as summer-fruiting, we now have autumn-fruiting varieties, also known as perpetual, everbearing, or remontant strawberries. Perpetual they're not, but they nevertheless usually produce a small crop in about June, then start cropping again from late summer right through to the first frosts of the autumn – or longer if you protect them by bringing them under cover. In addition, there are day-neutral strawberries, a relatively recent American innovation. These berries have been bred to take no notice of the length of the day, which means that it doesn't matter to them what time of year it is. As long as it's neither too cold nor too hot they should crop within about twelve weeks of planting. So, in theory at least, you can grow your own strawberries for Christmas and Easter.

Traditonal, summer-fruiting strawberries still have arguably the best flavour but their season is short. Modern perpetual varieties keep cropping right into the autumn – or even longer if you cover them to protect against frost.

Must-grow strawberries

1 'Flamenco'
Perpetual
Very high yields of up to 1kg (2.2lb) per plant. Excellent size and flavour. Suitable for growing in open ground, in containers, and under cover.
■ **Harvest** July to October

2 'Korona'
Summer-fruiting
A modern Dutch variety that can produce huge, intensely red berries with an excellent flavour. Heavy cropping, easy to grow, and resistant to most diseases.
■ **Harvest** early June to early July

3 'Cambridge Favourite'
Summer-fruiting
A long-standing, all-purpose favourite still widely grown. Reasonable flavour and reliable cropping.
■ **Harvest** mid-June to mid-July

4 'Symphony'
Summer-fruiting
A recent Scottish variety bred from 'Rhapsody'. Heavy crops of firm, well-formed berries with good flavour.
■ **Harvest** early July to early August

5 'Honeoye'
Summer-fruiting
One of the best of the early varieties. Heavy-cropping, medium-to-large, glossy-red, firm, juicy berries. Fairly good disease resistance.
■ **Harvest** early June to early July

6 'Florence'
Summer-fruiting
Good-sized, dark red berries with firm, juicy flesh. Easy to grow and resistant to many pests and dieases.
■ **Harvest** early July to early August

7 'Pegasus'
Summer-fruiting
Large berries with sweet, juicy flesh and bright, glossy skins. Good resistance to wilt.
■ **Harvest** mid-June to mid-July

8 'Elsanta'
Summer-fruiting
A Dutch variety with good flavour, often grown commercially as the berries are firm and retain their shape. Not the most disease-resistant, however.
■ **Harvest** mid-June to mid-July

9 'Mignonette'
Alpine
One of the heaviest cropping and best tasting named varieties of alpine or woodland strawberries. Small, scarlet, deep red berries with a characteristically intense, aromatic wild-strawberry flavour. Usually sold in the form of seeds.
■ **Harvest** July to October

'Alexandria' (not illustrated)
Alpine
Small, bright red fruits and the classic wild-strawberry flavour. Also available is a variety called 'Golden Alexandria', which has yellow or golden-green leaves. Seeds need warmth to germinate, so it's best to sow indoors or in a propagator, and plant out seedlings in late spring after you have hardened them off.
■ **Harvest** July to October

'Alice' (not illustrated)
Summer-fruiting
New variety with shiny, orange-red berries that have a good flavour. Heavy cropping and disease resistant.
■ **Harvest** mid-June to mid-July

'Aromel' (not illustrated)
Perpetual
One of the first modern, perpetual varieties, and still one of the best tasting and most popular – although it can be prone to mildew.
■ **Harvest** June and August–October

'Fern' (not illustrated)
Day-neutral
Large, bright red berries with good flavour. Firm enough to freeze reasonably well.
■ **Harvest** spring to autumn, 12 weeks after planting

'Gariguette' (not illustrated)
Summer-fruiting
An old-fashioned French variety worth seeking out for its super-sweet, aromatic, deep red berries.
■ **Harvest** early June to early July

'Hapil' (not illustrated)
Summer-fruiting
Reliably good crops of bright red, conical fruit. A good choice if you have light, sandy soil, as it tolerates dry conditions better than most other varieties. Suitable for sites prone to spring frosts because it flowers quite late.
■ **Harvest** mid-June to mid-July

'Mae' (not illustrated)
Summer-fruiting
A new variety perhaps set to become the top early-season strawberry. Arguably better than 'Honeoye' – heavier cropping and with an old-fashioned, traditional strawberry taste.
■ **Harvest** late May to late June

'Mara des Bois' (not illustrated)
Perpetual
Exceptional flavour. Sweet and aromatic – the variety that tastes most like a wild woodland or Alpine strawberry. Too easily bruised for the supermarkets, so it is a definite grow-your-own fruit.
■ **Harvest** June and August to October

'Rhapsody' (not illustrated)
Summer-fruiting
Bred in Scotland and descended from 'Cambridge Favourite'. Heavy-cropping, medium-sized fruits with good flavour.
■ **Harvest** early July to early August

'Royal Sovereign' (not illustrated)
Summer-fruiting
A 19th-century variety with a wonderful, old-fashioned flavour. Not particularly easy to grow, as it is prone to various diseases, but still popular. Perhaps best grown for nostalgic reasons.
■ **Harvest** early June to early July

'Selva' (not illustrated)
Day-neutral
Very heavy yields of large, firm berries. Perhaps not the best flavour but useful for out-of-season crops.
■ **Harvest** spring to autumn, 12 weeks after planting

Growing strawberries

Most people will tell you that strawberries are easy to grow, and in many ways they are. There's certainly no complicated training and pruning to worry about. But they're not quite as easy as you may think: they're prone to a lot of pests and diseases, and they need looking after carefully if they're to produce a satisfactory crop of good-sized, good-looking, tasty fruit. Easy to grow but difficult to grow well – that might be more accurate.

The year at a glance

	spring			summer			autumn			winter		
	M	A	M	J	J	A	S	O	N	D	J	F
plant summer-fruting / perpetual	▬		▬		▬		▬		▬			
plant cold-stored runners				▬		▬						
harvest summer-fruiting				▬		▬						
harvest perpetual						▬		▬				
harvest under cover	▬		▬				▬		▬			

Strawberries usually flower in mid-spring. The more flowers you get, the better the crop.

PLANTING STRAWBERRIES DIRECTLY INTO THE GROUND

Prepare the soil well in advance by digging in plenty of well-rotted manure or compost and by carefully removing all traces of perennial weeds. Fork in some general, compound fertilizer. Rake over the soil and level it out.

1 Use a line to measure out the positions of your planting holes, about 45cm (18in) apart.

2 Trim off any overlong, straggly roots from each runner and carefully spread them out over a small mound created in the bottom of each hole.

3 Check that the crown of the plant is at the same height as the surface of the soil, then backfill and firm down gently with your hands.

4 Water the young plants thoroughly, both now and at regular intervals over the next few weeks, especially if the weather is dry.

Choosing plants

Unless you're propagating your own strawberries (see p.190), you'll need to buy new, certified disease-free plants, since growing them from seed is difficult. They are available as either bare-root or container-grown plants. The strawberries you are most likely to get from a garden centre will be container-grown. Bare-root plants are less expensive but tend to come from specialist nurseries via mail-order. They will probably be open-ground or field-grown runners that have been dug up from the ground just before being dispatched. The first plants of the new season may be available as early as July. Alternatively, they may be cold-stored runners: these are put in storage after being lifted and kept at just below freezing point until they are ready for sale, between about May and July. All bare-root plants should be planted out as soon as they arrive.

When to plant

The timing varies according to the sort of plants available and the form in which you buy them. Do not attempt to plant in winter, between December and February, and certainly not if the ground is frozen or waterlogged.

■ SUMMER-FRUITING and PERPETUAL VARIETIES The best time is as soon as the first new plants become available – usually in July or August. Plant them then and you'll have a good chance of a decent crop the following year. If you can't plant bare-root runners until the autumn, or even until March or April the following spring, it's not a disaster: all it means is that you won't get any fruit in the first year. Good-sized pot-grown plants, however, may well crop in their first year whenever they're planted.

■ COLD-STORED RUNNERS Plant in May, June, or July. If all goes well, these recently thawed, unpromising-looking plants will burst into life and crop within 8–12 weeks.

■ DAY-NEUTRAL VARIETIES Plant outdoors in April–May for harvesting about 12 weeks later in July–September, and in August–October for harvesting the following summer. Plant in pots in June–September for autumn and winter crops under cover.

PLANTING STRAWBERRIES THROUGH A PLASTIC MULCH

Planting through slits cut in a plastic sheet stretched over a slightly raised bed has a number of advantages. The sheet warms the soil and acts as a mulch to suppress weeds. It also helps to retain moisture, and the berries won't get mud-splashed as they ripen. You can either install a length of trickle hose laid beneath the plastic to keep the plants moist, or water each plant with a watering can or hose.

1 Create a 1m (3ft) wide bed mounded up slightly in the centre. Cover it with a strip of plastic sheeting 1.2m (4ft) wide. Clear plastic warms the soil most effectively as it acts like a greenhouse, but opaque, black plastic suppresses weeds.

2 Bury the edges of the plastic sheet firmly into the soil along each side of the bed to anchor them.

3 Using a sharp knife or a pair of scissors, cut X-shaped slits in the plastic at 45cm (18in) intervals.

4 Plant the strawberries into the slits and firm down the soil around them. Fold back the edges of the plastic and water. The sloping bed will ensure the water drains away.

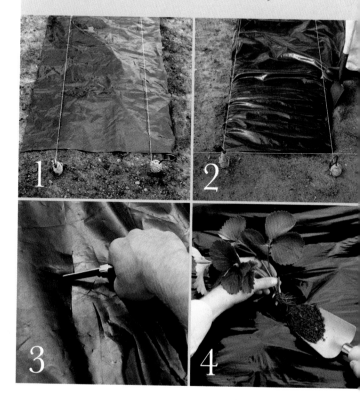

Where to plant

Strawberries grow best in full sun, though they will tolerate a few hours of shade during the day. Choose a sheltered site out of strong winds but avoid potential frost pockets. Don't plant where you've recently grown tomatoes or potatoes.

Soil type

Strawberries are not too fussy about soil, provided that it is free-draining. Damp, waterlogged conditions lead to root rots and other diseases. A slightly acid pH of 6–6.5 is ideal.

Planting distances

- PLANTS 45cm (18in) apart.
- ROW SPACING 75cm (30in) apart.

Routine care

- WATERING Newly planted strawberries need regular watering, as do established plants when the weather is hot and dry. However, the ripening fruits themselves dislike actually getting wet; this can trigger grey mould or botrytis (see p.325). If possible, water the soil rather than the plants, and water in the morning so that any moisture splashed on the fruits has evaporated by the evening.
- FEEDING In March or April, particularly if your soil is poor, sprinkle a little general, compound fertilizer around the plants, taking care that it doesn't touch the leaves. For an additional boost of potassium, give plants a high-potash feed after harvesting or at the start of the year, in late January.
- NETTING Nets are essential to keep birds off – certainly in summer as the strawberries begin to colour and ripen.
- FROST PROTECTION Early-flowering varieties may need covering with fleece or cloches overnight if there is a danger of frosts. Uncover the plants during the day to allow insects to pollinate flowers.
- MULCHING A mulch is necessary, not just to retain moisture and suppress weeds, but to keep

(left) **Protect strawberries** by surrounding them with a layer of straw when they are in flower or as soon as fruits begin to form.

the berries clean. Without a mulch, they actually sit on the soil and will soon be splashed with mud. "Strawing down" is the traditional method of protecting them (see opposite), but growing them through plastic sheeting or using special strawberry mats achieves the same result. Whichever you choose, weed thoroughly before mulching.

Straw mulch

Spread a generous layer of straw around each plant. Tuck it in carefully so the leaves and berries are lifted off the soil, and air can circulate beneath. Barley straw is the best, wheat straw is good, but oat straw may contain eelworms (see p.336).

Strawberry mats

Special fibre mats have a hole in the centre and a slit on one edge, enabling them to be slipped around the crowns of each plant, like a collar. They're neat and easier to install than laying straw, but in time they become dirty.

Plastic sheeting

Keep sheet mulches tightly anchored and stretched taut so that water runs off rather than collecting in puddles, which may cause fruits to rot.

Strawberry mats placed carefully around the crowns well before the fruits ripen will protect the berries.

(below left to right) **Remove surplus runners** that form on fruiting plants when they appear. Cut them off close to the parent plant with sharp secateurs. You can pot them up and grow them on (see p.190). **Netting** is vital to keep hungry birds off ripening fruit. In some areas, squirrels may also be a problem.

Harvesting and storing

Strawberries ripen quickly, and you'll need to check plants every day. For eating fresh, try to catch them at the point where they have turned completely red but before they begin to go soft. Pick them in the morning after the sun has dried them, and if possible, eat them immediately while they are at their very best. For storing, pick the berries while they are still slightly white at the end. They will probably continue to ripen and will keep in the fridge for a couple of days.

Strawberries do not freeze well – they almost invariably turn mushy when thawed. They are fine for cooking, but otherwise unappetizing.

Yield

Yields vary widely from variety to variety, but a healthy plant should produce something in the range of 225–450g (8oz–1lb) of fruit.

What to do at the end of the season

Although strawberries don't need pruning as such, they do need tidying up as soon as the last of the fruits have been picked if you want them to fruit again next year. Remove any old straw and used strawberry mats from around the plants, and pull out any weeds. Cut off all the old strawberry leaves and any unwanted runners, but leave at least 8cm (3in) of the crowns untouched, as new growth will already be forming there ready for next year.

The lifespan of strawberries

Strawberry plants don't last forever. Viruses and other diseases have a tendency to build up, and crops are likely to diminish as each year goes by. Perpetual and day-neutral strawberries are best replaced after two years or – even better – planted afresh each year and grown as annuals. Summer-fruiting varieties shouldn't be kept going for more than three or four years. It helps to rotate strawberry beds, just as you would with vegetables.

Growing in containers

Strawberries are ideal for container-growing. Indeed, there are a number of reasons why you may even prefer to grow them in containers. First, pots,

PROPAGATING STRAWBERRIES

Left to their own devices, most strawberries will virtually propagate themselves. Their natural behaviour is to throw out stems or "runners" on which plantlets form and take root where they come into contact with the soil. You can choose to cut them off and throw them away if they are unwanted, sever them and let them grow on where they have rooted, or pot them up and replant them elsewhere. A word of warning: strawberries are not immortal. To avoid the build-up of viruses and other diseases, propagate only from young, healthy plants.

1 Once runners have formed and young plantlets are starting to grow, carefully lift them from the soil – no more than four or five per plant. Don't separate them from the parent plant just yet.

2 Sink a small pot into the ground and fill it with potting compost. Plant the rooted runner, peg it down with a U-shaped wire peg, and keep it watered. In 4–6 weeks, once it has established, sever it from its parent. It is now ready for transplanting.

troughs, towers, hanging baskets, and growing bags are all economical in terms of space. Second, they are mobile, and can therefore be moved into a sunny, sheltered spot to take advantage of light and warmth or brought under cover for protection from cold. Third, they can be raised off the ground to protect them from slugs. And, lastly, they are less prone to soil-borne diseases.

Almost any kind of container is suitable, as long as it is deep enough and has sufficient drainage holes. Special terracotta or plastic strawberry pots have cup-shaped pockets around their sides in which individual plants are grown. Some have a central watering tube that helps prevent plants at the bottom from drying out. Tower pots are similar but are constructed from a number of stackable, self-contained units. Growing bags are particularly effective. They are best planted in spring and early summer with cold-stored runners or young, container-grown plants, and can be raised off the ground, either on planks or boxes or on a special "table-top" frame.

All containers should be watered regularly. Little and often is the mantra, so that the plants always remain moist, never becoming waterlogged, and never drying out. As soon as plants flower, start giving them a weekly liquid feed with a high-potash/low-nitrate fertilizer (tomato food, for example). After harvesting, when you remove all the old foliage, give them one last feed with a compound general fertilizer, then nothing more until next spring. Replace the plants every two or three years.

Growing strawberries under cover

The term under cover is used here to mean anything from a temporary cloche to a full-sized greenhouse. Whichever method you choose, the objective of growing plants under cover is always the same: to extend the season so that you can harvest fruits earlier or later than you would if you were growing strawberries outdoors.

Forcing outdoor strawberries for an early crop

Early varieties grown outdoors can be encouraged to fruit up to three weeks earlier than usual by covering the plants with glass or plastic cloches or

Greenhouse-grown strawberries will crop earlier than those grown outdoors without cover, but may not have as much flavour.

during the winter. It's best to plant up new runners in summer and leave them outdoors, exposing them to a certain amount of cold weather but protecting them from any severe, late-autumn or early-winter frosts and from heavy rain. Then bring them indoors, either into a heated greenhouse in about mid-December or into an unheated greenhouse in January. The plants should flower in February. As soon as they do, and because no insects will be around, hand-pollinate them every day using a small, soft brush. If pollination is successful and the fruit sets, begin watering regularly and feed with a liquid, high-potash fertilizer. On warm days, open doors or windows to keep the temperature at 20–24°C (68–75°F). You should have strawberries from a heated greenhouse as early as March or April, and from an unheated one in early May.

with low polythene tunnels in February or early in March. As soon as the flowers open, begin removing the covers on warm days so that insects can pollinate them. Remember that plants under cover will need watering by hand.

Forcing greenhouse strawberries for an early crop

Even earlier crops are possible by growing strawberries in containers brought under cover

Growing winter strawberries under cover

Day-neutral strawberries are the ones to choose if you really want to prolong the season. They will continue producing fruit completely irrespective of the length of day, as long as the temperature does not drop below 10°C (50°F). Plant them in pots at any time between June and September, bring them into an unheated greenhouse in autumn, and they may well fruit right up until Christmas. Perhaps not as delicious as an outdoor-grown strawberry in midsummer, they are welcome nonetheless.

ALPINE STRAWBERRIES

Like miniature versions of regular strawberries, Alpine strawberries (right) are closer to the original wild species than cultivated varieties. Also known as *fraises des bois*, meaning woodland strawberries, they produce tiny fruits – not much larger than peas – throughout the summer months. They have a fragrance and concentrated, intense flavour that makes them highly prized. They're easy to grow and can be bought as small, ready-grown container plants or raised from seed. Sow indoors or under cover in early spring, and plant out in May, in a partially shaded area if summers are hot. You may get a few berries in the first year, but you'll get a lot more in the second. Established plants are likely to self-seed and should spread readily.

Month by month

(left to right) **Flowers** begin to open in mid-spring. **Green fruitlets** soon follow on. **Ripe berries** are particularly attractive to birds as well as slugs.

March

■ Cover outdoor plants with cloches or tunnels in order to force an early crop.

■ Feed plants with a general, compound fertilizer.

■ Plant bare-root runners or new, pot-grown strawberries outdoors this month or next – though don't expect a crop this year.

■ Plant day-neutral varieties outdoors this month or next – they should crop in July-September.

April

■ Most varieties flower this month or next. Protect against frost damage if necessary, but uncover to allow pollination.

■ As fruits start to appear, put strawberry mats in place or spread a layer of straw around and underneath the plants.

■ Harvest greenhouse strawberries.

May

■ Water regularly as berries fatten up and ripen.

■ Protect plants against slugs, and net to keep off birds.

■ Plant cold-stored runners outdoors between now and July – they should crop within 8–12 weeks.

■ Harvest very early-season summer-fruiting varieties.

June

■ Harvest early- and mid-season summer-fruiting varieties.

■ Plant day-neutral varieties in pots between now and September – they will crop under cover from autumn through early winter.

■ Propagate by potting up young plantlets from runners between now and August.

July

■ Harvest mid- and late-season summer-fruiting varieties, and the first of the perpetual varieties.

■ New bare-root runners start to become available.

■ Plant new runners outdoors now or next month for a crop next year.

August

■ Plant day-neutral varieties outdoors between now and October – they will crop next summer.

■ Cut back and tidy up all plants that have finished fruiting.

September

■ Plant bare-root runners or new, pot-grown strawberries between now and November – though it is too late to expect much of a crop next year.

October

■ Harvest the last of the perpetual varieties until the first frost of winter – unless you cover them with cloches in order to prolong the season.

November

■ Last chance until next spring for planting new strawberries outdoors.

December

■ Bring pot-grown strawberries into a heated greenhouse for an early crop next March or April.

■ Harvest the last of container-grown, day-neutral varieties brought under cover earlier in the autumn.

What can go wrong

Flowers

Flower buds droop and fail to open
Tiny grubs hatch and feed inside young flower buds, preventing the flowers from opening. They may sever the stalks so that the buds droop, die, and fall off.
■ See **Strawberry blossom weevil** (p.340).

Green petals
Flowers are smaller than normal and petals are green instead of white or pink. Leaves turn yellow or red, and fruit may be misshapen or may simply not develop at all. A virus is probably the cause.
■ See **Strawberry green petal** (p.331).

Leaves and stems

1 Yellow-red blotches with grey centres
Irregular purple-red spots on leaves may spread and enlarge into grey-centred blotches with red and yellow margins. The blotches may turn into holes and an off-white mould may appear.
■ See **Fungal leaf spot** (p.327).

2 Yellow leaves with green veins
If leaves turn yellow with clearly visible, skeletal green veins, and if the plant is obviously growing poorly, then it's usually a sign that the soil is too alkaline and the plant is suffering from "lime-induced chlorosis", meaning that it is unable to absorb sufficient iron and manganese.
■ See **Iron deficiency** (p.320), **Manganese deficiency** (p.321).

Discoloured, wilted leaves and fine silk web
Green leaves mottle and turn bronze or pale yellow, wither, and die. A fine silk web spun over infested plants is the tell-tale sign that this might be spider mites. The problem can occur both under cover and outdoors.
■ See **Red spider mite** (p.339).

Curled, sticky leaves
Aphids are the most likely cause. The yellow- or greenfly are at their worst in spring, when they feed on new growth, especially if plants are growing under cover. Aphids spread viruses.
■ See **Aphids** (p.334).

Distorted, yellow-patterned leaves
Crumpled, crinkled, or stunted leaves with yellow margins, yellow spots and blotches, or yellow mosaic patterning are all symptoms of different viruses that can attack strawberries.
■ See **Strawberry virus** (p.331).

Dark patches and white powdery coating
Leaves develop dark, red-purple, blotchy patches on their upper surfaces, and a grey-white powder covers the undersides. The leaves curl upwards at the edges. Powdery mildew is caused by a fungus, and tends to be worse when the weather is hot and dry. Flowers and fruit may be affected too.
■ See **Powdery mildew** (p.329).

1

2

Leaves discolour and wilt

In summer, older leaves are red or brown, and young leaves are yellow. There may be black streaks on leaf stems, and the whole plant wilts and may die. The cause is likely to be verticillium wilt.
■ See **Verticillium wilt** (p.331).

Leaves wilt and base of stems rots

Leaves turn yellow and wilt, and the plant may die. Symptoms are similar to those of verticillium wilt but in this case the crown of the plant is also brown and rotten.
■ See **Crown rot** (p.326).

Stunted growth and red-brown leaves

Plants are smaller than normal. Inner leaves are red or orange, and outer leaves are brown and dry. The central cores of roots are red instead of white. The cause is the fungus known as red core.
■ See **Red core** (p.330).

Poor growth and small, wrinkled, brown leaves

Symptoms tend to appear in late summer, especially in hot, dry weather. Plants are small, and young leaves are brown and wrinkled. Tiny, pale brown strawberry mites may be the cause.
■ See **Strawberry mite** (p.340).

Crinkled leaves with thick stalks

Overall poor or stunted growth, crumpled, distorted leaves, and stalks either shorter and thicker than normal, or longer and coloured red, may be caused by an infestation of eelworms.
■ See **Eelworms** (p.336).

Leaves nibbled and roots eaten

Adult vine weevils eat notch-shaped holes out of the edges of the leaves and larvae feed underground on the roots. If severely attacked, plants may wilt and die.
■ See **Vine weevils** (p.340).

Fruit

3 Fluffy, grey or brown mould

In wet summers or in damp and humid conditions, fruits may become covered with mould and start to rot. The likely cause is the fungus, *Botrytis cinerea*.
■ See **Botrytis** (p.325).

4 Fruit partially or wholly eaten

Both birds and slugs find ripe strawberries absolutely irresistible and will attack them relentlessly.
■ See **Birds** (p.335), **Slugs** (p.339).

Strawberry seeds eaten out

If the fruits appear to have been nibbled and the seeds have been removed and eaten – especially on the undersides – suspect black strawberry beetles. They hide under leaves or straw in daytime.
■ See **Strawberry beetles** (p.340).

Fruit loses its shine

Berries that are dull rather than shiny and that are perhaps also stunted or distorted may be infected with powdery mildew.
■ See **Powdery mildew** (p.329).

4

Raspberries

The aroma and the flavour of a bowl of ripe, fresh raspberries captures the essence of midsummer. Traditionally, however, the raspberry season was woefully short. Most summer-fruiting raspberries lasted no more than three weeks or so, and were then over until next year. Admittedly, autumn-fruiting varieties were available that prolonged the season, but their yields were low and the berries lacked taste. Nowadays, modern autumn-fruiting cultivars are much improved, making it possible – at least in theory – to pick and eat fresh fruits from early July right through to the first frost of the autumn.

Once raspberries are established and you've got the hang of their basic pruning requirements, they're fairly easy to grow. They are vigorous plants and the summer-fruiting varieties, especially, will need sturdy supports as well as protection from hungry birds. For a reasonable crop, you'll need a row of canes 2–3m (6–10ft) long and if you are growing both summer- and autumn-fruiting varieties, make sure you keep them completely separate.

Picking perfectly ripe raspberries on a dry day is one of summer's great pleasures. You can still harvest the berries if the weather is wet but they won't keep as well. Red berries can be summer- or autumn fruiting, but the gold or yellow vareties tend to crop in autumn.

Which forms to grow

■ **Canes** Summer-fruiting raspberries grow tall and need supporting. Autumn-fruiting raspberries are shorter and can be grown without, though they too will do better with supports. Most support systems employ wooden posts and either a single or double row of wires.

Must-grow raspberries

1 'Glen Ample'
Summer-fruiting
Modern variety with very high yields and a longer season than most. Spine-free canes and good pest and disease resistance. A Scottish-bred offspring of 'Glen Prosen'.
■ **Harvest** late June to early August

2 'Tulameen'
Summer-fruiting
Large, bright red berries with excellent flavour. Crops generously, often for 4–6 weeks. Bred in Canada, it is hardy with good resistance to disease.
■ **Harvest** early July to mid-August

3 'Octavia'
Summer-fruiting
A late-cropping summer raspberry that produces a good harvest of large, well-flavoured berries throughout August, just before the first of the autumn-fruiting varieties are ready.
■ **Harvest** late July to late August

4 'Glen Moy'
Summer-fruiting
One of the earliest summer raspberries. In a good year fruit may even be ready for picking by the middle of June. Fine flavour, spine-free canes, aphid-resistant.
■ **Harvest** mid-June to late July

5 'Malling Admiral'
Summer-fruiting
A popular variety producing large, dark red berries with good flavour. Disease resistant and easy to grow. Medium yields.
■ **Harvest** mid-July to mid-August

6 'Allgold'
Autumn-fruiting
Perhaps the best of the yellow raspberries. Similar in growth habit to 'Autumn Bliss' but with sweeter, juicier berries. Sometimes confused with the very similar 'Fallgold'.
■ **Harvest** mid-August to early October

7 'Glencoe'
Summer-fruiting
New variety with unusual purple berries, intense flavour, and high yields. Canes are without spines, and tend to grow in a bushy clump, thus needing less support than most.
■ **Harvest** July to August

8 'Autumn Bliss'
Autumn-fruiting
The variety that launched the new generation of heavy-cropping, autumn-fruiting raspberries. Large, firm berries are well-flavoured and grow on short, stout canes.
■ **Harvest** mid-August to early October

9 'Joan J'
Autumn-fruiting
Widely grown for its bumper crops of sweet, juicy fruit – and also because it can produce continuously for two months or more. Berries are larger than those of 'Autumn Bliss'.
■ **Harvest** early August to early October

10 'Polka'
Autumn-fruiting
A recently introduced Polish variety, bred from 'Autumn Bliss' but capable of producing twice its yield. Large, aromatic berries that store well. Good disease resistance.
■ **Harvest** late July to early October

'Autumn Treasure' (not illustrated)
Autumn-fruiting
A modern English variety that produces large, conical berries of a bright red colour on sturdy, spine-free canes. Good pest and disease resistance, so it is a sensible choice for organic growers not wishing to use chemicals. Crops a little later than 'Autumn Bliss'.
■ **Harvest** late August to mid-September

'Belle de Malicorne' (not illustrated)
Autumn-fruiting
A French variety that produces large, bright red berries. Given the right growing conditions, it can fruit twice a year, once in midsummer and again in autumn – until very late if it is protected from frosts.
■ **Harvest** mid-June to late July and again mid-September to mid-November

'Cascade Delight' (not illustrated)
Summer-fruiting
Originally bred in the Pacific northwest region of North America, this raspberry is increasingly widely available in the UK. It is resistant to root rot and therefore ideal for damp conditions. Heavy crops of large fruits with excellent flavour.
■ **Harvest** early July to mid August

'Glen Fyne' (not illustrated)
Summer-fruiting
The most recent of the Scottish 'Glen' raspberries, introduced in 2008. Spine-free canes carry early crops of large, bright red berries with an outstanding flavour.
■ **Harvest** mid-June to late July

'Glen Prosen' (not illustrated)
Summer-fruiting
Smooth, spine-free canes and good crops of firm berries that have an excellent flavour. Resistant to viruses.
■ **Harvest** mid-July to mid-August

'Leo' (not illustrated)
Summer-fruiting
Not the heaviest of croppers but useful in that it's the latest of the summer-fruiting varieties: you may still be picking until almost the end of August.
■ **Harvest** late July to late August

'Malling Jewel' (not illustrated)
Summer-fruiting
An old favourite that fruits slightly earlier than 'Malling Admiral'. Plants are fairly compact and growth is not as rampant as others – a good choice for smaller plots.
■ **Harvest** early July to late July

Growing raspberries

Summer- and autumn-fruiting raspberries behave differently. Summer varieties fruit on last year's canes, and autumn varieties fruit on this year's. They are therefore pruned very differently. To get it right, you must know which you are dealing with, and you must keep them well separated. If they spread and the two types merge you'll get very confused, not knowing which canes to cut down and which to leave for next year.

(left) **Bare-root raspberry canes** are often sold in bundles by specialist nurseries and garden centres for planting out in late autumn until early spring. Container-grown canes may be available year-round but are still best planted in late autumn or in late spring when the soil is beginning to warm, allowing the plants to establish quickly.

The year at a glance

	spring			summer			autumn			winter		
	M	A	M	J	J	A	S	O	N	D	J	F
plant bare-root												
plant container												
prune												
harvest												

Choosing plants

Raspberries can be bought either as bare-root or container-grown plants, although bare-root forms are likely to be available only in autumn and winter. Each plant comes as a single cane not much thicker than a pencil, with its own root system. Look for small white buds on the roots from which new shoots or suckers will grow. It's important to buy certified virus-free plants.

When to plant

■ BARE-ROOT Plant between November and March, although not if the ground is frozen.
■ CONTAINER-GROWN Plant at any time of year – preferably in November to December, or in March, and not in hot, dry summer months.

Where to plant

Choose a sheltered site, out of strong winds, to prevent canes being damaged. Raspberries will tolerate some shade, but they ripen best in full sun, especially autumn-fruiting varieties, which crop late in the season.

Soil type

Raspberries need plenty of water, but they must have free-draining soil. If they become waterlogged, even for short periods of time, the roots are likely to die. If you garden on heavy soil, consider planting them in raised beds.

Raspberries like a slightly acidic soil with a pH of around 6.0-6.5. If your soil is alkaline (higher than 7.5, say) acidify it to help prevent lime-induced chlorosis (see p.320). If it is dry and sandy, add plenty of organic matter to help retain moisture, and water regularly.

How to plant

Prepare the soil thoroughly in advance and erect your post-and-wire supports. Weed meticulously. Dig a trench, add some well-rotted compost or manure, and mix it in with the soil.

Raspberries don't need planting very deeply. Spread out the roots at a depth of about 8cm (3in), firm down the soil, and cut off the top of each cane to a bud about 25cm (10in) above ground level. When new shoots start to emerge from below ground in spring, they'll grow more strongly if you cut the original cane right down to the level of the soil. It may feel drastic but it's worth it.

Planting distances

- CANES 38–45cm (15–18in) apart.
- ROW SPACING 2m (6ft) apart.

Growing in containers

Raspberries can be grown in pots, although they may not yield a large crop. Shorter, autumn-fruiting varieties are likely to be more successful. Plant two or three canes together in a single container about 30cm (12in) in diameter, and be prepared to support the canes as they grow, perhaps against a fence or trellis. Watering is crucial: they must never get waterlogged, nor must they ever be allowed to dry out.

(below, left to right) **Newly planted canes** will get off to a good start if you dig well-rotted compost into the planting trench to improve soil structure. **New shoots** soon begin to grow in spring and burst into leaf. Mulch the plants thickly to keep moisture locked into the soil, especially after feeding. **Cut down** the original cane to soil level, taking care not to damage the new growth. This will encourage the plant to produce more canes, as well as helping it to establish a strong root system.

Routine care

■ WATERING Water regularly, once or twice a week in a dry summer, especially when the berries are beginning to fatten up. Try to avoid splashing the canes or you may spread fungal infections.

■ FEEDING Raspberries are hungry plants and do need feeding. In March, top-dress the soil around the plants with a general, compound fertilizer to boost levels of nitrogen, phosphate, and potash.

■ MULCHING After feeding, water the soil thoroughly. Then spread a 5–8cm (2–3in) thick mulch of well-rotted manure or compost around the plants, without it touching the canes themselves.

■ NETTING Summer-fruiting raspberries need nets or a fruit cage to keep off birds. Autumn-fruiting varieties seem to generate less interest and can be grown without netting.

■ FROST PROTECTION Raspberries flower later in the year than most other soft fruits, so are less susceptible to frost damage.

Harvesting and storing

Most summer-fruiting raspberries ripen in July, though a few go on into August. Autumn-fruiting varieties start in August and may continue cropping until October, or when they are halted by the first frost of the winter. Unlike blackberries, the "plug" or core remains behind on the bush when you pick the fruit. So, if the berries don't come away easily, they're not ready. Ripe raspberries will keep for a few days in the fridge but, if you're not going to eat them promptly, freeze them soon after picking. Don't leave ripened fruits on the bush: they will rot and subsequent berries won't grow to their full size.

Yield

Crops tend to be heavier from summer-fruiting than from autumn-fruiting varieties. For each 1m (3ft) section of a row of canes, you might get 2–3kg (4.5–6.5lb) of summer raspberries and 1–1.5kg (2.2–3.3lb) of autumn raspberries.

Propagation

Young shoots can be lifted to make new plants very easily. Carefully dig up a healthy looking sucker with a fork so that it has some roots attached at its base, and cut it off from the main rootball. Replant it in a pot or elsewhere in the ground. Avoid propagating from old or unhealthy canes. It's safer to buy new, disease-free plants.

(top to bottom) **Correct watering** is important when the berries are ripening. Remove the rose attachment from the watering can so you don't splash the foliage and inadvertently spread fungal diseases. **Pick raspberries** when it's dry – although, if it's wet, you have the perfect excuse to eat them immediately as they won't keep. Slightly underripe berries are better for cooking or freezing.

Month by month

February
■ Plant bare-root canes if the ground is not frozen.
■ Tip-prune overwintering summer-fruiting canes.
■ Cut down and remove all last year's autumn-fruiting canes.

March
■ New young leaves start to appear on last year's summer-fruiting canes.
■ New canes start to shoot from below ground on autumn-fruiting varieties.
■ Feed with a general, compound fertilizer, then mulch around plants.
■ Plant new canes now if you didn't do so last autumn – it's your last chance to plant bare-root ones.

May
■ Flower buds form, and blossom opens ready for pollination.
■ Begin weeding and watering.
■ Net summer-fruiting berries against birds.

June
■ Water generously, at least once a week or more if the weather is dry.

■ Tie in new growth securely.

July
■ Harvest summer-fruiting berries.
■ Continue watering regularly as fruits ripen.

August
■ Harvest the last of the summer-fruiting and the first of the autumn-fruiting berries.
■ Cut down and remove summer-fruiting canes that have finished cropping. Tie in and loop over the new canes for next year.

September
■ Harvest autumn-fruiting berries.

October
■ Continue harvesting until the first frost.
■ New bare-root canes start to become available from specialist nurseries.

November
■ The best month for planting bare-root or container-grown canes.

Pruning and training raspberries

Summer- and autumn-fruiting raspberries are pruned very differently. Each needs pruning only once a year, but you need to know when – or you'll be in for a disappointing crop. Autumn-fruiting raspberries fruit on this year's canes. So, when they're finished you cut them down to the ground. Next year, the plants grow from scratch all over again. Summer-fruiting raspberries, however, fruit on the canes that grew the year before. You can, of course, remove those when all the berries have been picked, but you mustn't cut down the new canes that haven't yet fruited: you need those for next year.

Post-and-wire supports

A specially erected system of posts and wires is the best way to support raspberries, especially summer-fruiting varieties, which grow tall. Use 8 x 8cm (3 x 3in) treated wooden posts each 2.5m (8ft) in length. Sink them into the ground to a depth of 60cm (24in) and stretch horizontal lengths of heavy-gauge galvanized wire between them, either in a single row or in double rows attached to cross-pieces.

Single-wire supports

- Use three horizontal lengths of wire, at heights of about 75cm (30in), 1.1m (3 ½ft), and 1.5m (5ft).
- Tension them with straining bolts.
- As new canes grow, tie them in to the wires with string.

Double-wire supports

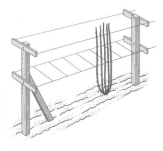

- Attach two cross-pieces 60cm (2ft) long to each of the wooden posts, one at a height of about 1m (3ft) and the other at 1.5m (5ft).
- Stretch parallel wires horizontally between them, and tie further wires or string crossways at regular intervals.
- Canes will grow up between the grid.

Summer-fruiting raspberries grow tall and definitely need supports. Autumn-fruiting raspberries are shorter and can be grown without, though they too will do better with supports.

Pruning summer-fruiting raspberries

Pruning mostly takes place in late summer, after all the fruit has been harvested. New canes, which will fruit next year, are tied in securely and merely tip-pruned lightly in winter.

1 In late summer, after harvesting, cut down to the base all canes that have fruited this year. This will let in light and air and reduce the risk of disease spreading from old growth.

2 At the same time, make sure that this year's new canes are tied in about 10cm (4in) apart. If they are overlong, arch them over and secure them in tall loops. It keeps them tidy and prevents wind damage.

3 In February, tip-prune the looped-over canes to about 15cm (6in) above the highest horizontal wire. These are the canes that will bear fruit this summer.

Pruning autumn-fruiting raspberries

After harvesting, the fruited canes are left in the ground over winter. Pruning does not take place until February, when all the old growth is cut down completely. New canes, which emerge in spring and grow up during the summer, will fruit from August until the first frosts.

1 Raspberries are hardy plants and can be left to overwinter without the need for protection.

2 In February, cut down to the base all the canes that grew last year.

3 New canes may need some support before they reach the height of the first wires. Hold them up by gathering them loosely together with string.

4 In early summer, prune out any new canes that are obviously spindly and weak, or are growing out at awkward angles.

What can go wrong

Leaves and canes

1 Yellow leaves with green veins
Yellowing of new leaves may indicate lack of iron, and of older, lower leaves lack of manganese. Called "lime-induced chlorosis", it is common in alkaline soils with a high pH.
■ See **Iron deficiency** (p.320), **Manganese deficiency** (p.321).

2 Leaves curled, brown, and dying
This may be a sign of either drought or lack of potassium, which often goes hand-in-hand with iron deficiency.
■ See **Potassium deficiency** (p.321).

3 Purple spots with white or grey centres
These signs of disease appear on both canes and on leaves. Serious infections can cause complete dieback.
■ See **Raspberry cane spot** (p.329).

White powdery coating on leaves
Powdery mildew is caused by a fungus, and tends to be more active when the weather is hot and dry. Leaves may yellow and die, and canes may wilt. Occasionally, fruits will spoil.
■ See **Powdery mildew** (p.329).

Curled, sticky leaves
Aphids cause leaves to become distorted and build up a sticky or sooty coating.
■ See **Aphids** (p.334).

Mottling or mosaic patterns on leaves
Blotchy, yellow-green patches, stunted growth, perhaps with downward curling at the edges, may be signs of a virus.
■ See **Raspberry virus** (p.329).

Pale yellow blotches on leaves
A sap-sucking mite is often responsible, but a more serious virus that produces similar symptoms may also be the cause.
■ See **Raspberry leaf and bud mite** (p.338).

Small holes eaten in leaves
Tiny, red-brown spots and holes with tattered, brown edges may be signs of attack by capsid bugs, which suck sap and are hard to spot.
■ See **Capsid bugs** (p.335).

Orange, rust-like patches on leaves
Rust is a fungus that affects many soft fruits. It is unlikely to be fatal.
■ See **Rust** (p.330).

Purple patches on canes around new buds
Blotches turn from purple–brown to silvery-grey in autumn and you may be able to spot tiny black fungal spores. New growth on infected canes may die the following spring.
■ See **Raspberry spur blight** (p.329).

Canes split and break
A fungal infection at the base of canes causes them to go dark brown, turn brittle, and snap off.
■ See **Raspberry cane blight** (see p.329).

Caterpillars or maggots
Red caterpillars burrowing inside new shoots are likely to be those of the raspberry moth. Small pink maggots, found just under the bark of canes, are the larvae of the raspberry cane midge.
■ See **Raspberry moth** (p.339), **Raspberry cane midge** (p.338).

Fruit

4 Fluffy, grey mould
Affected fruits become covered with powdery mould and start to rot.
■ See **Botrytis** (p.325).

5 Fruits eaten
Birds find raspberries irresistible, especially summer-fruiting varieties. Wasps and other insects are equally attracted to them.
■ See **Birds** (p.335), **Wasps** (p.341).

Maggots in fruits
Ripening berries may shrivel, discolour, and rot where they join the stalk. Inside, you may find the pale, creamy-brown grubs of the raspberry beetle, feeding.
■ See **Raspberry beetle** (p.338).

Blackberries and hybrid berries

These fruit all started out as wild brambles. In fact, provided you know where to look, it's still perfectly possible to pick as many wild blackberries as you're ever likely to need from hedgerows, woodland, and roadsides. However, in gardens and on allotments, you can grow specially bred, cultivated varieties. The fruit will be bigger and better quality, the yield will be higher, and new plants should be disease-free.

Hybrid berries – which include loganberries, tayberries, and a handful of other less familiar names – are the result of cross-breeding between blackberries and raspberries, and some of them date back to the 19th century. Plant-breeding programmes continue today, of course, though they now tend to concentrate on creating more compact, less rampant varieties, without thorns, and with larger, sweeter berries. All of these are welcome initiatives from the point of view of grow-your-own fruit gardeners.

Most blackberries have a long season. The first fruits may be ready for picking in July, and further berries should continue to grow and ripen well into the autumn – although they are likely to become increasingly "pippy" as time goes on.

Must-grow blackberries

1 **'Loch Ness'**
A compact, thornless variety that does not require a lot of space or complex training. Good-sized fruit, good yields, and good flavour.
■ **Harvest** from late August

2 **'Black Butte'**
Originally from the western United States, very large berries as much as double the size and weight of traditional fruits. Good for eating and cooking.
■ **Harvest** from mid-July

3 **'Silvan'**
Sometimes spelled 'Sylvan', an Australian variety with long, dark blue-black berries that ripen early. Good disease resistance.
■ **Harvest** from early July

4 **'Oregon Thornless'**
Originally bred from a wild European blackberry, it has distinctive, very attractive foliage. Harvesting can last into October.
■ **Harvest** from late August

5 **'Waldo'**
An early cropping, modern variety with large, exceptional-tasting berries. It is compact and thornless, so ideal for small gardens.
■ **Harvest** from mid–late July

'Fantasia' (not illustrated)
Heavy crops of large, delicious berries – though the thorny, fast-growing canes need strict taming if they're not to run out of control.
■ **Harvest** from late August

'Helen' (not illustrated)
Recent, compact, thornless variety that may be ready to pick very early and is resistant to disease.
■ **Harvest** from early July

'Karaka Black' (not illustrated)
A New Zealand variety with long, cylindrical, well-flavoured fruits. It crops from July through to September.
■ **Harvest** from mid-July

Must-grow hybrid berries

1 Loganberry
Hybrid raspberry × blackberry. Originally created in California in the 19th century. The berries are sharp-tasting and better for cooking than eating fresh.
■ **Harvest** from mid-July

2 Boysenberry
Hybrid loganberry × blackberry. Large, juicy, red-purple fruits that taste distinctly of blackberries.
■ **Harvest** from late July

3 Tayberry
Hybrid raspberry × blackberry. First bred in Scotland in the 1960s. The berries are red-purple, have a fine flavour, and are larger and sweeter than loganberries.
■ **Harvest** from mid-July

4 Japanese wineberry
A species in its own right. Clusters of unusual, small, red berries are sweet and juicy, and all ripen at the same time.
■ **Harvest** August

Dewberry (not illustrated)
Also a species in its own right rather than a hybrid. Grown widely in the US as a trailing bramble, less common in Europe.
■ **Harvest** July

Marionberry (not illustrated)
Sometimes classed as a hybrid, sometimes as a true 'Marion' blackberry, this US cultivar certainly has loganberry in its parentage. Very long, trailing canes and berries with a superb flavour.
■ **Harvest** from late July

Tummelberry (not illustrated)
A Scots-bred variant on the tayberry. Hardier but not so sweet. Closer in flavour to a loganberry.
■ **Harvest** from mid-July

Other hybrid berries that you may be able to obtain from specialist nurseries include:
King's Acre Berry
Sunberry
Veitchberry
Youngberry

Growing blackberries

Most blackberries and hybrid berries grow vigorously and do not require a lot of attention. If anything, you'll find they need taming rather than encouraging. Pruning them once a year, after you've finished harvesting the fruit, is important as it will clear out old canes that have no further use and create space for the new growth that will bear fruit the following year.

The year at a glance

	spring			summer			autumn			winter		
	M	A	M	J	J	A	S	O	N	D	J	F
plant bare-root	▬	▬					▬	▬	▬	▬	▬	▬
plant container	▬	▬	▬	▬								
prune						▬	▬	▬				
harvest				▬	▬	▬	▬					

Blackberry bushes will produce heavier crops if you train the new canes along horizontal wires, and keep tying in the long fruiting stems. Some of the best varieties are thornless, which makes for much easier harvesting.

Choosing plants

Blackberries and hybrid berries can be obtained bare-root but they are usually sold as container-grown plants. They don't look very impressive – you're most likely to get just a single cane, not much thicker than a pencil. For healthy plants, make sure you buy certified virus-free stock and of a recognized variety or cultivar.

When to plant

■ BARE-ROOT Plant between October and March,

PLANTING A BLACKBERRY BUSH

This container-grown blackberry is to be trained across a wooden fence. If you plan to use a system of posts and wires, it's best to construct it before you plant. If possible, dig some well-rotted compost or manure into the soil a month or two beforehand. And remember to remove all perennial weeds.

1 Dig a hole deep enough and wide enough to accommodate the plant's rootball comfortably, allowing for an additional 10cm (4in) all round.

2 Give the plant a good soaking with water, remove it from its container or wrapping, and place it in the hole.

3 Check the depth to ensure that the top of the rootball is level with or slightly below the surface of your soil.

4 Carefully firm down the soil. Water generously and spread an organic mulch around the plant, keeping it clear of the stem. If necessary, shorten the cane to a bud at a height of about 22–25cm (8–10in), and cut it off completely in midsummer once other new canes emerge.

---

although not if the ground is frozen or waterlogged.
■ CONTAINER-GROWN Plant at any time of year – preferably in November or March, and not in hot, dry summer months.

Where to plant

Choose a sheltered site, out of strong winds. Hybrid berries need full sun in order ripen successfully in summer. For blackberries this is not so crucial; most varieties are still productive in partial shade.

Soil type

Blackberries are tolerant of most soils as long as they are free-draining. Hybrid berries are a little fussier: they appreciate a deep, rich, fertile soil. Both will grow best if your soil has had plenty of organic matter added to it to help provide nutrients and retain moisture. Add some lime if the pH of your soil is below 5.5.

Planting distances

■ LEAST VIGOROUS 2.5–3m (8–10ft) apart.
■ FAIRLY VIGOROUS 3–4.5m (10–13ft) apart.
■ VERY VIGOROUS 4.5–5m (13–16ft) apart.
■ ROW SPACING 2m (6ft) apart.

Routine care

■ WATERING In a dry summer water generously, at least once a week, particularly when the berries are turning from red to black. Try not to splash the new canes or the fruit to minimize the risk of spreading fungal infections.
■ FEEDING In late February or early March, top-dress the soil around the plants with a general, compound fertilizer.
■ MULCHING About a month after feeding, pull rather than hoe out any weeds and water the ground well. Then spread a 5–8cm (2–3in) mulch of well-rotted manure or compost around the plants,

PROPAGATION BY TIP LAYERING

Blackberries and hybrid berries are easy to propagate. New shoots will quickly develop roots if they come into contact with the soil. Indeed, in the case of dense, overgrown bushes, you may well find it happening naturally, without your help.

1 Between July and September, bend over the tip of a new shoot and bury it in the soil to a depth of about 10cm (4in). Firm it down and water it in.

2 By the end of the year, the tip should have rooted. Cut it free from its parent, and either pot it up or leave it until spring, then transplant.

without letting it touch the canes.

■ NETTING Hybrid berries are more likely to need nets to keep off birds than are blackberries.

■ FROST PROTECTION Blackberries and hybrid berries flower relatively late in spring, and are less prone to frost damage than most other soft fruits.

Harvesting and storing

Blackberries are ready to pick when they are plump and shiny-black. They should pull away easily in your hand, with the plug or core still in the fruit. If they resist, they're not ready, and if they squash easily then they are overripe. Ripe blackberries will keep for a few days in the fridge but, if you're not going to eat them promptly, they freeze well.

Hybrid berries should be left to ripen as long as you dare, to develop maximum flavour and sweetness. It's tempting to pick them too soon. The best time to harvest them is in the morning, after the dew has dried and before it gets too hot, or in the evening. Wet berries won't store well.

Yield

It's hard to generalize about yields, as the size and vigour of bushes vary so greatly. However, expect something in the range of 5–15kg (11–32lb).

(below left to right) **Pick ripe fruits** while they are still firm to the touch. They should come away easily, with the plug, which is edible, still in the fruit. **Freeze ripe berries** if you have a surplus and use them for cooking during the winter months.

Month by month

February
- Plant bare-root canes if the ground is not frozen.
- Spread out and tie in last year's new canes if you didn't do so the previous autumn.
- Feed with a general fertilizer at the end of this month or do it early next month.

March
- Leaf buds begin to burst and new young leaves start to appear.
- Weed and mulch around plants to suppress weeds.
- Along with November, March is the best month for planting – and it is the last chance to plant bare-root canes.

May
- Blossom should be fully open, and pollinating insects will be at work.
- First young fruitlets start to form as the blossom drops.
- Weed and water if necessary.

June
- Water more generously if the weather is dry – once a week or more.
- Net hybrid berries against birds.
- Train new growth away from fruiting canes and tie it in neatly. These new canes will fruit next year.

July
- Harvest early-season fruits.
- In hot weather continue watering regularly as fruits ripen.
- Over the next three months, propagate new plants by tip layering.

August
- Harvest mid-season fruits.

September
- Harvest late-season fruits.
- Cut down and remove canes that have fruited this summer – either this month or at any time before the end of the year.
- Spread out and tie in this year's new canes in place of the fruited canes you have just removed. These new canes will fruit next year.

October
- New bare-root canes start to become available from specialist nurseries.

November
- This month and March are the best times for planting bare-root or container-grown canes.
- Uproot new plants propagated by tip layering and transplant.

(top to bottom) **New buds** emerge early in spring. **Blossom** appears a couple of months later, when frosts are usually over. **Pollinated flowers** form fruitlets. **Berries** soon start to ripen.

Pruning and training blackberries

Blackberries and hybrid berries all fruit on one-year-old canes from the previous summer. Training separates last year's canes (the ones bearing fruit this summer) from this year's canes (the new shoots that will fruit next summer). Pruning after harvesting removes all the old canes that have just fruited.

Wire-training methods

Use 8 x 8cm (3 x 3in) treated wooden posts each 2.5m (8ft) tall and sink them to a depth of 60cm (24in). Stretch 4 horizontal lengths of heavy-gauge wire between them, 35–45cm (14–18in) apart.

Upright fan This year's fruiting canes are fanned out, and the new ones grow up the centre. In autumn or winter, the fruited canes are cut out and new canes take their place.

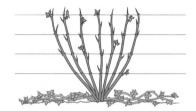

Trailing fan New canes trail on the ground on either side of this year's fan. When old fruited canes are cut down, new canes are raised up and tied in position as a new fan.

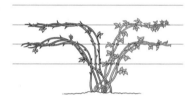

Alternate bay This year's fruiting canes are tied to one side, and all new growth is tied to the other side. So, one side fruits and the other doesn't. Next year everything swaps.

Pruning and training an established blackberry

Pruning takes place in autumn, when you simply cut out all the canes that have finished fruiting. Thereafter, it's a matter of tying in new growth to keep new and one-year-old canes separated.

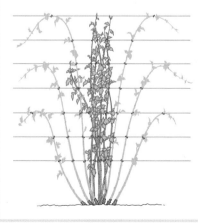

1 In autumn, after harvesting, cut down to the base all canes that have fruited this year.

2 During the winter or next spring, move last year's new canes into position for fruiting in the coming season and tie them in place.

3 As the new season's shoots emerge and form new canes, carefully tie them in too, training them out of the way of this year's fruiting canes. They will fruit next year.

What can go wrong

Leaves and canes

1 Purple spots with white or grey centres
These appear on leaves and on canes, and can cause complete dieback. Both blackberries and hybrid berries (particularly loganberries) may be affected.
■ See **Blackberry cane spot** (p.325) or **Raspberry cane spot** (p.329).

2 Brown spots on leaves
Small, irregular brown spots surrounded by yellow patches appear on leaves, which may then die.
■ See **Fungal leaf spot** (p.327).

Purple patches on canes around new buds
By autumn the patches turn silvery-grey and you may be able to spot tiny black fungal spores. Hybrid berries such as loganberries are most at risk.
■ See **Raspberry spur blight** (p.329).

Yellow, mosaic patterns on leaves
Downward curling at the edges and stunted leaf growth may be signs of a virus.
■ See **Raspberry virus** (p. 329).

White powdery coating on leaves
The powdery mildew is caused by a fungus, and tends to be worse when the weather is hot and dry. Leaves may yellow and die, and canes may wilt. Occasionally, fruits will spoil.
■ See **Powdery mildew** (p.329).

Orange-red, rust-like patches
Rust is a fungus that affects many soft fruits. It is unlikely to be fatal, but it is advisable to pick off and destroyed infected leaves.
■ See **Rust** (p.330).

Small holes eaten in leaves
Tiny red-brown spots and holes with tattered brown edges may be signs of capsid bug damage.
■ See **Capsid bugs** (p.335).

Fruit

3 Berries do not ripen fully
Parts of berries remain hard and stay red (hence the name "redberry"), especially later in the summer. Tiny insects called blackberry or redberry mites are the reason.
■ See **Blackberry mite** (p.335).

4 Maggots in fruits
Yellow-white grubs of the raspberry beetle feed inside the ripening berries. They may or may not cause visible damage to the fruits.
■ See **Raspberry beetle** (p.338).

5 Fluffy, grey mould
Affected fruits become covered with mould and start to rot.
■ See **Botrytis** (p.325).

Gooseberries

Only if you grow your own are you ever likely to taste the mouthwateringly sweet, muscat-like flavour of a perfectly ripe, freshly picked gooseberry. Fruit that you buy in the shops has a short season and the berries will probably be hard and unripe. They're fine for cooking, but they'll be too sour to eat raw.

Gooseberries are generally classified as either culinary or dessert varieties. Culinary fruit is sour but when cooked with added sugar makes wonderful jams, jellies, pies, and fruit fools. Dessert fruit is sweet enough to eat straight from the bush. Some varieties offer the best of both worlds: pick half the berries when they are young and use them for cooking, then let the other half ripen and eat them freshly picked. The berries themselves may be green, yellow, or red, and smooth or slightly hairy. Their dimensions can vary greatly: the giant berries traditionally grown for competition can reach the size of hens' eggs.

Most gooseberries grow very vigorously and need regular pruning to keep them under control, although if you train them as cordons against a wall or fence, you'll be able to fit two or three different varieties into a limited space.

Which forms to grow

■ **Bushes** Probably the easiest form to grow, although they can reach 2m (6ft) in height and spread.
■ **Cordon** Needs regular pruning but is economical on space and the fruit is easy to pick.
■ **Standard** Grown on a long leg and will need stakes at either side for support.
■ **Fan** Less common, but ideal for a sheltered, sunny fence or wall.

Must-grow gooseberries

1 'Greenfinch'
Culinary/dessert
Bushes don't grow too large so this is a good choice if space is limited. Less prone to mildew and leaf spot than most other varieties. Good flavour.
■ **Harvest** July

2 'Lancashire Lad'
Culinary/dessert
This traditional 19th-century variety with dark red berries has a loyal following. Some resistance to mildew but needs a fertile soil.
■ **Harvest** July to Aug

3 'Leveller'
Culinary/dessert
Large yellow berries with a superb flavour; often grown competitively. However, it crops heavily only if grown in fertile, well-drained soil and is susceptible to mildew.
■ **Harvest** July to Aug

4 'Hinnonmaki Red'
Culinary/dessert
Sometimes called 'Hino Red', this variety is very hardy, easy to grow, and also resistant to mildew. The red berries are sweet and aromatic.
■ **Harvest** July

5 'Hinnonmaki Yellow'
Culinary/dessert
Like the red, the yellow variety originally comes from Finland. It too can withstand cold winters and is resistant to mildew. The fruit is sweet and aromatic, with a slight apricot flavour.
■ **Harvest** July

6 'Careless'
Culinary/dessert
One of the earliest of the green varieties, 'Careless' is a traditional berry that dates back to the 19th century. The flavour is good and crops are heavy, though it is prone to mildew.
■ **Harvest** July

7 'Invicta'
Culinary/dessert
Bushes grow strongly and produce bumper crops of firm, smooth-skinned fruit ideal for cooking and preserving. Good mildew resistance.
■ **Harvest** June to July

8 'Langley Gage'
Dessert
A sweet, aromatic, old-fashioned variety that can be eaten straight off the bush when fully ripe. Worth searching out from specialist nurseries.
■ **Harvest** July to Aug

9 'Whinham's Industry'
Culinary/dessert
A traditional variety first bred in Morpeth, northern UK. It grows well in most conditions, although it is prone to mildew. Use green berries for cooking or eat raw when they ripen to dark red.
■ **Harvest** July

'Captivator' (not illustrated)
Dessert
A European–American hybrid producing good crops of berries sweet enough to eat raw when fully ripe. This almost thornless variety is mildew-resistant.
■ **Harvest** July to Aug

'Martlet' (not illustrated)
Culinary/dessert
A new, mildew-resistant variety with high yields of smooth, sweet, red berries that can be eaten raw or cooked.
■ **Harvest** July to Aug

'Remarka' (not illustrated)
Culinary/dessert
Early ripening red variety with good flavour and some resistance to mildew.
■ **Harvest** July

'Pax' (not illustrated)
Culinary/dessert
A recently introduced red variety with large, tasty berries and fewer thorns. Easy to grow and fairly resistant to mildew.
■ **Harvest** July

'Xenia' (not illustrated)
Culinary/dessert
A new variety from Switzerland. Large, red, sweet berries ripen very early. Strong-growing and mildew-resistant.
■ **Harvest** June

Growing gooseberries

Gooseberries are not difficult to grow. Tolerant of most weather and soil conditions, they are natural survivors. In fact, you'd have to be extremely unlucky – or very neglectful indeed – to succeed in killing them off. However, there's a big difference between a plant that produces a handful of small berries and one that is laden with a bumper crop of ripe, juicy, delicious fruit. The secret lies in a little tender loving care: feeding, watering, mulching, and pruning, plus nets to keep off birds, and a watchful eye for mildew and gooseberry sawfly.

The year at a glance

	spring			summer			autumn			winter		
	M	A	M	J	J	A	S	O	N	D	J	F
plant bare-root	■							■	■			■
plant container	■	■	■	■	■	■	■	■	■	■	■	■
winter-prune	■								■	■	■	■
summer-prune					■	■						
harvest				■	■	■	■					

PLANTING A GOOSEBERRY BUSH

Gooseberry bushes either grow on a short, single "leg" from which lateral branches spread out or they grow as stooled bushes, in which case the branches all emerge in a cluster straight from the rootball. Bushes with a leg should have a clean main stem, without any shoots or side branches, to a height of 10–15cm (4–6in) above soil level. Standard bushes, which grow on a leg 60–90cm (2–3ft) high, need staking for support.

1 Dig a hole deep and wide enough to accommodate the plant's roots comfortably. Add some well-rotted compost or manure and work it into the soil. Make a small mound of earth in the centre of the hole and gently spread the roots of the bare-root plant over it. Check the depth to ensure that the old nursery soil mark on the stem is level with the surface of your soil.

2 Carefully fill the hole with soil, firming it down around the roots as you go. Water generously and at regular intervals over the next few weeks. For initial pruning, see page 226. Spread an organic mulch around the plant to help retain moisture and suppress weeds.

Choosing plants

Gooseberries are sold as either bare-root or container-grown plants. If you buy them from specialist nurseries, where the choice is wider, they will probably be bare-root, though they may be available only in autumn and winter, between about October and March. Gooseberries are self-fertile.

When to plant

■ BARE-ROOT Plant in October–November or February–March. The ground is likely to be too cold in December–January.
■ CONTAINER-GROWN Plant at any time, though autumn is best. Avoid hot, dry summer months.

Where to plant

Gooseberries are cool-climate plants. They are happy in partial shade but appreciate being sheltered from the wind. Avoid frost pockets: although gooseberries are hardy and will survive severe winters, new leaves and flowers appear early in spring and can be vulnerable to frost damage.

Soil type

Gooseberries are fairly tolerant and don't mind soil that is a little alkaline. However, a slightly acid pH of 6–6.5 is ideal. They dislike being waterlogged and will grow more vigorously, and produce heavier crops, if your soil is well-drained and you have added plenty of well-rotted compost or manure to it.

Planting distances
■ BUSHES 1.2–1.5m (4–5ft) apart.
■ CORDONS 30–45cm (12–18in) apart.
■ ROW SPACING 1.5m (5ft) apart.

Growing in containers

It is possible to grow gooseberries in containers although, because their roots spread widely, they may be happier in the ground. A standard or a double cordon supported with a stake, is a better option than a bush. Choose a container with a minimum diameter of 30cm (12in) and fill it with multi-purpose, soil-based compost mixed with some sand or gravel to improve drainage. Feed with a high-potash fertilizer in spring, and above all keep the pot well-watered.

Routine care
■ WATERING Gooseberries need plenty of water throughout their growing season. Take special care to water regularly and often when the weather is hot and dry, or the skins of the fruits may split as they swell.
■ FEEDING Gooseberries need potassium. You should be able to supply them with as much as they require by sprinkling sulphate of potash over

the soil at a rate of about 15g/sq m (½oz/sq yd) in February or March. At the same time, add a general fertilizer, such as blood, fish, and bone. Avoid high-nitrogen fertilizers: the leaf growth that they stimulate invites mildew.

■ MULCHING After feeding, spread a mulch around the plants to help keep down weeds. Pull out by hand any weeds that do appear; using a hoe risks damaging the roots of the gooseberries.

■ NETTING Use nets to keep off birds. Bullfinches, in particular, will eat the fruit buds in winter, and blackbirds and others will eat the berries in summer.

■ FROST PROTECTION Gooseberries flower early in the year and may need covering with fleece overnight if there is a danger of hard frosts.

Harvesting and storing

Gooseberries will grow larger if you thin out the crop. Start picking alternate berries from about the end of May onwards, using them for cooking and leaving the remaining fruit to swell up and ripen fully as the summer progresses.

Ripe, dessert gooseberries are best eaten soon after picking, when the flavour and sweetness are at their height. However, they will keep in the fridge for up to ten days or so, and they also freeze well.

Yield

Yields can vary widely, not just from variety to variety and even from bush to bush but also from one year to the next, depending on the weather. With luck, these are roughly the kinds of quantities you can expect:

■ BUSH 3.5–4.5kg (8–10lb).
■ CORDON 0.9–1.4kg (2–3lb).

Harvest gooseberries by going over each bush two or three times, searching for berries that are just slightly soft and therefore ready for picking. Leave a short length of stalk attached to prevent the skins from tearing.

JOSTABERRIES AND WORCESTERBERRIES

Here are two unusual fruits worth tracking down from specialist nurseries. The jostaberry is a hybrid cross between a gooseberry and a blackcurrant, originally developed in Germany. The Worcesterberry is actually a native American species. They are both grown in the same way as gooseberries.

■ **Jostaberries** (far left) bear purple-black fruits that are larger than blackcurrants but a little smaller than gooseberries. The taste combines elements of both, and the berries can be cooked or eaten raw when fully ripe. The plants are vigorous, resistant to most pests and diseases, and mercifully free of sharp thorns.

■ **Worcesterberries** (left) are smooth-skinned fruits that start off green and gradually turn red–black as they ripen. They are unlikely to become sweet enough to eat raw, but are good for cooking and for making jam. But beware when picking: the plants are armed with truly vicious spines.

Month by month

February
■ This year's new buds should be visibly swelling by now.
■ Plant bare-root gooseberries if the ground is not frozen.
■ Winter-prune newly planted and established gooseberries.
■ Apply sulphate of potash (to boost potassium) and a general fertilizer around existing plants.

March
■ Buds begin to burst and new young leaves start to appear.
■ Mulch around plants to suppress weeds.
■ Last chance to plant bare-root gooseberries.
■ Last chance for winter pruning.
■ Prune newly planted gooseberries.

April
■ Blossom opens. Be ready to protect against frost.
■ If necessary, spray against capsid bugs after blossom has fallen.

May
■ Fruitlets form and begin to swell.
■ At the end of the month, start thinning out unripe fruits by picking every other berry to use for cooking.
■ Weed and water regularly.
■ Inspect the centre of bushes for larvae of gooseberry sawfly. Pick them off and destroy them.

June
■ Harvest early-season fruits.
■ Summer-prune this month and next.

■ Watch for any signs of American gooseberry mildew, leaf spot, rust, or dieback.

July
■ Harvest mid-season fruits.
■ Complete summer pruning by mid-month.

August
■ Harvest late-season fruits.

October
■ Take cuttings to propagate new plants.
■ New bare-root gooseberries start to become available from specialist nurseries. Plant this month or next.

November
■ Buy and plant bare-root gooseberries.
■ Winter pruning can start this month, though it may be better left to February or March.

Pruning and training gooseberries

The main aim of pruning gooseberries is first to create an open, uncrowded structure so that light and air can circulate freely, thus reducing the risk of disease. The second – because gooseberries fruit on older wood – is to keep cutting back stems and sideshoots to encourage them to be productive. Gooseberries, redcurrants, and whitecurrants are all pruned in the same way.

Pruning a gooseberry bush

For the first two or three years of their lives, newly planted gooseberries need formative pruning to train them into the shape required.

1st winter pruning
FEBRUARY–MARCH

- Whatever time of year you plant, February or March are the best months to begin pruning.
- Select 4–5 main stems and cut each back by a half or three-quarters of its length – unless the job has already been done by the plant nursery. Cut to a bud that faces outwards and upwards, in the direction you want the stem to grow.
- Remove all other stems, especially any that are crowding the centre, and, if the bush is growing on a short leg, any shoots lower than 10–15cm (4–6in) above the ground.

2nd winter pruning
FEBRUARY–MARCH

- Cut each of the main stems back by about a quarter or a half of the growth they made last year.
- Select enough new shoots to give a total of 8–10 strong, healthy, equally spaced stems and prune those back by a quarter, too.
- Cut back any unwanted new shoots to 4 buds or about 5cm (2in).

Winter pruning an established bush
NOVEMBER–MARCH

- If the plant is overgrown, prune out up to a quarter of the oldest branches and any tangled growth from the centre by cutting the stems down to the base.
- Shorten long stems by cutting them back by about half of the previous year's growth. For upright bushes, cut to an outward-facing bud. For arching bushes with stems prone to droop, cut to an inward-facing one.
- Prune crowded growth and any suckers from around the base. If the bush is growing on a short leg, make sure it is clear.
- If the plant is not overgrown, simply tip-prune main stems and cut back hard any new sideshoots to 1–4 buds.

Summer pruning an established bush
JUNE–JULY

- Prune all new sideshoots so that only 5 leaves remain on each.

Pruning a gooseberry cordon

Cordons require a regular routine of both summer and winter pruning in order to maintain their shape. Pruning them hard and regularly should produce good crops, and the neat, decorative form of the plant will also make for easy access when it's time to harvest the berries.

1st winter pruning
ON PLANTING

- Plant in winter and prune straight away – unless the nursery has already done so.
- Prune the main leader by a half of the new growth it made during the previous summer.
- Cut back all sideshoots to just 1 or 2 buds.

1st summer pruning
JUNE–JULY

- Prune all new sideshoots so that they have only 5 leaves left.

(from top to bottom) **With established bushes,** shorten any long stems in late winter using sharp secateurs. **Prune these** stems to an outward-facing bud. **Weak stems** and suckers should be removed from the base of the bush, as well as any overcrowded growth, to leave the centre clear.

Winter pruning an established cordon
NOVEMBER–MARCH

- Prune the main leader by a quarter of last summer's new growth. Cut to a bud facing in the opposite direction from last year's. Continue tying in the leader as it grows. When it reaches the top of the cane, cut it off to just 1 new bud each year.
- Prune back all sideshoots to 1 or 2 buds in order to keep generating new fruiting spurs.
- Remove any shoots that grow at the base of the stem.

Summer pruning an established cordon
late JUNE–JULY

- Prune all new sideshoots so that only 5 leaves remain.

What can go wrong

Buds and blossom

New buds stripped by birds

Birds are a continual nuisance. Bullfinches, in particular, eat the buds during winter, and will come back in summer, as will blackbirds, to take the fruits.
■ See **Birds** (p.335).

Blossom dies

Although gooseberries are hardy, they blossom early in the year and there is always a danger of a severe frost scorching young leaves and damaging or destroying flowers.
■ See **Frost** (p.316).

Leaves

1 Leaves turn brown and fall off

This may be the first sign of gooseberry dieback, usually caused by a form of the fungus, grey mould. As the infection takes hold, entire branches die off, and unless you cut them out and destroy them promptly you may lose the plant completely.
■ See **Gooseberry dieback** (p.328).

2 Curled, distorted leaves

Gooseberry aphids hatch in spring from eggs that have overwintered on the bushes. The small greenfly will be visible feeding on new shoots. Leaves that they have infested appear curled and twisted.
■ See **Aphids** (p.334).

3 Leaves being eaten

The most likely culprits are the caterpillar-like larvae of the gooseberry sawfly. They have pale green bodies up to 20mm (³/₄in) long, often covered with small black spots, and a black head. In the case of a bad attack a whole bush can be stripped in a few days. Look for tiny, pale green eggs underneath the leaves.
■ See **Gooseberry sawfly** (p.336).

4 White or grey powdery covering

This is most likely to be American gooseberry mildew, a fungal disease that regularly attacks gooseberries, though some varieties are more resistant than others. New shoots are affected first, then the leaves and berries. As the infection worsens, the powdery coating turns brown.
■ See **American gooseberry mildew** (p.324).

Brown spots on leaves

Small, irregular brown spots surrounded by yellow patches appear first on older leaves at the bottom of the plant. Affected leaves die and the disease spreads upwards to attack new growth. The cause is fungal leaf spot.
■ See **Fungal leaf spot** (p.327).

Brown, curled edges on leaves

Leaves that are curled and scorched yellow or brown at the edges may be an indication of potassium deficiency, especially if there are also purple–brown spots on the undersides.
■ See **Potassium deficiency** (p.321).

Leaves turn yellow between veins

A deficiency of iron or manganese can cause a distinctive yellowing of the leaves. These elements are likely to be present in the soil but high alkalinity (a pH of more than 7.0) is probably preventing the plants from absorbing them – a disorder known as lime-induced chlorosis.
■ See **Iron deficiency** (p.320) or **Manganese deficiency** (p.321).

Orange or red blisters on leaves

Blisters or pustules, which are more likely to appear after a dry spring, are caused by a fungal infection called gooseberry rust or cluster cup rust. They may spread to fruits and stems.
■ See **Gooseberry rust** (p.328).

Small holes in leaves

Tiny red-brown spots and holes with tattered brown edges are signs of capsid bugs. The insects feed on the sap in young leaves, infecting and killing the plant tissue with their saliva. They are difficult to see and may have departed by the time you spot the damage.
■ See **Capsid bugs** (p.335).

Fruit

5 Dried, shrivelled fruits

Severe attacks of gooseberry dieback affect both fruits and leaves, causing berries to dry out and shrivel up.
■ See **Gooseberry dieback** (p.328).

6 Cracked skin

Scars and cracks in the skin of the fruit may be caused by birds, or may be evidence of attack by capsid bugs, especially if leaves are also holed and tattered.
■ See **Birds** (p.335) or **capsid bugs** (p.335).

7 Brown, felt-like patches

The brown covering is a fungal growth caused by American gooseberry mildew. Strictly speaking, the berries are still edible but they will probably be stunted, lacking in flavour, and distinctly unappetizing. Cut out and destroy all affected parts of the plant. Prune regularly to encourage air circulation and reduce damp, humid conditions.
■ See **American gooseberry mildew** (p.324).

Fluffy, grey mould

Affected fruits become covered with grey-white or grey-brown mould and may start to rot. Botrytis is to blame – the same fungus that can also cause gooseberry dieback.
■ See **Botrytis** (p.325).

Redcurrants and whitecurrants

Red- and whitecurrants have a tendency to be unfairly overlooked. Even today they are disappointingly uncommon in shops, most likely because they have a fairly short season, they are fragile to transport, and when ripe their shelf life is limited. If you manage to track them down, they will probably be sold at high prices and in tiny quantities. However, as a grow-your-own crop they have a great deal going for them. Once established, they are very productive, and neither bushes nor cordons require a lot of attention: a feed every spring, a simple prune twice a year, in summer and in winter, a spot of weeding and watering, and protection from birds.

Of the red and white varieties, redcurrants have the sharper, more acidic flavour. Whitecurrants, which are in fact a creamy yellow or even a faintly flushed pale pink, may look less glamorous and jewel-like, but they tend to be naturally sweeter.

Fully ripe fruit may be sweet enough to eat raw, but for cooking and for making jellies, harvest the berries when they are slightly unripe and still retain some acidity. If you want to store fresh currants for as long as possible, pick them when they're dry, not when they're wet.

Which forms to grow

- **Bushes** are the easiest form to grow and produce the most fruit, though they can reach 2m (6ft) in height and spread.
- **Standard** A good choice for growing in a container.
- **Cordon** Needs regular pruning but is economical on space and the berries are easy to pick.
- **Fan** Less common but worth considering for a sheltered wall or fence.

Must-grow redcurrants & whitecurrants

1 'White Versailles'
Whitecurrant
Popular, long-established, and widely available with early cropping, sweet, pale-yellow berries that are perfect for eating raw when fully ripe.
■ **Harvest** early July

2 'Stanza'
Redcurrant
A late-flowering variety, so a good choice for regions prone to frost. The dark red fruits have a sharp but good flavour.
■ **Harvest** late July

3 'Rovada'
Redcurrant
This modern Dutch variety can produce extremely heavy yields of bright-red, attractive berries on long strigs (trusses).
■ **Harvest** late July–August

4 'Red Lake'
Redcurrant
Widely grown, reliable, disease-resistant, and heavy cropping. Like 'Rovada', the fruits are on long strigs but ripen earlier.
■ **Harvest** late July

5 'Blanka'
Whitecurrant
Sometimes spelled 'Blanca', a new variety that may challenge 'White Versailles'. The creamy yellow-white fruits are equally sweet but heavier cropping and ripen slightly later.
■ **Harvest** late July–August

6 'Jonkheer van Tets'
Redcurrant
Popular, tried-and-tested, Dutch variety that ripens early and produces high yields of excellent fruit. Vigorous, so if space is limited, this is a good choice for cordons.
■ **Harvest** early July

'Junifer' (not illustrated)
Redcurrant
A recently introduced French variety, it is one of the earliest and heaviest cropping.
■ **Harvest** early July

Growing redcurrants and whitecurrants

Although red- and whitecurrants are closely related to blackcurrants, they are in fact grown much more like gooseberries. These cool-climate plants do well in northern regions and will happily tolerate partial shade, though the berries will ripen more quickly and taste sweeter with the help of some summer sunshine.

The year at a glance

		spring		summer			autumn			winter		
	M	A	M	J	J	A	S	O	N	D	J	F
plant bare-root	▬							▬	▬	▬	▬	▬
plant container	▬	▬	▬	▬	▬	▬	▬	▬	▬	▬	▬	▬
winter prune	▬								▬	▬	▬	▬
summer prune				▬	▬	▬						
harvest					▬	▬						

Choosing plants

Red- and whitecurrants are sold as either bare-root or container-grown plants. Buying them from a specialist nursery will give you a wider choice, but they are likely to be bare-root and therefore available only in autumn and winter.

When to plant

■ BARE-ROOT Plant between October and March, although not if the ground is frozen or waterlogged.
■ CONTAINER-GROWN Plant at any time of year, although autumn is best. Avoid hot, dry summer months.

Where to plant

Choose a sheltered site, out of strong winds, but avoid frost pockets, and incorporate well-rotted organic matter into the soil before planting. Redcurrants are hardy enough to survive most winters, and although they come into blossom fairly early in spring, the flowers are reasonably frost-resistant – more so than blackcurrants. They are one of the few fruits that will grow against a shady north-facing wall, although in summer they ripen earlier in sunshine, provided they don't get too hot.

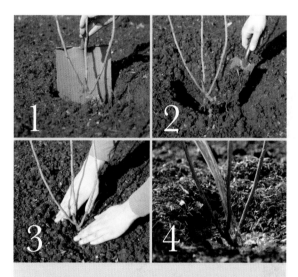

PLANTING A REDCURRANT BUSH

Red- and whitecurrant bushes grow best on a short "leg" from which lateral branches or stems spread out. The leg should be free of any sideshoots to a height of 10–15cm (4–6in) above soil level. Standard bushes grow on a longer leg, 60–90cm (2–3ft) high.

1 Check the depth of your planting hole to ensure that the old nursery soil mark on the main stem is level with the surface of your soil.

2 Work some well-rotted compost or manure into the soil around the roots, taking care not to damage them.

3 Carefully fill the hole with soil, firming it down around the roots as you go.

4 Water generously now (and at regular intervals over the next few weeks), then spread an organic mulch around the plant to keep moisture in.

Soil type

Red- and whitecurrants do best in fertile soil with a pH of 6.5–7. However, it must be free-draining: they really dislike being waterlogged.

Planting distances

- BUSHES 1.5m (5ft) apart.
- SINGLE CORDONS 38–45cm (15–18in) apart.
- ROW SPACING 1.5m (5ft) apart.

Growing in containers

Currants grow well in containers because they are quite shallow-rooted and don't seem to mind the restriction. Use a container with a minimum diameter of 30cm (12in) filled with multi-purpose soil-based compost mixed with some sand or gravel to improve drainage. Feed with a general compound fertilizer in spring, and make sure you water regularly, especially when the weather is dry.

Routine care

- WATERING Water regularly and often when the weather is hot and dry. Don't let plants dry out.
- FEEDING In February or March, apply a general fertilizer such as blood, fish, and bone, and, to ensure a good supply of potassium, sprinkle sulphate of potash over the soil at a rate of about 15g/sq m (½ oz/sq yd). Be wary of high-nitrogen fertilizers: the vigorous leaf growth may invite mildew.
- MULCHING After feeding, water the ground well and spread a mulch around the plants to help keep down weeds. Pull out any weeds that do emerge.
- NETTING If necessary, use nets to keep off birds – both in winter when they will eat the buds and in summer as the fruits colour and ripen. A fruit cage is recommended.
- FROST PROTECTION Plants are hardy but may need covering with fleece on very frosty nights.

Harvesting and storing

Fruit is usually ready for picking in July and August. The currants don't all ripen at once, so you'll have to go over the plant several times. It's a lot easier to cut entire trusses (or "strigs") than it is to pick individual currants. You can then eat the perfectly ripe ones raw, and use the less ripe, firmer ones for cooking or preserving. Ripe currants won't keep for long, even in the fridge, but they do freeze well.

Yield

Yields can vary from variety to variety and from year to year, depending on the weather, but you should be able to expect:

- BUSH 4–5kg (9–11lb).
- CORDON 1kg (2.2lb).

(far left to right) **Single, double, or triple cordons** are an economical way of getting a lot of fruit from a relatively small space. They need regular pruning and tying in. **Tie in cordons** to 1.5 or 2m (5 or 6ft) bamboo canes supported by a post-and-wire structure or secured against a wall or fence. You'll need at least two horizontal wires, one at a height of 60cm (2ft) and the other at 1.2m (4ft). **A fruit cage** or nets are the only sure way of protecting fruit from birds. **Testing for ripeness** is easy with redcurrants, which are ready to pick when plump and bright scarlet. It's harder to tell with whitecurrants as their colour change is more subtle; taste is the best test.

Month by month

February
- New buds should be visibly swelling.
- Plant bare-root currants if the ground is not frozen.
- Winter-prune both newly planted and established gooseberries.
- Apply sulphate of potash and a general fertilizer.

March
- New young leaves and flowers start to appear. Protect against frost if necessary.
- Mulch around plants to suppress weeds.
- Last chance to plant bare-root currants.
- Last chance for winter pruning.

April
- Blossom is fully open, and pollinating insects should be at work.
- If necessary, spray against capsid bugs after blossom has fallen.

May
- Fruitlets form and begin to swell.
- Weed and water regularly.

June
- Summer-prune this month and next.
- Watch for any signs of leaf spot, grey mould, or dieback.

July
- Harvest early and mid-season fruits.
- Complete summer pruning by mid-month.

August
- Harvest late-season fruits.

October
- Take cuttings to propagate new plants.
- New bare-root currants start to become available from specialist nurseries. Plant this month or next.

November
- Buy and plant bare-root currants.

(left to right) **New buds** form at the base of last year's stems. **Long strings** of tiny flowers appear, usually in mid spring. Plants are self-fertile and pollination should take place without the need for a partner. **Taste berries** for ripeness before picking.

Pruning and training redcurrants and whitecurrants

Prune redcurrants and whitecurrants in the same way as gooseberries (see pp.226–27). They fruit on buds that form at the base of last year's new shoots and also on older spurs. Both bushes and cordons need pruning quite hard every winter to encourage the formation of spurs, and again in the summer to cut back the new growth on sideshoots.

(top to bottom) **In summer** shorten the new sideshoots so the plant concentrates its energy back on the main stem. **From late autumn** cut back the shoots you shortened in summer to one bud.

Winter-pruning an established bush

Prune between November and March. If the centre of the bush is overgrown and crowded, aim to open it up to let in light and air. Remove any old, unproductive, or crossing stems, and cut back sideshoots to encourage the development of the short spurs that will bear the currants.

1 Cut down to the base up to a quarter of the oldest branches and any tangled growth that is crowding the centre. Use a pruning saw if stems are thicker than a pencil.

2 Cut out any weak, low-growing stems from around the base of the bush. If the bush is growing on a short leg, leave it clear.

3 Remove about half of the previous year's growth from the end of each main stem, cutting just above an outward-facing bud.

4 Prune back sideshoots to just one bud, which will encourage the spurs to produce new growth, flowers, and then fruit.

Pruning an established cordon

Cordons need pruning in both summer and winter. In June or July, prune all new sideshoots back to just five leaves. Between November and March, cut back the main leader to leave just one bud of last year's growth, and prune all all sideshoots to one or two buds to keep generating new fruiting spurs.

What can go wrong

Buds and blossom

New buds stripped by birds
Birds eat the buds in winter, and then return in summer to take the fruit.
■ See **Birds** (p.335).

Blossom dies
Currants flower early in spring and frosts can destroy flowers and scorch young leaves.
■ See **Frost** (p. 316).

Leaves and stems

1 Leaves being eaten
The most likely culprits are gooseberry sawfly larvae. They have distinctive caterpillar-like, pale-green bodies, often covered with small black spots, and a black head.
■ See **Gooseberry sawfly** (p.336).

2 Pink spots on stems and branches
Small, pink or orange pustules appearing on stems and branches that have died back indicate coral spot, a fungal disease. The problem is likely to be worse if the weather is damp.
■ See **Coral spot** (p.326).

3 Entire stems die
Leaves turning brown and whole stems dying may be a sign of gooseberry dieback, which can also affect currants. It is usually caused by a fungus, botrytis or eutypa.
■ See **Gooseberry dieback** (p.328).

4 Curled, blistered leaves
Currant blister aphids are pale yellow and should be easily visible feeding on new shoots. Leaves that they have infested appear twisted and develop red or yellow blisters. Other types of aphid may also attack the leaves.
■ See **Currant blister aphids** (p.336).

5 Brown spots on leaves
Small, irregular brown spots surrounded by yellow patches appear on leaves, which may then die.
■ See **Fungal leaf spot** (p.327).

Small holes in leaves
Tiny red-brown spots and holes with tattered brown edges may be signs of capsid bug damage.
■ See **Capsid bugs** (p.335).

Fruit

Fluffy, grey mould
Affected fruits become covered with grey-white or grey-brown mould, skins may split, and they may start to rot.
■ See **Botrytis** (p.325).

Blackcurrants

Blackcurrant bushes are tough and self-reliant. Usually, they'll go on for year after year even if neglected. But put in just a bit of extra effort and it will certainly be repaid. If you weed, feed, and water them, and if you learn to prune them properly so that the plant is continually producing new healthy growth on which the following year's fruit will be carried, then you'll get bigger, better blackcurrants, and a lot more of them.

In recent years, modern varieties (those whose names begin with 'Ben') have been bred to resist frost damage, mildew, and other pests and diseases. There has been a move, too, towards developing larger, sweeter berries – not as intensely flavoured for cooking perhaps, but perfect for picking and eating fresh, straight from the bush.

Ripe blackcurrants will keep for a few days provided they are firm when picked, and can be made into delicious puddings, jams, jellies and juices. The fruit's popularity owes much to its high vitamin C content and blackcurrants are widely grown commercially.

Which forms to grow

■ **Bushes** Blackcurrants are always grown as "stooled" bushes, which means that all the stems emerge directly from ground level instead of branching out from a single trunk or leg. Bushes can reach a height and spread of up to 2m (6ft).

Must-grow blackcurrants

1 'Ebony'
Perhaps the sweetest of all varieties, as well as one of the earliest. Its larger-than-average berries are perhaps the best for eating fresh, straight from the bush.
■ **Harvest** early to mid-July

2 'Ben Lomond'
Launched in 1975, this was the first of the specially bred Scottish blackcurrants with the prefix 'Ben'. It was crossed with Scandinavian varieties to delay flowering and thus be less prone to frost damage.
■ **Harvest** late July

3 'Ben Sarek'
Compact, smaller-than-average bushes that can be planted slightly closer together or squeezed into limited spaces. Yields can be so high that fully laden branches may droop and require supporting with canes and string. Reasonable frost and disease resistance.
■ **Harvest** mid–late July

4 'Big Ben'
A new variety that that can be eaten fresh or used for cooking. Its huge berries can be twice the average size, and have a good sugar/acid balance.
■ **Harvest** from mid-July

5 'Ben Connan'
Produces an early crop of large berries that are sweet and juicy. Some resistance to frost, mildew, and leaf spot.
■ **Harvest** from mid-July

6 'Baldwin'
A long-established variety with medium-sized berries that are fairly tart in flavour, so best for cooking. Growth is compact and the fruits are not usually prone to splitting.
■ **Harvest** late July

'Titania' (not illustrated)
A variety that originates from Scandinavia. Good frost and mildew resistance. Tall, productive bushes produce high yields of large berries.
■ **Harvest** late July

Growing blackcurrants

Blackcurrants are cool-climate plants and grow well in northern regions, provided you give them a sunny position and protect them from hard frosts when in blossom. They don't stay productive forever, so it's wise to think about replacing established bushes after eight to ten years.

The year at a glance

	spring			summer			autumn			winter		
	M	A	M	J	J	A	S	O	N	D	J	F
plant bare-root	▬						▬	▬	▬	▬	▬	▬
plant container	▬	▬	▬				▬	▬	▬	▬	▬	▬
winter-prune	▬									▬	▬	▬
summer-prune				▬	▬							
harvest				▬	▬	▬						

Choosing plants

Blackcurrants are sold as either bare-root or container-grown plants. Buy certified disease-free, two-year-old plants to minimize the risk of reversion disease (see p.330). Specialist nurseries offer a wider choice of varieties than most garden centres, but their plants will probably be bare-root and therefore available only in autumn and winter.

When to plant

■ BARE-ROOT Plant between October and March, though not if the ground is frozen or waterlogged. November is the best month.

■ CONTAINER-GROWN Plant at any time – autumn is ideal. Avoid hot, dry summer months.

Where to plant

Choose a sheltered site, out of strong winds, but avoid frost pockets: blackcurrants are hardy enough to survive most winters, but they flower early in spring and are vulnerable to frost damage.

Soil type

Blackcurrants are tolerant of most soils, though a pH of 6.5–7 is ideal. They are hungry, thirsty plants,

PLANTING A BLACKCURRANT BUSH

Plant deeply – at least 5cm (2in) deeper than the previous nursery soil marks on the stems – to encourage new, underground stems.

1 Dig a hole deep enough and wide enough to accommodate the plant's roots. If you haven't already done so, add some well-rotted compost or manure and work it into the soil.

2 Check the depth to ensure that the old nursery soil marks on the stems are sitting below the surface of your soil.

3 Carefully fill the hole with soil, ensuring that there are no air pockets among the roots.

4 Firm down the soil. Water generously, and if possible, mulch around the plant. Prune newly planted bushes immediately (see p.244).

and appreciate rich, fertile soil that has had plenty of organic matter added to it to help provide the nutrients and retain the moisture they need.

Planting distances

- BUSHES 1.5m (5ft) apart.
- ROW SPACING 1.5m (5ft) apart.

Growing in containers

Blackcurrant bushes usually do well in containers, and bringing them in undercover at night to protect them from frost is particularly helpful. Plant them in a pot with a diameter of 30–45cm (12–18in), filled with multi-purpose soil-based compost mixed with some sand or gravel to improve drainage. Feed with a general compound fertilizer in spring, and water regularly, especially in dry weather. Be prepared to repot at least once every three years, replacing some of the old compost with fresh.

Routine care

- WATERING Blackcurrants need a lot of water, especially when the fruits are starting to fatten up. Water regularly and often, and try not to splash water on the stems, which spreads fungal infections.
- FEEDING In March, apply a general fertilizer and, to boost nitrogen, sprinkle sulphate of ammonia over the soil – about 25g/sq m (1oz/sq yd).
- MULCHING After feeding, water the ground well and spread a thick organic mulch around the plants. Pull rather than hoe out any weeds.

- NETTING You will have to use nets to keep birds off– certainly in summer as the fruits colour and ripen. A fruit cage is recommended.
- FROST PROTECTION Plants are hardy but may need covering with fleece overnight if there is a danger of frost when they are in flower.

Harvesting and storing

Depending on the variety, fruits are usually ready for picking from early July to late August. Traditional, old-fashioned blackcurrants ripen first at the top of the "strig" (truss), so you must pick individual currants as they become ready to harvest. Modern varieties, however, are bred to ripen simultaneously, so you can snip off an entire strig in one go. Ripe blackcurrants won't keep for long – no more than a few days in a sealed container in the fridge – but they can be frozen successfully.

Yield

Yields can vary from variety to variety and from year to year, but from an average bush you should expect 4.5–5.5kg (10–12lb) of fruit.

(below, left to right) **After feeding** water the ground well and spread a thick organic mulch around the plants to conserve moisture and keep down weeds. **Support heavy-fruiting** varieties as they grow with bamboo canes and thick string. **Blackcurrants are ready to pick** when plump and shiny blue-black. Try to get the timing just right, as the longer they are left on the bush the sweeter they taste.

Month by month

February
■ Look out for abnormally swollen "big buds", a possible sign of gall mite and the serious reversion disease.

■ Plant bare-root blackcurrants if the ground is not frozen.

■ Winter-prune established bushes.

March
■ New young leaves and flowers start to appear. Protect against frost if necessary.

■ Feed with sulphate of ammonia and a general fertilizer.

■ Mulch around plants to suppress weeds.

■ Last chance to plant bare-root bushes.

■ Last chance for winter pruning.

April
■ Blossom is fully open, and pollinating insects should be at work.

May
■ Fruitlets form and begin to swell.

■ Weed and water regularly.

■ Inspect bushes for sawfly caterpillars and destroy any you find.

June
■ Watch for any signs of leaf spot or mildew.

■ Continue weeding and watering as fruits ripen.

■ Net against birds.

July
■ Harvest early- and mid-season fruits.

■ Give established bushes a summer prune if they are overcrowded and the fruit is shaded.

August
■ Harvest mid- and late-season fruits.

October
■ Take cuttings to propagate new plants.

■ New bare-root currants start to become available from specialist nurseries.

■ Plant bushes this month or next.

November
■ The best month to plant bare-root or container-grown blackcurrants.

■ Prune new bushes after planting.

■ Winter-prune established bushes between now and March.

Pruning and training blackcurrants

Blackcurrants fruit mainly on lengths of stem that grew the previous summer – in other words, on one-year-old wood. New growth put on in the current year will fruit next year. Stems three years old or older are less productive and should therefore be cut out. So, the aim of pruning is, in effect, to renew the whole bush every three or four years.

Pruning a newly planted blackcurrrant

The most important function of pruning now is to encourage the roots to establish, ready for the emergence of strong new growth in spring. So, as soon as you've planted a new bush you should prune the stems almost to the base. This might sound a little bit harsh but actually it will get the bush off to the right start.

1st winter pruning
OCTOBER–MARCH

BARE-ROOT
- If planting in December–March, cut all stems back to about 2.5cm (1in) above the level of the soil. Only 1 or 2 buds should remain on each stem.

CONTAINER-GROWN
- No need to prune, provided the established root system is intact during planting.

2nd winter pruning
NOVEMBER–MARCH

- Very little pruning is required. If any of the new stems are weak or if they are growing parallel with the ground, cut them out entirely.

Pruning an established blackcurrant

An established, overgrown bush may need opening up to let in light and air. You should also remove some older, dark-coloured stems, so they can be replaced by newer, paler, fruit-bearing ones. You can leave this job until autumn or winter, or start it as early as July to allow sunlight to reach ripening fruits.

Summer/winter pruning
JULY and NOVEMBER–MARCH

- Cut to one bud above ground level as many as one-third of the dark, three-year-old or older stems.
- Remove any weak, crossing, damaged, or diseased stems, as well as any growing too close to ground.
- Leave healthy, one- and two-year-old stems untouched; they will bear fruit next year.

Cut out up to a third of old, unproductive wood in winter. This will open up the bush, prevent overcrowding, and make it easier to pick the fruits when they ripen next summer.

What can go wrong

Buds and blossom

Blossom dies
Blackcurrants flower early in spring and frosts can destroy flowers and scorch young leaves.
■ See **Frost** (p.316).

Abnormally swollen buds
Unusually large, rounded "big buds" that fail to produce leaves or flowers are the classic signs of the gall mite or big bud mite, responsible for the spread of reversion disease.
■ See **Blackcurrant gall mite** (p.335) and **Reversion disease** (p.330).

Leaves and stems

1 White or grey powdery mould on leaves
This is an indication of American gooseberry mildew. Leaves are usually affected first, then the fruit.
■ See **American gooseberry mildew** (p.324).

2 Curled, blistered leaves
Leaves that appear twisted and develop red or yellow blisters are usually infested with currant blister aphids. The insects are pale yellow and should be visible feeding on new shoots.
■ See **Currant blister aphids** (p.336).

3 Sticky leaves covered in greenfly
Blackcurrant aphids cover upper surfaces of leaves in a coating of sticky honeydew, which may develop into grey mould. The aphids can be found on the undersides of the leaves.
■ See **Aphids** (p.334).

4 Entire stems die
If leaves turn brown and whole stems die, suspect gooseberry dieback, which can also affect currants. The usual cause is a fungus, botrytis or eutypa.
■ See **Gooseberry dieback** (p.328).

5 Yellow leaves with green veins
This probably indicates lack of iron or manganese. Called "lime-induced chlorosis", it is common in alkaline soils with a high pH.
■ See **Iron deficiency** (p.320), **Manganese deficiency** (p.321).

Unopened, distorted new leaves
Young, furled leaves that fail to open properly then shrivel and die may be the result of an infestation by the white, maggot-like larvae of tiny gall midges.
■ See **Blackcurrant gall midge** (p. 335).

Brown spots on leaves
Small, irregular brown spots surrounded by yellow patches appear on leaves, which may then die.
■ See **Fungal leaf spot** (p.327).

Small holes in leaves
Tiny red-brown spots and holes with tattered brown edges may be signs of capsid bug damage.
■ See **Capsid bugs** (p.335).

Leaves being eaten
The most likely culprits are blackcurrant or gooseberry sawfly larvae.
■ See **Gooseberry sawfly** (p.336).

Small, slightly misshapen leaves
Leaves that turn faintly yellow, are smaller than normal and possibly with fewer lobes and veins, can indicate reversion disease. Diagnosis is difficult but there may also be fewer flowers and a smaller crop.
■ See **Reversion disease** (p.330).

Fruit

Fluffy, grey or brown mould
Affected fruits become covered with mould and start to rot.
■ See **Botrytis** (p.325) or **American gooseberry mildew** (p.324).

Berries stripped by birds
Birds find the ripening fruits irresistible.
■ See **Birds** (p.335).

Blueberries

Blueberries are native to North America, and, via a complex web of cross-breeding, the cultivated varieties grown in the UK and elsewhere in Europe all derive from there. The most common form is known as the Northern highbush, which is a tall, upright plant adapted to cold winters. You may also come across the Southern highbush, which was bred for southern states where the summers are hot. In the UK, it may also be the best choice for mild, southern areas. Less common but still worth looking out for are so-called half-high blueberries, a cross between Northern highbush and wild American blueberries. They are very hardy and relatively low-growing.

As long as you grow them in the acid soil they require, blueberries are fairly trouble-free. Because they are not indigenous to Europe, they seem not to be troubled by many of the pests and diseases that afflict them in North America.

If their wonderful, sweet, juicy flavour were not reason enough to grow them, blueberries also have a reputation as a "superfood", as they are very high in the antioxidants that are claimed to help combat the ageing process, and improve memory and coordination.

Leave blueberries to ripen fully – making sure they come away easily from the stalk – if you want them to be sweet enough to eat raw. Pick over the bushes several times as the berries don't all ripen at once. Blueberries keep for longer than most soft fruits and also freeze well.

Which forms to grow

■ **Bushes** Blueberries are always grown as multi-stemmed or "stooled" bushes – like blackcurrants. Bushes can reach a height and spread of up to 2m (6ft). Don't attempt a cordon, fan, or standard.

Must-grow blueberries

1 'Berkeley'
Tall bushes producing generous crops of large, pale, powder-blue berries. Fruits are less likely to split than some other varieties.
■ Harvest August

2 'Spartan'
Flowers late but fruits early, so ideal for areas where frost may be a problem. Large, pale-blue berries with good flavour.
■ Harvest July

3 'Earliblue'
Reckoned to be one of the earliest-fruiting of all the varieties, its large, pale-blue, sweet berries may be ready to pick in mid-July.
■ Harvest July

4 'Coville'
Heavy crops of large berries with a slightly tart flavour. Named after the 19th-century American botanist who pioneered domestic blueberry growing.
■ Harvest August

5 'Jersey'
A hardy variety that is good for cooler regions. Medium to large juicy berries with a sweet flavour. Not self-fertile, so plant with a partner.
■ Harvest August

6 'Bluetta'
Compact, smaller than normal bushes and early cropping. Plenty of medium-sized, high-quality fruit.
■ Harvest July

7 'Brigitta'
Tall, upright variety originally bred in Australia. Pale-blue berries are firm and crisp, and store well in the fridge.
■ Harvest August–September

8 'Herbert'
If 'Earliblue' is the earliest to ripen, then 'Herbert' has earned an equal reputation as the best-tasting berry. Large fruits with a wonderful flavour.
■ Harvest August

9 'Chandler'

Huge blue-black berries that when ripe may be almost as large as cherries. The harvest period is long and may last for up to six weeks.
■ **Harvest** August–September

10 'Bluecrop'

Popular, widely grown variety with vigorous, upright growth, producing large berries with a good flavour. Ensure berries ripen before picking.
■ **Harvest** July–August

11 'Top Hat'

A dwarf variety even smaller than 'Sunshine Blue': average height and spread may be as little as 40–60cm (16–24in). Perfect for containers and areas where space is tight. Medium-sized, purple berries with excellent flavour.
■ **Harvest** July–August

'Duke' (not illustrated)

Mild-tasting, medium-sized berries that store well. Attactive yellow-orange leaf colour in autumn. This variety may not be as easy to find as it once was, but it is still prized because it flowers late and fruits early.
■ **Harvest** July

'Northsky' (not illustrated)

A "half-high" cultivar originally crossbred from a Northern highbush and a wild American blueberry. Grows to only 30–45cm (12–18in) high and 60–90cm (2–3ft) across. It will survive extremely cold winters. Small, pale, sky-blue fruit with distinct flavour of wild blueberries.
■ **Harvest** August

'Ozarkblue' (not illustrated)

A so-called Southern highbush blueberry that will survive cold winters but tolerate hotter summers than most other varieties. A good choice for warmer regions.
■ **Harvest** August–September

'Sunshine Blue' (not illustrated)

Compact, bushes that are smaller than most, rarely growing more than 1m (3ft) tall. Good for small gardens and for container growing. Distinctive red buds and bright-pink flowers.
■ **Harvest** August

Growing blueberries

Blueberries are very easy to grow. In fact, they're amongst the easiest of all soft fruits. That said, you must grow them in the very acid soil that they need in order to thrive. They then require a minimum of care, no training, and only a little, simple pruning. New, young plants can seem slow to get going but, once established, they are productive and long-lived. They can last for twenty years or more – indeed, they may even outlast you.

The year at a glance

	spring			summer			autumn			winter		
	M	A	M	J	J	A	S	O	N	D	J	F
plant	▬	▬							▬	▬	▬	▬
prune	▬	▬								▬	▬	▬
harvest					▬	▬	▬					

Choosing plants

Blueberries can sometimes be bought bare-root but container-grown plants are more common and less likely to dry out before planting. If possible, buy certified disease-free, two- or three-year-old plants in containers. They will establish more quickly than bare-root plants.

Flowering and pollination

Many blueberries are what's called partially self-fertile, which means that they are capable of setting fruit from their own pollen – at least, in theory. However, it's a lot safer to plant more than one bush so that they cross-pollinate each other. Ideally, a minimum of three different varieties should ensure that pollination is successful.

When to plant

■ PLANTING IN THE GROUND Plant either bare-root or container-grown plants between November and March, at any time after the leaves have fallen but before the plant awakes from its winter dormancy in the spring. Do not attempt to plant if the ground is frozen or waterlogged.

■ PLANTING IN CONTAINERS Container-grown plants can be purchased and potted up at any time of year, though the best time for potting them on into a new container is in spring. Avoid re-potting in midwinter and in hot, dry summer months.

Not all blueberry varieties flower at the same time. Some as early as March, others not until May. To guarantee cross-pollination it's best to plant varieties that will blossom more-or-less simultaneously.

PLANTING A BLUEBERRY BUSH

Only attempt to grow blueberries in acid soil. If yours is naturally neutral or alkaline, consider creating a raised bed filled with soil that you can ensure has the correct level of acidity. Prepare the ground several months in advance by digging in composted sawdust, composted pine bark, or special ericaceous compost.

1 Mark out your planting position, allowing a space of up to 1.5m (5ft) all round.

2 Give the plant a good soaking with rainwater, and remove it from its container.

3 Dig a hole deep enough and wide enough to accommodate the plant's rootball, with an additional 10cm (4in) all round. Check the depth to ensure that the top of the rootball is level with, or slightly below, the surface of your soil.

4 Carefully firm down the soil, ensuring that there are no air pockets among the roots.

5 Water generously, preferably with rainwater and not with alkaline water from a tap, unless tap water is your only option.

6 Spread a mulch of composted sawdust, leafmould, or pine bark around the plant.

Where to plant

Choose a sheltered site, out of strong winds. Most blueberries are very hardy and relatively resistant to frost damage, although those that come into flower very early in the spring are most at risk, and may need protecting. In summer all blueberries like plenty of sunshine but most will tolerate partial shade for a few hours a day.

Soil type

The nature of the soil is the most important aspect of growing blueberries. They will grow only in very acidic soils, those with a pH of 4–5.5. If you are successful with rhododendrons, azaleas, camellias, heathers, and other acid-loving plants, then you'll probably succeed with blueberries, too. If not, then employ raised beds or containers, where it is easier to manage the acidity of the soil.

Neutral or slightly alkaline soils were once acidified by adding peat. Eco-friendly alternatives to peat include composted sawdust, composted pine bark or needles, sulphur dust or chips, and loam-based ericaceous compost. Beware of some peat substitutes: they may be too alkaline. Blueberries also need free-draining soil. They won't do well in heavy clay soils that are prone to waterlogging.

Planting distances

- BUSHES 1.2–1.5m (4–5ft) apart.
- ROW SPACING 1.8m (6ft) apart.

Routine care

- WATERING Blueberries need a lot of water. Water regularly and often, using rainwater if possible. If using tap water is unavoidable, you may need to apply additional quantities of acidic mulch or use special ericaceous fertilizer in order to maintain the low pH level.
- FEEDING In March, after pruning, apply a lime- free general fertilizer. Don't use tomato or other general vegetable fertilizers. For an additional boost of nitrogen, you might also sprinkle sulphate of ammonia over the soil at a rate of about 15g/sq m (½oz/sq yd).
- MULCHING A thick organic mulch spread around the plants after feeding will help retain moisture and keep down weeds. Use only acidic material: composted sawdust, chipped or composted pine bark, pine needles or leafmould. Avoid farmyard manure and ordinary compost.

- NETTING You will have to use nets to keep birds off – certainly in summer as the fruits colour and ripen. A fruit cage is recommended.
- FROST PROTECTION Plants are hardy but early-flowering varieties may need covering with fleece overnight if there is a danger of frost once buds have burst.

Harvesting and storing

Blueberries have a relatively long harvest period. Early varieties should be ready to pick in July, late varieties may last into early September. The berries don't all ripen at the same time, so you may have to go over each bush several times looking for the ones that are ripe. Blueberries keep for longer than most soft fruits – for a week or more in the fridge. They also freeze particularly well.

Yield

Yields depend on the age of the bush, the variety, and of course the weather, but you should expect 1.5-2.5kg (3.3-5.5lb) from a four-year-old bush, and up to 5kg (11lb) or even more from a fully established, mature bush.

GROWING BLUEBERRIES IN CONTAINERS

Blueberries usually do well grown in tubs or containers, particularly if you take care to maintain the soil at the right level of acidity. The trick is to use special lime-free ericaceous compost formulated for other acid-loving plants, such as rhododendrons and camellias. Mix the compost with coarse grit to improve drainage, and mulch the surface with acidic, organic material. Feed with a lime-free general fertilizer in spring, and water regularly, especially in dry weather. Blueberries should never be allowed to dry out, nor should the container be allowed to sit in water.

Start off young plants in a pot with a diameter of 30–35cm (12–14in). Check the rootball and be prepared to pot on to a larger-sized container every couple of years. Remember that in open ground blueberry bushes can grow to a height of 2m (6ft), so unless you choose a compact variety you may eventually graduate to large containers (left), with diameters of 60cm (24in) or more.

PROPAGATING BLUEBERRIES

You can propagate blueberries from softwood cuttings taken in midsummer. Always insert them into ericaceous potting mix.

1 Select a healthy shoot and cut it off just above a leaf joint, so you have a cutting 10cm (4in long).

2 Make holes with a dibber in a small pot of compost before inserting your cuttings around the edge. Water, and put the pot in a propagator.

(right) **Don't pick** the berries as soon as they turn blue. Wait until they develop a powdery white bloom on their skins and turn slightly soft. They should pull way easily between your finger and thumb, leaving the stalk behind.

Month by month

(above, left to right) **Buds** are already beginning to burst in late winter. **Bell-like flowers** appear early in spring and may need protecting from frost. **Small fruits** begin to form as soon as the blossom starts to drop. From now on, keep watering with rainwater. (right) **Berries** ripen in stages rather than all at the same time.

February
- Fruit buds are visibly fattening up.
- Plant new bushes if the ground is not frozen.
- Winter-prune blueberry bushes this month or next.

March
- Complete any winter pruning early this month.
- On early-flowering varieties, young leaves and blossom start to appear.
- Protect against frost if necessary.
- Feed with a lime-free general fertilizer and sulphate of ammonia.
- Spread an acid organic mulch around plants to suppress weeds.
- Last chance to plant new bushes.

April
- On most bushes, blossom is fully open, attracting pollinating insects.
- Pot on blueberries growing in containers if necessary.

May
- Late-flowering varieties are in flower now.
- As blossom drops, small green fruitlets form and begin to swell.
- Weed and water regularly.

June
- Continue weeding and watering as fruits ripen.
- Net against birds.

July
- Harvest early- and mid-season fruit.
- Take softwood cuttings in order to propagate new plants.

August
- Harvest mid- and late-season fruit.

September
- There may still be a few late-season fruits for picking.

November
- Plant new bushes between now and next March.

Pruning blueberries

Most of the fruit is produced on stems that are between one and three years old. In addition, young new stems that shoot up from the soil in the current summer, from about July onwards, may produce a second crop of fruit at the end of the season. These berries may even be larger than the first crop. Wood that is older than three years won't fruit as well or as plentifully as newer wood. Prune it out gradually.

Pruning a blueberry bush

Blueberries are always pruned in the winter, when the plants are in their dormant phase. You can do it at any time between November and early March but, if you wait until February or March, the fruit buds will have fattened up visibly. You'll then be able to see which stems are going to fruit heavily and should therefore be left untouched.

1st and 2nd winter pruning
NOVEMBER–MARCH

- Very little pruning is required in the first 2 years after planting.
- Remove any damaged or diseased stems.
- Thin any obviously weak or crossing stems from the centre of the bush.
- Prune out any thin stems growing parallel with, or too close to, the ground.

Winter pruning an established bush
NOVEMBER–MARCH

- If the bush has become overgrown, aim to open up its centre to let in light and air.
- Remove any dead, damaged, or diseased stems.
- Cut 1 or 2 of the oldest, thickest, least productive stems right down to the base. Aim to leave 4 to 6 main stems.
- Remove any lateral shoots growing too close to the base of the main stems.
- Tip-prune the twiggy ends of the stems that produced fruit last year. Always cut back to a strong sideshoot or to a bud that is facing upwards.
- Don't prune out more than a quarter of the bush at once.

(top to bottom) **Use loppers** to cut old, unproductive stems down to the base in winter. **Prune out** any diseased or damaged stems, cutting back to a strong, healthy shoot.

What can go wrong

Leaves and stems

1 **Scorching on edges of leaves**
Leaves turning brown and curling at the edges, and the tips of new shoots dying back, are the classic signs of drought. If not lacking moisture, the plant may be in need of potassium, which an annual feed with a lime-free, general fertilizer will provide.
■ See **Potassium deficiency** (p.321).

2 **Small, brown, shell-like insects on stems**
Scale insects are sometimes found on plant stems. They are elliptical in shape and covered with a domed shell. Some may excrete a white waxy or fluffy substance that encourages grey sooty mould to develop.
■ See **Scale insects** (p.339).

3 **Multicoloured, mottled patches on leaves**
Irregular pale green, yellow, and red markings are often signs of one of the several viruses that can attack blueberries. They may also be a symptom of a lack of magnesium.
■ See **Blueberry virus** (p.325), **Magnesium deficiency** (p.321).

Yellow leaves with green veins
If leaves turn yellow with clearly visible, skeletal green veins, and if growth is poor, it's usually a sign that the soil is too alkaline. This produces lime-induced chlorosis, meaning that the plant is unable to take up sufficient iron and manganese from the soil.
■ See **Iron deficiency** (p.320), **Manganese deficiency** (p.321).

Dead brown leaves remain on stems
Clusters of leaves turning brown, dying off, and failing to drop may look like "flags" against otherwise normal green foliage. When they finally do fall the dead stem is likely to have turned almost black.
■ See **Blueberry stem blight** (p.325).

Fruit

4 **Berries eaten**
Birds are very partial to the ripening fruits and begin eating the berries as soon as they start to change colour from green to blue. Any damaged fruits also attract wasps and flies.
■ See **Birds** (p.335), **Wasps** (p.341).

Fluffy, grey or brown mould
In wet summers or on sites where conditions are damp and humid, fruits may become covered with mould and start to rot, sometimes after harvesting. Flowers, leaves and stems may also be affected. The cause is likely to be the fungal infection, botrytis.
■ See **Botrytis** (p.325).

Cranberries and lingonberries

Cultivated cranberries originate from North America, where their natural habitat is boggy, peat-rich moorland. They are low-growing, sprawling, evergreen plants that are not hard to grow yourself – provided that you are able to recreate their natural growing conditions.

Wild cranberries found in Europe and Japan are a different species: they are slightly smaller, and tend not to be grown commercially.

Cranberries ripen in the autumn, later than blueberries. Although the deep-red fruits look appetizing, they are far too sharp to be eaten raw and, after the addition of generous quantities of sugar, are usually used for juices, jellies, cakes, and the cranberry sauce, without which a Thanksgiving or Christmas turkey would be almost unthinkable.

Ripe cranberries can stay on the bush, so pick them as and when you need them. Frosts will, however, damage the berries so harvest before night-time temperatures drop.

Growing cranberries

Cranberries are not hard to grow provided you can give them the conditions they need. If you can't, you should probably not bother. The two most important things are an acid soil and plenty of water – in other words, the sort of environment that mimics their natural habitat.

The year at a glance

	spring			summer			autumn			winter		
	M	A	M	J	J	A	S	O	N	D	J	F
plant	▬	▬	▬	▬								
trim	▬							▬	▬			
harvest cranberries							▬	▬				
harvest lingonberries				▬			▬					

Planting cranberries

Because they have such specific requirements, cranberries are usually best grown in containers or in specially constructed beds. They are sold as container-grown rather than bare-root plants. Unlike blueberries, they are self-fertile so you don't need more than one plant to guarantee pollination.

When to plant

Plant at any time of year, except in the extreme cold of midwinter or heat of midsummer. Spring is best.

Must-grow cranberries

1 **'Pilgrim'**
One of the most popular and widely grown varieties. Rightly so, because plants are heavy cropping and the berries are among the largest. They are dark red and can grow to the size of cherries.

2 **'Early Black'**
Not actually black but rather a rich, dark red-purple. This variety produces generous crops of medium-sized berries that are ready for picking earlier than most other varieties – perhaps even in August. Originally from Massachusetts in northeast USA.

ALSO TRY

'CN'
A vigorous, spreading variety that produces heavy crops of large, juicy red berries. It is widely grown commercially.

'Franklin'
A cross between 'Early Black' and another long-established US cranberry, 'Howes', this compact variety is ideal for container-growing. It crops slightly more heavily than 'Early Black' and ripens almost as early.

Where to plant

Choose a sunny site, but not an enclosed, south-facing one that gets too hot. Cranberries do best in a raised or sunken bed, where you can control the acidity of the soil and the drainage.

Soil type

Cranberries, like blueberries, will only grow in very acid soils, those with a pH of 4–5.5 or even lower. And they need the right balance between being constantly moist yet not becoming waterlogged.

Planting distances

- PLANTS 30cm (12in) apart.
- ROW SPACING 30cm (12in) apart.

Growing in containers

Use a pot or container with a diameter of at least 38–45cm (15–18in), and fill it with a mix of ericaceous compost and coarse, lime-free grit to improve drainage. Stand the pot in a non-porous dish or tray and keep it topped up with rainwater so that the soil never dries out.

Growing in special beds

Cranberries can be grown in either raised or sunken beds filled with acid soil to a depth of 15–20cm (6–8in). If possible, when constructing

(left to right) **Cranberry flowers** are tiny and appear in early summer, by which time insect pollinators are plentiful. **A purpose-built bed** made from an old ceramic sink, set into the ground, is ideal for growing cranberries. Fill it with ericaceous compost and keep the soil moist.

the bed, line it with polythene mesh or with plastic sheeting that has been perforated with plenty of drainage holes. Fill with lime-free, ericaceous compost or a suitably light, low-pH soil. Cover the surface with a layer of lime-free grit or sand to act as a mulch. Once established, plants will spread to form a mat-like ground cover.

Routine care

■ WATERING Cranberries need a lot of water and must be kept constantly moist, using rainwater if possible.

■ FEEDING Not usually necessary, but if crops are disappointing try applying a little liquid, lime-free general fertilizer in about April.

■ MULCHING A top-dressing of grit or sand will help retain moisture and keep down weeds.

Harvesting and storing

Cranberries usually start to ripen at the end of September, but there is no need to pick them straight away. They will happily stay on the bush for another month or two. You will almost certainly collect your cranberries by hand, but when grown commercially in the United States they are harvested by flooding entire fields so that the berries float. They can then be "combed" from the plants by machine. Cranberries store well – for as long as two or three months in a fridge. They also freeze well.

Pruning

Cranberries don't really need pruning as such, though they benefit from an annual trim, immediately after harvesting, or in spring to remove any straggly, untidy stems or runners, and to encourage bushy growth.

What can go wrong

Diseases and disorders are rare, although if the soil is not acid enough plants may suffer from lime-induced chlorosis (see p.320). Few pests seem to, target cranberries, and neither birds nor slugs find them to their taste.

GROWING LINGONBERRIES

Like cranberries, lingonberries grow as low, spreading, evergreen bushes. They have pale-pink and white flowers that appear in May or June, and they usually produce two harvests of small red berries, the first at the end of July and the second in September. Lingonberries also need acid soil and are therefore best grown in containers filled with special, lime-free ericaceous compost. They don't need quite such boggy conditions as cranberries, but they must nevertheless be kept well watered.

Must-try unusual berries

These berries push the boundaries of what is usually defined as grow-your-own fruit. If you are curious and have the space, give them a try.

1 Goji berry

Originating in the foothills of the Himalayas, goji berries are among today's fashionable superfoods, owing to their very high concentrations of minerals, vitamins, and antioxidants. The plants are very hardy, and will survive severe winters as well as hot, dry summers. Grow them in a sheltered, sunny spot with plenty of room. Once established, purple-and-white flowers are followed by small, red berries in autumn. The berries are usually eaten dried, like raisins, or used in juices.

2 Chokeberry

Chokeberries are sometimes referred to as aronia berries. In the wild, they grow in damp, acid soils, often near the edges of woodland. In gardens, they are grown as ornamental shrubs for their white or pink flowers and vibrant autumn leaf colour. The small, redcurrant-sized fruits of the red, black, and purple chokeberry are edible, and can be used for juices and jams. They are very high in antioxidants.

3 Huckleberry

In North America, huckleberries, like blueberries, grow wild in acid, boggy soils, often at high-altitudes. The garden huckleberry is unrelated to them and, although a member of the deadly nightshade family, it is edible, not poisonous. Sow seeds in pots indoors in March or outdoors under cover in May, and treat them much like tomatoes or aubergines. Pick the berries when they turn black, and use in tarts and jams.

1

5

6

4 Honeyberry

The honeyberry is in fact an edible form of honeysuckle. Native to northern Europe, Asia, and America, it grows to a height of 1–2m (3-6ft) and produces purple-blue berries from early summer onwards. The fruits taste rather like wild blueberries. Honeyberries are worth searching out from specialist nurseries and are easy to grow. You'll need to buy at least two as they need a neighbouring plant for successful pollination. Honeyberries are extremely hardy, drought-resistant, and, unlike blueberries, they don't need acid soil.

5 Oregon grape

Despite its name, this isn't a grape but actually a type of mahonia (*Mahonia aquifolium*), and often grown as a decorative garden shrub. It is closely related to the once-popular but now out-of-fashion barberry, a member of the *Berberis* genus. The Oregon grape produces yellow flowers in spring and small blue-black berries that ripen in July or August. They can be eaten raw but are usually cooked, sweetened, and made into preserves.

6 Bilberry

In Europe and northern Asia, bilberries are traditionally a wild food. Known in the UK as whortleberries or whinberries, in Scotland as blaeberries, and in France as *myrtilles*, they grow in acid, boggy soils, often on high moorlands. They taste like blueberries but are smaller, with purple flesh and juice. Unfortunately, they are difficult to buy commercially and very hard to grow. It might be better to think of them as a fruit for foraging. Confusingly, in North America, the so-called bog bilberry is actually a form of huckleberry.

7 Elderberry

Strictly speaking, the elderberry is a tree fruit rather than a soft fruit, and one that usually grows wild. It is not normally cultivated. However, if you have plenty of space it's worth planting an elder, and an annual winter-prune should keep it from becoming too large. Harvest the sweet-smelling flowers for making cordials and other soft drinks – or for flavouring a gooseberry fool – and use the berries in pies, tarts, jams, jellies, as well as home-made wine.

Grape vines

Not so long ago, there were strict rules about growing your own grapes, at least in cool temperate climates. Grapes for winemaking were grown outdoors, and dessert grapes – those sweet enough to be eaten fresh from the vine – were grown under cover, in glasshouses or conservatories. However, today's modern varieties have blurred the distinction and, depending on your particular site and microclimate, it's now possible to grow both types of grapes either outdoors or under cover.

Pruning a grape vine has the reputation of being a black art. The various different techniques are rich in complexity and excite strong opinions. Yet, in all honesty, it's only as hard as you want to make it. There's nothing wrong with growing a vine informally, allowing it to scramble up over a trellis or pergola. You'll almost certainly get some grapes, though perhaps not as many as you might hope for. But, if you want to train a grape vine properly – as it's done in a commercial vineyard or in traditional glasshouses – then you must get to grips with either cordon pruning or the guyot system. Take heart: neither is as difficult as it initially appears.

Grapes may ripen slightly unevenly, depending on how much sun they receive. Wait until they are all ready, then cut off the entire bunch with a sharp pair of secateurs.

Must-grow grapes

1 'Buckland Sweetwater'
Dessert
A greenhouse vine that usually crops early and reliably if watered regularly and fed from time to time. Pick the grapes as soon as they turn amber-gold or the skins may thicken.
- **Grow** under cover
- **Colour** white-amber
- **Harvest** September to October

2 'Dornfelder'
Wine and dessert
A hybrid German variety that can be eaten fresh or used to make red wine. It is one of the few red wine grapes suitable for cool temperate climates.
- **Grow** outdoors
- **Colour** purple-red
- **Harvest** early October

3 'Brandt'
Dessert
This is an attractive, easy-going vine that doesn't need complex pruning and is therefore a good choice for training over a pergola or up a wall. The grapes are perhaps not the largest, but they have a good, sweet flavour nevertheless.
- **Grow** outdoors
- **Colour** purple
- **Harvest** mid-October

4 'Müller-Thurgau'
Wine and dessert
This is a perennially popular grape for home winemaking. It is easy to grow, should ripen in most sheltered spots, and usually produces a good crop.
- **Grow** outdoors
- **Colour** pale yellow-green
- **Harvest** mid-October

5 'Flame'
Dessert
A red seedless grape often sold in supermarkets. It can be raised under glass or outdoors in a warm, sheltered spot and tastes far better home-grown.
- **Grow** outdoors or under cover
- **Colour** red
- **Harvest** late September to early October

6 'Lakemont'
Dessert

A relatively modern, white seedless grape that can be grown outdoors in a warm, sheltered location or in a greenhouse in cooler regions. It has a wonderful, sweet, muscat-flavour.
- **Grow** outdoors or under cover
- **Colour** gold-yellow
- **Harvest** late September to early October

7 'Perlette'
Dessert

A French grape that can usually be grown outside or under cover. It produces good crops of sweet, juicy, seedless grapes.
- **Grow** outdoors or under cover
- **Colour** yellow-green
- **Harvest** late September

8 'Muscat of Alexandria'
Dessert

Not the easiest of grapes to grow, as ideally the fruits need a heated greenhouse and a long period on the vine in order to ripen fully. Definitely worth trying, though, because its flavour is so outstanding.
- **Grow** under cover
- **Colour** gold-yellow
- **Harvest** November to December

9 'Black Hamburgh'
Dessert

Also known as 'Schiava Grossa' and 'Trollinger', this is a long-established, popular greenhouse grape. It is sweet and juicy, with a good flavour, and is reliable and easy to grow.
- **Grow** under cover
- **Colour** purple-black
- **Harvest** September to October

'Boskoop Glory' (not illustrated)
Dessert

This black grape is reliable as well as heavy cropping. It does best in a sheltered spot against a warm, sunny wall but is one of the few sweet black grapes that can be successfully grown outdoors in cool climates.
- **Grow** outdoors
- **Colour** blue-black
- **Harvest** September to October

'Regent' (not illustrated)
Wine and dessert

Originally bred in Germany for growing in cool temperate climates, this is a red-wine grape that crops heavily and is disease-resistant. When fully ripe, the grapes are sweet enough to eat fresh.
- **Grow** outdoors
- **Colour** blue-black
- **Harvest** early October

'Phoenix' (not illustrated)
Wine and dessert

A good choice for organic growers, as it is fairly resistant to mildew and may not need spraying. The grapes have a slight muscat-flavour, and can be eaten fresh or used to make wine.
- **Grow** outdoors
- **Colour** pale green
- **Harvest** early to mid-October

'Siegerrebe' (not illustrated)
Wine and dessert

Sweet, golden grapes that ripen early. They have a slight muscat-flavour when eaten fresh and can also be used to make wine. Vines are usually heavy-cropping, but they tend not to grow well on chalky, alkaline soils.
- **Grow** outdoors
- **Colour** gold-amber
- **Harvest** late August to early September

Growing grapes outdoors

In order to crop successfully, grapes need the following: a cold spell during the winter (though not so cold that they are killed off), warmth in spring when they flower and set fruit, and heat and sunshine in summer to ripen the grapes. So, it's no surprise that growing them outdoors in cool temperate regions is always going to be a bit hit and miss. That said, it's not impossible. With global warming, it may even be becoming easier. Choose your site and your varieties carefully, and keep your fingers crossed for good weather.

The year at a glance – outdoors

	spring			summer			autumn			winter		
	M	A	M	J	J	A	S	O	N	D	J	F
plant bare-root	▇								▇	▇	▇	▇
plant container	▇	▇	▇	▇	▇	▇	▇	▇	▇	▇	▇	▇
summer-prune		▇	▇	▇	▇	▇						
winter-prune									▇	▇	▇	▇
harvest							▇	▇				

Flowering and pollination
Most grapes are self-fertile, and are pollinated by the wind rather than by bees or other insects.

Choosing grape vines
Young plants are available bare-root from some specialist nurseries, but they are more commonly supplied container-grown and can be bought all year round. They are likely to have been either grown from cuttings or grafted onto disease-resistant rootstocks.

When to plant
■ BARE-ROOT November–March, when vines are dormant, unless the soil is waterlogged or frozen. November or December are best since you will be

For top-quality plants visit a specialist supplier who will also be able to offer advice about suitable varieties for your garden.

able to prune straight away (see right). March is good for planting, too, after the worst of the winter is over.

■ CONTAINER-GROWN In theory, you may plant at any time of year, although late April or May are best, when the danger of frost has gone. Avoid summer months if it is hot and dry.

Where to plant

Grapes need full sun. If you're going to train them on post-and-wire supports, choose a south-, southwest-, or southeast-facing slope, somewhere protected from strong winds, and orient the rows north to south. Alternatively, grow them against a sunny, sheltered wall or fence. In both cases, avoid frost pockets.

Soil type

The roots of grape vines are very long, penetrating deep into the earth, and spreading widely. For this reason, they are able to survive in most soils, including extremely dry and stony ground. Soils with a pH in the range of 6.0–7.5 should be suitable. The few sites on which they will struggle are thin, shallow soils and heavy, poorly drained ones prone to waterlogging. In soils that are very rich vines may produce too much foliage and too few grapes.

(above) **Grapes grown outside** require two good summers in a row: the first so new shoots ripen and buds form, the second to ensure fruit sets and ripens.

(below) **Prune a new vine** planted in November or December straight away. Cut it down to a strong, healthy bud about 30cm (12in) above ground level. At any other time, wait until the autumn to prune, or the sap will weep.

Cut away some of the foliage from time to time during the summer so that air can circulate freely and sun can get to the ripening bunches of grapes.

Planting distances outdoors
- CORDONS 1–1.2m (3–4ft) apart.
- SINGLE GUYOTS 1m (3ft) apart.
- DOUBLE GUYOTS 1.5–2m (5–6ft) apart.

Routine care
WATERING Water both newly planted vines and those grown against walls regularly throughout the spring and summer.
- FEEDING Each February, before growth starts, apply a general compound fertilizer. Between May and August, give dessert grapes a diluted, high-potassium liquid feed every couple of weeks. If signs of magnesium deficiency appear (see p.321), spray with a solution of Epsom salts.
- MULCHING In March, after feeding, remove any weeds and mulch around the base of wall-trained vines.
- NETTING Birds can be a problem in summer as fruit ripens, and nets may be necessary.
- THINNING Dessert grapes usually crop better if thinned (see p.272), although it's not necessary with grapes grown for winemaking. Removing some of the leaves in summer will help ripen the grapes.

Harvesting and storing
For the best flavour and maximum sweetness, it's important to leave grapes on the vine until they are absolutely ripe. They may not actually reach that point, however, until several weeks after they've developed their full colour. The only failsafe method is to taste them. When they're ready, cut off the whole bunch using sharp scissors or secateurs (see p.273). If they were dry when picked, grapes will keep in a cool place for a few days but they're far better eaten straight away.

Yield
It's difficult to generalize about yields. The heaviness of the crop varies according to many factors, including how the vine is grown, trained, and pruned. An established cordon may produce two or three bunches of wine grapes, but perhaps only one bunch of dessert grapes, per lateral. A guyot-trained vine may well produce twice as many. It really depends on how many flower trusses you leave in place to develop.

How to plant
Prepare the site a month or two in advance by weeding carefully and digging in plenty of well-rotted compost or manure. Construct a post-and-wire support for cordon (see p.276) or guyot (see p.278) vines. If you're growing your vine against a wall or fence, attach the necessary wires.

Dig a hole and plant the vine so that the old nursery soil mark on the stem is level with the surface of your soil. Insert a cane or thin stake into the hole and tie the vine to it for support. If the vine is completely dormant prune it immediately (see p.269).

Growing grapes under cover

In cool temperate climates, growing vines under cover opens up a much wider choice of varieties, including grapes that need higher temperatures and a longer growing season than you could ever offer them outdoors. There are a number of options. The simplest is to grow vines in containers and move them indoors or out, according to the weather and the season. The second is an unheated greenhouse, conservatory, polytunnel, or even a porch. And the third is a heated greenhouse, where you have complete control over the microclimate.

The year at a glance – indoors

	spring			summer			autumn			winter		
	M	A	M	J	J	A	S	O	N	D	J	F
plant bare-root												
plant container												
summer-prune												
winter-prune												
harvest												

Flowering and pollination

Although grapes are usually self-fertile, outdoor-grown vines are pollinated by the wind, so those grown under cover may need a little help. Once the flowers are open, give the vines a gentle shake or gently cup your hand and run it over them to help transfer pollen. This method is more likely to be successful in the middle of the day, when the atmosphere is warm and dry.

Planting under cover

Indoors, grapes are usually grown as cordons (see p.276). The way in which they are trained will depend on the design of your greenhouse or conservatory. In the case of a south-facing lean-to, the vine can be attached either to the back wall or to wires strung across the front, nearer the glass. In a tall, ridge greenhouse the vine can be trained up into the roof space, leaving room for other plants beneath. In all cases, it's important not to crowd the vine. Good air circulation is vital.

Grapes grown in greenhouses or conservatories need a support system of strong, horizontal wires to take the weight of the sideshoots that bear the fruit. It's also important to provide plenty of ventilation.

When to plant

■ BARE-ROOT November–March, when vines are dormant. The best time is November or December, since your new vine will be dormant and you will be able to prune it back as soon as it is in the ground, without causing the cut to weep sap.

■ CONTAINER-GROWN In theory, you may plant at any time of year, although November or December are best, for the same reason.

(top to bottom) **Thinning bunches** of dessert grapes encourages the fruits that remain to develop their full size and flavour. Use sharp, long-nosed scissors and remove first any diseased grapes, then the smallest, and finally some from the middle. In all, reduce the size of the bunch by about a third.

Where to plant

You have two choices. The first is to plant your vine in a specially prepared soil bed inside the greenhouse. The second is to plant it directly into the soil outside, then to train it through a hole in the wall so that it grows and fruits under cover. What are the pros and cons? Planting inside gives you more control and is probably better for a heated greenhouse, but it can involve more work. You must ensure that the soil is kept in top condition, that the bed has good drainage, and that the vine is regularly watered. Without rainfall, the only moisture it will receive is the watering you provide. Planting outdoors is easier, but it will take longer for the soil to warm up in spring, so tender vines will not get off to such an early start.

Soil type

For an indoor soil bed, use a loam-based compost, such as John Innes No. 3. For outdoor soil requirements, see page 269.

How to plant

Before planting, put up a system of strong, horizontal wire supports spaced 25–30cm (10–12in) apart. Make sure they are at least 30cm (12in) away from the wall or glass, in order to avoid sun scorch and to allow air to circulate.

Plant the vine so that the old nursery soil mark on the stem is level with the surface of your soil and tie it to a cane for support, at least initially. In November or December, prune it immediately (see p.269). Otherwise, wait until autumn.

Planting distances under cover

It's unlikely that the average-sized greenhouse will be large enough for more than one vine, although it can of course be trained as either a single or multiple cordon. If you have more space, plant cordons 1–1.2m (3–4ft) apart.

Routine care

■ HEATING AND VENTILATING Open vents between November and January to give vines the period of winter chill they need while dormant. In a heated greenhouse, gradually increase the temperature from February or March onwards in order to stimulate vines into growth. An unheated greenhouse should begin to warm up from April onwards. Open and shut vents as required in order to keep air circulating freely, and don't let spring temperatures fall below 5°C (41°F) at night or rise above 20°C (68°F) during the day.

■ WATERING Water regularly during the growing season if the vine is planted inside. Ease off as the grapes ripen, and avoid any sudden overwatering that may cause skins to split.

■ FEEDING For vines planted outside, see page 270. Vines planted inside may need a more frequent liquid feed – perhaps once a week between flowering and the grapes starting to colour. They also need a top-dressing of fresh compost each autumn or winter.

■ MULCHING In March, after the first good watering of the year, mulch around the base of the vine with well-rotted compost or manure.

■ THINNING Greenhouse grapes grow larger and are healthier if thinned (see opposite). It's a fiddly job, and one you may have to do more than once, but it's worthwhile for dessert grapes. For wine grapes, it's not necessary.

■ SCRAPING BARK In winter, use a blunt knife to scrape away any old, loose bark. It harbours pests, such as mealybugs (see p.337) and red spider mites (see p.339. If necessary, spray with a suitable insecticide.

Harvesting and storing
As with grapes grown outdoors, it's important to leave fruit on the vine until it's absolutely ripe. In the case of late-season dessert varieties this "finishing" or "holding" period may last several weeks, meaning that grapes in a heated greenhouse can be harvested as late as December.

Yield
Yields vary according to variety, method of training, and growing conditions. As a rough guide, you might expect 10 bunches of grapes per 4m (12ft) of cordon. A single bunch can weigh about 500g (1.1lb).

Pick dessert grapes by cutting off the whole bunch, suspending it from an 8–10cm (3–4in) wide "handle" of lateral stem at the top. Try not to touch dessert grapes with your fingers or you'll spoil the bloom on the surface.

GROWING IN CONTAINERS
Container-grown grapes can live indoors or out. Indeed, you can easily give them the best of both worlds if you move them outside into the garden or onto a terrace during winter, when they need a spell of cold, and then bring them back under cover at other times of the year when they need warmth.

A standard is the form most commonly grown in pots. One-year-old vines can be started off in pots as small as 19cm (7in) in diameter. In the autumn of the following year, pot them on into 30–38cm (12–15in) pots. Use loam-based compost mixed with some sand or gravel to improve drainage. Feed with a general liquid fertilizer in spring and summer, and keep the pot well-watered. Each winter, top-dress with fresh soil and pot on to a larger container only when necessary.

An established standard vine should have a clear stem of about 1–1.2m (3–4ft) topped with a "head" of fruiting spurs. Restrict cropping to just one bunch of grapes per spur, by pruning them as you would those on a cordon (see p.277).

Month by month

(left to right) **Buds** burst and leaves unfurl as spring temperatures rise. **Flowers** bloom from tight clusters of tiny buds. **Fruitlets** set and begin to swell.

January
■ Untie established cordons and let the central leader or "rod" hang down to stimulate new growth.

February
■ Close greenhouse vents once the winter chill period is over, and start to increase the temperature in heated greenhouses.
■ Apply a general compound fertilizer around indoor and outdoor vines.

March
■ Last chance to plant bare-root vines, as they are now coming out of their dormant period.
■ Re-tie cordons that have been allowed to hang horizontally.
■ Weed and also mulch indoor and outdoor vines.

April
■ Temperatures in unheated greenhouses should be rising now.
■ Plant young container-grown vines this month or next.
■ Prune established cordons this month and next, thinning to two shoots on each spur.

May
■ Flowers usually open this month.
■ Begin weeding and watering regularly.
■ Give vines a regular liquid feed while grapes are developing, between now and August.

June
■ Thin bunches of dessert grapes.
■ On established cordons, start pruning back laterals and pinching out unwanted growth.
■ Begin to tie in new vertical shoots on guyot vines and remove unwanted growth.

August
■ Net outdoor vines against birds.
■ Prune out excessive foliage to let sun and air reach ripening grapes.

September
■ Start harvesting early-season grapes.

October
■ Harvest mid- and late-season grapes.

November
■ Late-season grapes grown under cover may still be ripening on the vine this month or even next.
■ After harvesting, open greenhouse vents to give vines their necessary period of winter chill.
■ This is the best month to buy and plant new vines: the soil is still warm, you can prune them without the sap bleeding, and their roots should establish before growth starts next year.
■ Winter-prune established cordons this month and next.
■ On guyot vines, remove all the growth that fruited this year, and prune and tie in the three main shoots required for next year.

December
■ Top-dress greenhouse vines with fresh compost.
■ Scrape away loose bark from the base of vines to expose pests.

Pruning and training grapes

Pruning is essential. Without it, vines very quickly grow out of control and you'll end up with a straggly plant that is all foliage and little or no fruit. The cordon and guyot methods are the most commonly used. Both will keep vines neat and orderly, as well as encouraging the new growth that will fruit in the current year. All major pruning is carried out in winter when vines are dormant; otherwise they weep sap so freely they may actually be weakened. Only minor pinching out is done in summer.

Post-and-wire supports

Outdoors, both cordon and guyot systems need a structure of sturdy post-and-wire supports. Use 8 x 8cm (3 x 3in) treated wooden posts each 2.5m (8ft) in length. Drive them into the ground to a depth of 60cm (24in) at intervals of 4–5m (12–16ft), and brace the posts at either end of the row with diagonal struts. Stretch horizontal lengths of heavy-gauge galvanized wire between them: single wires at 40cm (16in) and 60cm (2ft) from the ground, and double wires at 90cm (3ft), 1.2m (4ft), and 1.5m (5ft).

Indoors, in a greenhouse or conservatory, attach single horizontal wires to the wall or frame of the building, ensuring they are spaced 25–30cm (10–12in) apart and at least 30cm (12in) away from the brickwork or glass.

This cordon-trained indoor vine is putting on healthy new growth in spring. The flower trusses, which are visible towards the top of the vine, will bear fruit during the coming summer.

Pruning a single cordon vine

The method shown here is most often used for greenhouse grapes, though it is also widely employed outdoors. Growth consists of a single upright stem (the cordon) from which horizontal, fruit-bearing laterals shoot out left and right, like arms. It is sometimes known as the "rod-and-spur" system, because the central cordon is termed the rod and because the laterals grow from spurs that form on it. The laterals are pruned back and grow afresh each year.

1st winter pruning
NOVEMBER–DECEMBER

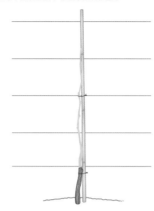

- If you planted in November or December, cut down the leader to a strong, healthy bud about 30cm (12in) above ground level.
- If you planted any later, leave the vine to grow or it will weep sap.

1st summer pruning
MAY–AUGUST

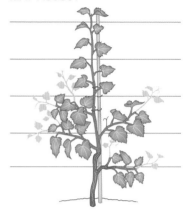

- Keep pruning to a minimum. Let the central leader grow. It may reach a height of 3m (10ft) or more. Tie it in to a cane or thin stake.
- Cut back all laterals growing directly from the leader so that they have only 5–6 leaves left.
- Pinch out any new sideshoots growing from the laterals to just 1 leaf.

2nd winter pruning
NOVEMBER–DECEMBER

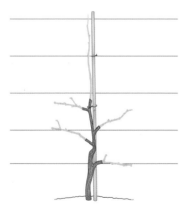

- Prune when the vine enters dormancy – as soon as the leaves have fallen.
- Cut back the central leader by about two-thirds of the growth it made last year. Only brown stem that has ripened should remain.
- Prune laterals back to 1–2 healthy-looking buds.

2nd summer pruning
MAY–AUGUST

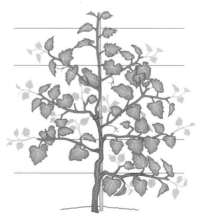

- It's best not to let the vine produce any grapes this year, so pinch out any flowers that form.
- Tie in the central leader as it grows.
- Cut back all laterals to 5–6 leaves.
- Pinch out sideshoots growing from the laterals to just 1 leaf.

3rd winter pruning
NOVEMBER–DECEMBER

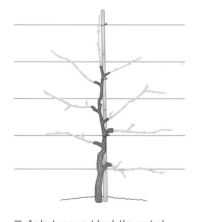

- As last year, cut back the central leader by about one-half or two-thirds of the growth it made last year. Remove wood that is still green, leaving only brown, ripened stem remaining.
- Prune laterals back to 1–2 healthy-looking buds.

Spring pruning an established cordon
APRIL–MAY

Summer pruning an established cordon
JUNE–AUGUST

Winter pruning an established cordon
NOVEMBER–DECEMBER
and JANUARY–FEBRUARY

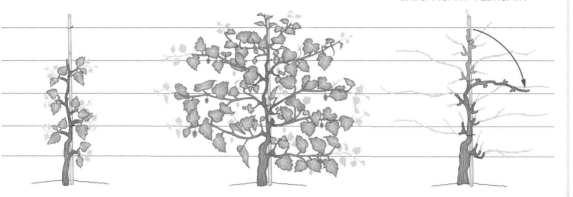

- In spring, new shoots will emerge from the spurs on the central leader.
- Remove all except 2 shoots from each spur. The 1st (the strongest) will form the lateral that bears this year's fruit. The 2nd is for back-up, in case the 1st is damaged or dies.
- Once the 1st new lateral is growing strongly, pinch back the 2nd to just 2 leaves.

- Tie in the central leader as it grows.
- Cut back all laterals without flower trusses to 5–6 leaves.
- Cut back laterals with flower trusses to 2 leaves beyond the furthest truss and tie them in to horizontal wires.
- Remove surplus flower trusses. Leave just 1 per lateral for dessert grapes, and 1 per 30cm (12in) for wine grapes.
- Pinch out sideshoots growing from the laterals to just 1 leaf.

- Prune back the laterals that fruited last summer to 1–2 healthy-looking buds.
- Thin out old, congested spurs by removing surplus wood with a pruning saw.
- Cut back the central leader to a bud facing in the opposite direction from last year's. It should be just below the topmost wire.
- In January or February, before growth begins, release the top half of the central leader so that it bends over horizontally. Tie it loosely to one side. Doing this ensures new shoots form on all the spurs, not just the upper ones.
- In spring, when shoots start to emerge, lift the central leader back into position and re-tie it.

In spring, restrict sideshoots to two per spur. Once you can tell which is the stronger, start training it horizontally, then remove the weaker one, along with any other new growth.

Pruning a double guyot vine

The method shown here is most often used for grapes grown outdoors, supported on posts and wires. It's also the system you're likely to see in commercial vineyards. It differs from the cordon method in that there is no tall, single upright stem. Instead, each year just three shoots are grown from a short, stubby trunk or leg. Two are trained horizontally as arms, one to the left and one to the right. From these two arms, shoots grow vertically to carry the current summer's fruit. The third, central shoot is cut back hard. Its job during the summer is not to bear fruit at all but to produce the three main shoots required for the following year.

1st winter pruning
NOVEMBER–DECEMBER

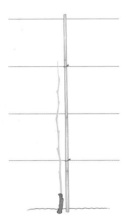

- If you planted in November or December, cut down the leader to a strong, healthy bud about 15cm (6in) above ground level.
- If you planted any later, leave it to grow on or it will weep sap.

1st summer pruning
MAY–AUGUST

- Keep pruning to a minimum. Let the central leader grow, and tie it in to a cane or thin stake as it does so.
- Cut off completely any strong laterals growing upwards in competition with the leader.
- Prune back all other laterals so that they have only 5–6 leaves left.

2nd winter pruning
NOVEMBER–DECEMBER

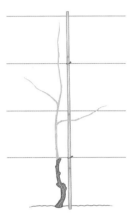

- Prune as soon as the leaves have fallen, when the vine enters its dormant period.
- Cut back the central leader to about 38cm (15in) above ground level – just below the bottom wire. Ensure at least 3 strong, healthy buds remain.

Winter pruning an established guyot
NOVEMBER–DECEMBER

- Untie and remove completely the two horizontal arms, together with all their vertical shoots. Having fruited in the summer they are no longer required.
- Of the 3 remaining shoots, cut back the central one to 3–4 buds in preparation for the following year.
- Prune back the other 2 shoots to about 60cm (2ft), with 8–12 buds on each.
- Gently bend them down either side of the main stem and tie them in place so they will produce vertical shoots next summer.

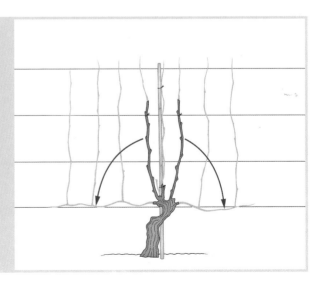

2nd summer pruning
MAY–AUGUST

- 3 strong shoots should grow from the buds you left last winter.
- As they grow, gather them together with string and tie them loosely to the cane or stake.
- Repeatedly pinch out all other new shoots growing from the base or leg of the vine.

3rd winter pruning
NOVEMBER–DECEMBER

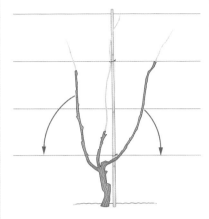

- Cut back the central shoot to 3–4 strong, healthy buds. Growth from these buds should form the 3 main shoots for the year after next.
- Prune back the other 2 shoots to a length of about 60cm (2ft). Each should have 8–12 strong, healthy buds.
- Gently bend these shoots down in an arc on either side of the main stem and tie them to the lowest horizontal wire. New shoots will grow vertically from them during the summer.

3rd summer pruning
MAY–AUGUST

- As shoots grow vertically from the two horizontal arms, thread them between the double wires or tie them in. Remove the growing tips when they reach the top wire, and pinch out completely any small new sideshoots.
- As last year, 3 strong new shoots should grow from the buds you left on the central stem last winter. If there are more than 3 remove them.
- As the 3 central shoots grow, tie them in. Remove any flowers and pinch out sideshoots to just 1 leaf.

Summer pruning an established guyot
MAY–AUGUST

- Thread or tie in vertical shoots. Remove the growing tips when they reach the top wire, and pinch out completely any new sideshoots.
- Restrict bunches of grapes to 1 per 30cm (12in).
- Remove any more than 3 new shoots growing from last winter's central stem. As they grow, tie them in, remove any flowers, and pinch out any young sideshoots they produce to just 1 leaf.

What can go wrong

Leaves, shoots, and stems

1 Leaves mottled and bronzed
Glasshouse red spider mites can cause upper surfaces of leaves to become speckled or mottled with pale yellow-bronze spots, to dry up, and die. Fine silk webbing may also be visible.
■ See **Red spider mite** (p.339).

2 Blisters and felt-like patches on leaves
Microscopic mites cause blistering on the upper surface of leaves and hairy, felt-like patches that turn from white through yellow to brown, usually on the undersides but sometimes above as well.
■ See **Vine leaf blister mite** p.340).

3 Yellow leaves with green veins
Gradual yellowing of the leaves is usually a sign of a mineral deficiency in the soil, one that interferes with the plant's ability to produce green chlorophyll. When the margins of leaves are affected (as shown here), a shortage of magnesium is likely. If the yellowing is all-over and the veins stand out prominently in green, it may be due to a lack of iron or manganese.
■ See **Common mineral deficiencies** (pp.320–21).

4 Small, white, wax-covered insects on stems
Mealybugs feed on sap that they suck from stems and branches. They are recognizable by the fluffy, white wax with which they are coated. They are more of a problem on vines grown under cover.
■ See **Mealybugs** (p.337).

5 Leaves curled and distorted
Leaves that curl up at the edges and are twisted or stunted may be a symptom of accidental contamination by hormonal weedkiller – to which grape vines are particularly sensitive. Plants are seriously damaged only rarely; they should recover the following year, and fruit is still safe to eat.

6 Leaves and roots eaten
Adult vine weevils feed on vine leaves, leaving distinctive notches along the edges. They are usually active at night. Worse, their fat, white larvae (shown here) live in the soil feeding on roots; they can seriously damage young plants, especially those in containers.
■ See **Vine weevils** (p.341).

7 Small, brown, shell-like insects on stems
Scale insects – sometimes called brown scale – may be found on stems and branches, especially under glass. They are elliptical in shape and covered with a domed shell.
■ See **Scale insects** (p.339).

White powdery coating on leaves

Grey-white powdery mildew appears on the leaves and can develop into dark blotchy patches. Fruit can be affected too. The cause is a fungus, which tends to be worse in hot, humid conditions.
■ See **Powdery mildew** (p.329).

Yellow blotches on leaves with mildew beneath

Pale green or yellow blotches appear on the upper surfaces of leaves with corresponding patches of grey-white mildew underneath. Leaves may dry up and die. Infected fruit may shrivel too.
■ See **Downy mildew** (p.327).

Galls on leaves and roots

Pink or yellow, round galls form on leaves and roots. Inside can be found tiny insects called phylloxera that feed on sap, rather like aphids. Most grapes grown these days are now resistant to them.
■ See **Phylloxera** (p.338).

Leaves sticky with honeydew

An infestation of glasshouse whitefly can cover foliage in sticky honeydew and often patches of black, sooty mould too.
■ See **Whiteflies** (p.341).

Fruit

8 Fruit shrinks and fails to ripen

A proportion of grapes in the bunch do not ripen properly – black grapes may go red, and green ones are translucent. They wither and taste unpleasant.
■ See **Shanking** (p.330).

9 Fruit rots on the vine

Furry grey–brown mould appears on the skins of grapes. As the infection takes hold, they wither and rot. The cause is a fungus that attacks both indoor and outdoor grapes. It is worse in wet or humid weather.
■ See **Botrytis** (p.325).

10 Powdery coating and splits in fruit

Grapes develop a covering of grey-white powdery mould. Later, the mildew turns brown, and grapes become leathery, harden, and split open.
■ See **Powdery mildew** (p.329).

Fruit eaten or stripped

Birds, wasps, and other insects feed on ripening grapes, making holes in the skin, aggravating existing ones, or even stealing the fruits entirely.
■ See **Birds** (p.335) and **Wasps** (p.341).

Tender and exotic fruit

This chapter includes a range of fruit from warm temperate, tropical, or subtropical climates. Many of them require high temperatures, high humidity, and consistently high levels of sunlight. Even those that are not so demanding need hot summers and mild winters. Admittedly, a few are hardy enough to survive all but the coldest of winters, but the principal challenge for the fruit grower isn't simply keeping them alive, but coaxing them into flowering and producing fruit. In cool temperate climates many won't. Even if they could, tender flowers and new shoots may be killed by spring frosts, and ripening fruit may well be damaged by autumn frosts.

In cool regions, such as the UK, the only worthwhile strategy is to grow these fruits in a greenhouse, a conservatory, or a polytunnel, where the microclimate can be controlled precisely. Plants can then be grown under cover permanently, or they can be grown in containers and moved in and out as the weather dictates. A few may still prove impossible – but, hopefully, you'll have fun trying.

A full-sized mandarin tree such as this one may thrive outdoors in a warm, frost-free climate, but in cooler regions it must be grown in a large glasshouse or polytunnel to crop so generously.

Citrus fruits

Let's be honest. Unless you live in southern California, Florida, the Mediterranean, or another similarly warm part of the world, you're unlikely to face a glut of home-grown citrus fruit. They are, by nature, subtropical plants that need a lot of heat and light, and won't tolerate frosts – hardly a natural choice for cool temperate climates, then. Having said that, don't rule them out. In fact, there is a long tradition in northern Europe of growing citrus fruit in glasshouses – it's where the name "orangery" comes from. And there are all sorts of techniques for coaxing a crop from trees grown partly outdoors and partly under cover.

The citrus family includes a wide range of different fruits – including oranges, lemons, limes, grapefruits, pummelos, citrons, mandarins, tangerines, clementines, satsumas, kumquats, and more. The way in which they are classified is complex, and names can be confusing. There are plenty of hybrids, too, such as the mandarinquat (mandarin/kumquat), tangor (tangerine/orange), and tangelo (tangerine/pummelo).

Kumquats resemble oranges but are smaller and slightly more elongated in shape. Unlike oranges, ripe kumquats can be eaten whole, including the skin, though the flesh can be rather tart. All citrus make very attractive plants for a sheltered garden and work well in pots.

Which forms to grow

■ **Bushes** Suitable outdoors only for warm climates.
■ **Dwarf bushes and dwarf standards** The best choice for growing in a container under cover.

Must-grow citrus fruit

1 'Calamondin'

Thought to be a cross between a mandarin and a kumquat, 'Calamondin' is widely available as a dwarf container-grown tree for growing indoors. Outdoors in hot climates it grows into a large tree. The fruits are small, rounded, and when completely ripe may be sweet enough to eat raw. Otherwise, use for marmalade or cooking.

2 'Buddha's Hand' citron

Not an easy plant to grow as it needs high temperatures, but it's worth trying purely for its bizarre, alien-like fruits. Each "finger" is a separate segment of fruit, individually covered with skin. Although inedible, this fruit is traditionally prized in the Far East for its wonderful fragrance.

3 Lime

Although we think of limes as green-skinned, that's purely because they are usually harvested and sold before they are ripe. Given time, they turn yellow, like lemons. There are two main types: West Indian (also known as Mexican or Key lime) and Persian, which is slightly hardier and more compact.
■ **Varieties to try** 'Tahiti', 'Bearss'.

4 Mandarin

Cross-breeding and hybridization of mandarins has been taking place for centuries and there are scores of different varieties – including satsumas (which originated in Japan), tangerines (named after Tangier in Morocco), tangors (mandarin-orange hybrids), and clementines (probably the best choice for cool, temperate climates).
■ **Varieties to try** Mandarin 'Fortune', 'Nova'; Clementine 'De Nules', 'Fina'; Tangerine 'Dancy'; Tangor 'Ortanique'; Satsuma 'Okitsu', 'Owari'.

5 Kaffir lime

Grow this for its leaves. They have a lovely, distinctive fragrance and are a key ingredient in Thai cooking. The knobbly fruits look intriguing but are in fact almost inedible, and are more likely

to be used in shampoos, insecticides, and air fresheners, than in the kitchen. Alternative names include keiffer, k-lime and 'Makrut' lime.

6 Grapefruit

These are amongst the largest of citrus fruit and take the longest to ripen – up to 18 months from flowering. They need a lot of heat and are not easy to ripen in cool temperate climates. They are heavy, too, and only fairly large trees with strong branches will support them.
■ **Varieties to try** 'Marsh', 'Star Ruby' (or 'Sunrise'). New Zealand grapefruits – crossed with pummelos – require less heat. Try 'Golden Special', 'Wheeny'.

7 Kumquat

Smaller than most citrus fruits, oval-shaped kumquats are juicy, thin-skinned, and when ripe can be eaten raw, as well as being used for cooking. The trees are hardier, too. Botanically speaking, kumquats are classified separately from other citrus fruits, but are regularly crossed with them to produce hybrids, such as limequats and orangequats.
■ **Varieties to try** 'Nagami', 'Eustis', limequat.

8 Lemon

The fastest growing of the citrus fruits, this is also the one most likely to need pruning to keep it tidy. Most lemons flower more than once a year, and so may carry fruits that will ripen at different times. Pick them when they are fully sized and fully coloured.
■ **Varieties to try** 'Garey's Eureka', 'Lisbon', 'Meyer', 'Variegated Eureka', 'Verna', 'Villafranca'.

9 Orange

Oranges are classified as either sour or sweet. Sour oranges, of which 'Seville' is probably the best known, are used for making crystallized fruit, drinks, and marmalades. Sweet oranges require more heat to ripen fully. They include navel oranges which feature a little hole at the end of the fruit (the so-called navel), and blood oranges which have pink or red flesh.
■ **Varieties to try** 'Salustiana', 'Valencia'; Blood orange 'Moro', 'Sanguinelli'; Navel orange 'Navelina', 'Lane Late', 'Washington'; Sour orange 'Chinotto', 'Seville'.

Growing citrus fruit

Citrus trees need a consistently warm, sunny climate. Their natural habitat provides them with year-round temperatures that rarely drop below about 15°C (59°F) and an optimum 60–70 per cent humidity. Elsewhere, they may be able to survive short periods of cold, but they are likely to be damaged, perhaps even killed, by a frost. They are very difficult, then, to grow outdoors in cool temperate regions. They can, however, be grown under glass – at least during the times of the year when they need protection.

When buying a young container-grown tree, look for a healthy plant with plenty of shiny, deep green leaves. Avoid plants with bare stems where leaves have dropped and check for signs of scale insects or mealy bugs; they are difficult to eradicate. Mature plants in pots will crop well, given the right conditions.

Flowering and pollination

Although citrus trees usually flower in spring, blossom can appear at any time of year, provided conditions are warm and moist, and the tree is not dormant. Once set, the fruit takes a long time to ripen – a minimum of about six months, and in the case of grapefruits up to 18 months – so it's not unusual to see both fruit and blossom on trees at the same time. Almost all citrus are self-fertile, so a single tree can be grown on its own.

Choosing trees

Don't be tempted to grow citrus from seed. It's perfectly possible but it takes too long. Instead, buy container-grown, two- or three-year-old plants from a nursery or garden centre that can guarantee they are virus-free. For trees whose permanent home will be in containers, choose plants that have been grafted on to dwarfing rootstocks, and if possible buy named varieties.

When to plant

Outdoors, spring is the best season to plant. It's also the best time to pot up or repot container-grown trees, but don't pot them on too often or plant them in containers that are too large.

Where to grow

Trees planted outdoors need a sunny, sheltered site where there is no danger of frost. If grown permanently under glass, they need a position where they receive plenty of light, especially during summer, coupled with good ventilation.

Trees in containers can be moved outdoors

onto a warm, sunny terrace or patio in summer, and brought under cover into a heated greenhouse or cool conservatory during winter. Beware: bringing them indoors into a centrally heated conservatory or garden room doesn't usually work. The chances are that it will be too hot, too dry, and too dark. If you have no alternative, turn the heating down to no higher than 15°C (59°F), keep the air humid by misting or spraying, and make sure the plants are close to large, bright windows.

Soil type

Citrus trees are tolerant, though they grow best in reasonably fertile, free-draining soil with a slightly acid pH in the range 6.0–7.0. For containers, use a loam-based compost or a proprietary citrus compost, available from most garden centres.

Routine care

■ TEMPERATURE CONTROL Citrus trees hate sudden changes in temperature and may respond by dropping their leaves. This doesn't necessarily mean that they've died, and they will probably regrow the following spring, but the shock is not good for the plants. Try to acclimatize them gradually to any kind of change in their growing conditions.

■ FROST PROTECTION Container-grown trees need covering overnight or moving indoors if there is any risk of frost. If the tree freezes it will die.

■ WATERING Outdoors, water regularly during spring and summer, to avoid flower or fruit drop. Plants growing in pots should be soaked thoroughly each time you water, to the point where the compost is fully saturated and water drains freely out of the base – but don't let the pot sit in water or the roots may rot. Let the soil almost dry out before you water again. In winter, when trees are dormant or semi-dormant, you can water a lot less frequently. Getting the balance right is tricky: it's a fact that as many, if not more, citrus plants die from overwatering as they do from underwatering.

■ FEEDING Outdoors, use a general compound fertilizer two or three times a year between early spring and early autumn. For container-grown plants, use special citrus fertilizer. There are two different types: one for winter, and one for summer.

■ MULCHING Outdoors, a layer of mulch around

Citrus blossom is strongly fragrant and if grown under cover is capable of perfuming a whole conservatory or greenhouse.

the base of the tree will help retain moisture in the soil and reduce weed growth.

■ THINNING FRUIT Large, freestanding trees growing outdoors do not need thinning, but don't allow plants in pots to carry more fruit than they are able to support. Remove some if the crop becomes too heavy.

Harvesting and storing

Fruits need plentiful sunlight and high temperatures and humidity in order to ripen fully. The only sure way to tell if fruits, such as sweet oranges and mandarins, are ripe is to taste them. Timing is less critical with lemons, limes, and other sour citrus fruits. Pick and use them when they are fully coloured and no longer seem to be growing in size.

Fruits should keep for a few weeks in a fridge, fewer if left at room temperature. If you're not ready to use them straightaway, it's better to leave them on the tree until you are.

Yield

Yields are hard to quantify as they vary according to the type of fruit, how the tree is being grown, and the climatic conditions. From an average-sized, container-grown tree in a cool temperate region, you might expect 10–20 fruits per year. Large, container-grown trees ten or more years old may even produce up to 100 fruits per year.

Pruning and training citrus fruit

Unlike most other fruit trees, citrus require very little pruning. When trees are young, remove any low-growing lateral shoots in order to keep the main trunk clear, and cut out any over-vigorous shoots that grow vertically upwards in the centre of the tree; they are called water shoots and are unlikely to fruit. Thereafter, prune back to a healthy bud any dead, damaged, or diseased growth as soon as you spot it. Watch out for sharp thorns.

Pruning a citrus bush

Full-size trees can be grown outdoors only in warm, frost-free climates. The bush form is the most common. Trees have a short main trunk or central leader, then an open-centred crown made up of a handful of laterals that form the main framework of branches, not unlike an apple or pear.

Pruning is best carried out before new spring growth starts, but in warm climates you can prune at any time of year. It's difficult to say how long the early stages of shaping a young tree will take; it depends on how quickly the tree grows.

Outdoors in warm temperate or subtropical climates, lemon trees (seen here) can grow up to 6m (20ft) in height. Grapefruits can reach 10m (30ft) or more but limes tend to be smaller.

1st pruning
FEBRUARY–MARCH cool climates
ANY TIME of YEAR warm climates

- Newly planted trees should comprise just a single main stem. They do not need staking.
- When the stem reaches 90–120cm (3–4ft) high, prune it back to about 60cm (2ft). Cut just above a leaf.
- Pinch out any shoots sprouting from the rootstock, below the graft union.

2nd pruning
FEBRUARY–MARCH cool climates
ANY TIME of YEAR warm climates

- Laterals will have formed below your last pruning cut.
- Choose the 3 or 4 strongest and best placed, and prune each back to about 30cm (12in) from the main stem.
- Pinch out new shoots growing low down on the main stem, below the laterals.

Subsequent pruning
NOVEMBER–MARCH cool climates
ANY TIME of YEAR warm climates

- Laterals will now be starting to form the main branch leaders.
- Cut them back by one-third of the growth they put on since you last pruned them.
- Tip-prune sub-laterals or sideshoots by 3–4 leaves.
- Open up any crowded growth in the centre.
- Pinch out new shoots growing from the main stem.

Pruning an established citrus bush
NOVEMBER–MARCH cool climates
ANY TIME of YEAR warm climates

- While trees are still relatively young, tip-prune main branch leaders if they become too long.
- Prune out any shoots growing into the crown of the tree, in order to keep a fairly open centre.
- After harvesting the fruits, cut the shoots that bore them back to a healthy sideshoot that does not have any fruit.
- Once trees are mature, restrict pruning to the removal of any dead, damaged, or diseased growth, and any suckers that grow from the rootstock itself.

Pruning a citrus standard

The standard or half-standard form is probably the best choice for citrus grown in containers. It's not difficult to train a young plant – though you should be patient; don't remove too much growth in one go. The aim is to create a clean, straight main stem and a bushy, rounded crown. You will need to stake the tree until its roots are well established and its trunk is able to support its own weight.

1st pruning

FEBRUARY–MARCH
cool climates
ANY TIME of YEAR
warm climates

- Start with a young plant that has a strong, straight, single main stem.
- Tie it in to a vertical cane or stake.
- Prune back each lateral or sideshoot by about one-third.

2nd year pruning

FEBRUARY–MARCH
cool climates
ANY TIME of YEAR
warm climates

- Once the tree is tall enough, cut off the central leader or main stem, pruning just above a bud.
- Remove completely the laterals that you pruned last time.
- Leave untouched any new laterals or sideshoots that have appeared above them.
- There is no need to remove single leaves that appear on the main stem. They will drop off naturally.

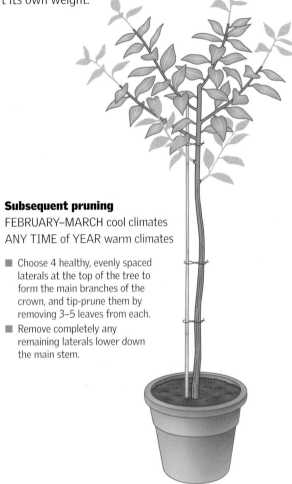

Subsequent pruning

FEBRUARY–MARCH cool climates
ANY TIME of YEAR warm climates

- Choose 4 healthy, evenly spaced laterals at the top of the tree to form the main branches of the crown, and tip-prune them by removing 3–5 leaves from each.
- Remove completely any remaining laterals lower down the main stem.

Pruning an established citrus standard

FEBRUARY–MARCH cool climates
ANY TIME of YEAR warm climates

- Once established, trees should require very little pruning.
- Tip-prune laterals if they become overlong in order to retain a rounded shape to the crown.
- Remove any shoots that appear on the main stem.
- Cut out any dead, damaged, or diseased growth.

What can go wrong

1 Small, brown, shell-like insects on stems

Scale insects – sometimes called brown scale – may be found on stems and branches, especially under glass. They are elliptical in shape and covered with a domed shell.
■ See **Scale insects** (p.339).

2 Small, white, wax-covered insects on stems

Mealybugs feed on sap that they suck from stems and branches. They are recognizable by the fluffy, white wax with which they are coated.
■ See **Mealybugs** (p.337).

3 Leaves are mottled and yellowed

If upper surfaces of leaves become speckled or mottled with pale yellow-bronze markings, then begin to dry up and die, the cause may be the red spider mite. In severe cases, you may also see fine silk webbing.
■ See **Red spider mite** (p.339).

Leaves are curled and sticky

Both aphids and whiteflies feeding on sap on the undersides of leaves cause them to curl up and become misshapen. Foliage may be sticky with honeydew, on which grey mould may grow.
■ See **Aphids** (p.334) and **Whiteflies** (p.341).

Leaves are yellowed or silvered with black specks

The discolouration is likely to be caused by sap-sucking insects called thrips. The black specks are their excrement.
■ See **Thrips** (p.340).

Leaves drop unexpectedly

A number of things can cause leaves (and sometimes flowers) to fall. Sudden changes in temperature or humidity, overwatering, and underwatering are the most likely causes. Leaves may re-grow in time.
■ See **Routine care** (p.289).

Leaves and stems wilt and die back

Citrus trees planted in poorly drained soil are very prone to fungal infections that cause rot – as are container-grown plants that are overwatered or allowed to stand in water.
■ See **Foot and root rots** (p.327).

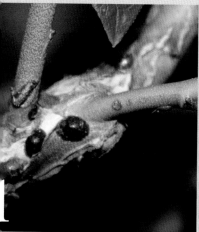

Melons

There are hundreds, if not thousands, of different melons in cultivation around the world, many of which are notoriously difficult to classify and name with any consistency. However, the main distinction is between sweet melons and watermelons. Sweet melons usually have pale green, yellow, or orange flesh that is dense, meltingly sweet, and wonderfully aromatic. They include cantaloupes, musk melons, and yellow or green, thicker-skinned winter melons, such as honeydews. Watermelons are usually larger and have red or pink flesh that is crisper and juicer.

Melons are tropical or subtropical plants and need high temperatures and high humidity to grow properly. In cool temperate climates, it's best to accept the fact that you can grow them with confidence only in cold frames or greenhouses. Having said that, recent years have seen the introduction of new cantaloupe varieties bred to tolerate cooler outdoor conditions. Even so, they're unlikely to ripen fully unless the summer is long, hot, and sunny.

When melons are about the size of grapefuits, support them in nets or string bags. The heavy fruits contain a lot of water and may split and spoil if they ripen and fall to the ground.

Must-grow melons

1 'Charentais'

These melons are referred to as either a named variety or a type. They are cantaloupes and originate from France, where they are widely grown for their sweet, scented, dark-orange flesh.

2 Cantaloupe melons

Most are round or slightly flattened with ridged grey-green or pale yellow-brown skin that may or may not have lacy, net-like patterning. The flesh is pale green, orange, or pink. The best choice for cool climates.

■ **Varieties to try** 'Amber Nectar' (or 'Castella'), 'Antalya', 'Emir', 'Hearts of Gold', 'Sweetheart'.

3 Winter melons

This group includes honeydew and casaba melons. They usually start to ripen as temperatures begin to fall. Oval with yellow or green skins, their flesh is sweet but they aren't as fragrant as cantaloupes and musk melons.

■ **Varieties to try** 'Honeydew Green Flesh', 'Jade Lady', 'Rocky Ford'.

4 Musk melons

Their smooth yellow, green, or pale brown skins have distinctive net-like markings, and the flesh is usually orange or pink and very sweet. A heated greenhouse is vital in cool climates.

■ **Varieties to try** 'Blenheim Orange', 'Hale's Best Jumbo', 'Hero of Lockinge'.

5 'Ogen'

Reputedly named after the kibbutz in Israel where the prototype was first bred, several slightly different forms of 'Ogen' exist. Most have smooth, slightly netted skins, turning from light green to yellow when ripe. The flesh is pale green.

6 Watermelons

These need the warmest, most humid climate. Given the right growing conditions, they can be enormous – up to 45kg (100lb) in weight. Flesh is red, pink, or orange, crisp, and juicy.

■ **Varieties to try** 'Blacktail Mountain', 'Charleston Grey', 'Sugar Baby'.

Growing melons

Melons are annuals and need growing afresh each year. They are usually available as ready-potted seedlings from garden centres, but you'll get a much wider choice if you buy seeds and raise them yourself. Sow the seeds in pots and plant them out when the soil is warm enough. Where you grow them depends entirely on your climate: outdoors in the open, under cloches or in cold frames, or in a greenhouse.

The year at a glance

	spring			summer			autumn			winter		
	M	A	M	J	J	A	S	O	N	D	J	F
sow seeds	▬	▬	▬									▬
plant greenhouse	▬	▬	▬									
plant outdoors			▬	▬								
harvest greenhouse				▬	▬	▬	▬	▬				
harvest outdoors					▬	▬	▬					

When to sow and plant

For plants that will be grown outdoors, sow seeds in pots in April and germinate them indoors or under cover. They should be ready to plant out in May or June, when the soil is warm and frosts are over. For plants to be grown in a heated greenhouse, you can sow earlier – in February and March for crops in June and July. And in an unheated greenhouse, sow in May or June for crops in September and October.

Melons need heat to get them off to a good start. Seeds are unlikely to germinate at all if the

SOWING MELON SEEDS

Germination can be hit and miss, so it's always best to sow seeds in pots and keep them warm until seedlings appear. You can then plant them out when conditions are favourable.

1 Sow seeds into damp potting compost at a depth of about 1cm (½in), two or three to a pot.

2 Put a clear plastic bag over each pot and secure it with an elastic band.

3 Place the pots indoors on a sunny windowsill, each in its individual propagation tent.

4 Once seedlings have emerged – in a week to ten days – move the plants outdoors during the day to harden them off.

Fit a collar around the stem so you can water the surrounding soil without wetting the plant. This reduces the risk of foot and root rots. Special terracotta collars are available but improvised plastic ones work just as well.

temperature is below 18°C (64°F). Thereafter, 25–30°C (77–86°F) is ideal, though some varieties will tolerate cooler conditions.

Where to plant

Outdoors, choose a sheltered, sunny site. In cool climates, you'll need a warm sun-trap and a long, hot summer. You may also need to protect plants with cloches. Even a mild frost will kill them.

Melons can be grown in cold frames filled with a pre-prepared mix of good soil and well-rotted compost or manure. Mound up the earth slightly and plant seedlings at the top to prevent waterlogging.

In greenhouses, melons can be planted either directly into borders or in growing bags. Plant them in small mounds in the soil to ensure they don't get waterlogged, or use special collars to help keep water off the stems (see left).

Soil type

Melons like deep, fertile soil with a pH of 6.5–7. It should be free-draining but constantly moist, with plenty of organic material incorporated before planting.

GROWING MELONS IN A POLYTHENE COLD FRAME

In truth, most traditional cold frames used for growing melons outdoors in cool temperate climates are too small. You'll be lucky to get more than one plant in each. However, the large, polythene "polytents" shown here are more like small, low polytunnels, and offer a lot more space.

1 Prepare the ground with a mulch of well-rotted compost or manure. Clear a number of planting holes in the soil and water thoroughly.

2 Cover the area that will form the base of the polytent with plastic sheet mulch.

3 Cut holes in the plastic above the pre-prepared planting holes.

4 Plant pot-grown melons through the holes in the sheet mulch. The mulch retains moisture, inhibits weeds, and keeps the growing melons dry and clean.

Planting distances

■ OUTDOORS IN OPEN GROUND 90cm (3ft) apart.
■ IN A GREENHOUSE single cordons 40cm (16in), double cordons 60cm (24in) apart.

Flowering and pollination

When grown outdoors in warm climates, insects usually pollinate melons quite readily. If you can time the opening and closing of the lid or window on a cold frame to coincide with a spell of warm weather, and the moment when the flowers are all fully open, they may do the same. If not, plants will need pollinating by hand. Melons grown in a greenhouse certainly require it.

Melons are self-fertile. They produce both male and female flowers, which will pollinate one another. They are not difficult to tell apart. Use a soft, dry brush to collect pollen from the male flowers and transfer it to the female ones. Alternatively, remove a male flower, pick off the petals, and push it carefully into the centre of each of the female flowers. Repeat every day for a week or so.

Routine care

■ WATERING Regular watering is important once plants have become established. The soil must remain constantly moist – not too wet, not too dry. Water carefully since splashing the stems can cause them to rot.
■ FEEDING Once fruits have formed, feed weekly with a liquid tomato fertilizer. Stop when the fruits are almost ripe.
■ VENTILATION Melons need the right mix of high humidity and good ventilation. As long as it's not too cold, take particular care to open cold-frame

(clockwise from top left) **Female flowers** have a rounded swelling at the base of their petals. It is where the fruit will develop if fertilization takes place. **Male flowers** are slender and straight, without any visible bulge. They are always the first to appear. **Greenhouse melons** sown and planted at different times will give you an early and a late crop. The main stems are trained up canes, with the laterals or sideshoots supported on horizontal wires.

Cut back shoots to two leaves beyond the melon you want to grow and ripen.

(below, left to right) **Tie in to horizontal wires** the lateral shoots that grow from either side of the main stem or cordon, using flexible plant ties. **Pinch out** any tendrils that grow from the shoots. Now that you've tied them in, they're not needed for support and simply divert energy from developing fruits.

lids and greenhouse windows when the flowers are ready for pollination and at the end of the growing season, when the fruits are ripening. That's when the plants need a dry atmosphere. At other times, spray or damp down to raise the humidity. If necessary, paint or shade panes of glass to prevent sun scorch.

Pruning and training

Melons are vines and so naturally trail or climb. Outdoor melons and those grown in cold frames are usually left to sprawl over the ground. Greenhouse melons, however, need training to help them climb. The usual technique is to construct a support system from canes and wires, and to train them vertically up towards the roof of the greenhouse.

Melons don't really need pruning as such, but their growth does need controlling. For outdoor and cold-frame melons pinch out the tip of the main stem once five leaves have appeared, and do the same for greenhouse melons once the main stem reaches a height of about 1.5–2m (5–6ft). This encourages the growth of the sideshoots that will form the main laterals. Traditional wisdom has it that melons grown outdoors or in a cold frame should be allowed only four laterals or main shoots each, and greenhouse melons no more than six. Once these have formed, you should pinch out the

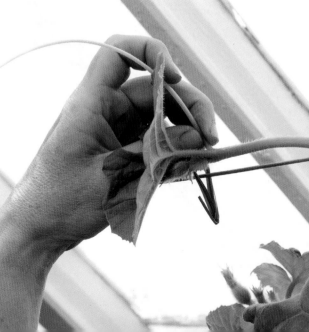

growing tip of each lateral when it has five leaves. This will stimulate the growth of sub-laterals or sideshoots on which flowers appear. If pollination is successful, fruits will begin to develop. When they reach the size of golf balls, choose the healthiest-looking melon on each lateral, pinch out the shoot two leaves beyond it, and remove all other flowers and fruit. You should now have a maximum of either four or six melons per plant. If you have fewer that's fine. In fact, plants with only one or two are likely to produce larger fruits.

Harvesting and storing
Leave melons on the vine for as long as possible to ripen. The longer you leave them, the sweeter and more aromatic they will become. But leave them too long, and they will start to rot – if they don't fall off first. Tell-tale signs include slight cracking at the end attached to the stalk, softening at the other end, and a gradually intensifying fragrance. As the optimum moment approaches, apply a gentle squeeze-and-sniff test a couple of times a day.

You can store melons in the fridge but don't serve them too cold or they won't release their full aroma.

Yield
- OUTDOOR MELONS maximum 4 per plant.
- GREENHOUSE MELONS maximum 6 per plant.

Support ripening melons with nets or string bags. Otherwise the heavy fruits will snap the stems they are growing on, or fall to the ground and become bruised and damaged.

WHAT CAN GO WRONG

Leaves are curled and sticky
Both aphids and whiteflies feed on sap and cause leaves to curl up and become distorted. They may also be sticky with honeydew, on which grey mould will grow. See **Aphids** (p.334) and **Whiteflies** (p.341).

Leaves are mottled and yellowed
Spider mites cause upper surfaces of leaves to become speckled or mottled with pale yellow-bronze markings, and then to dry up and die. In severe cases, you may be able to see their fine silk webbing.
- See **Red spider mite** (p.339).

Leaves distorted with yellow patterning
Misshapen, stunted leaves with a yellow, mosaic pattern may be a sign of cucumber mosaic virus. Flowers may

not open, and even if they do, any melons that form will be small and hard.
- See **Cucumber mosaic virus** (p.326).

Powdery white coating on leaves
This is a very common fungal disease. It's always worse if the soil is allowed to dry out, yet the air remains humid and plants are poorly ventilated.
- See **Powdery mildew** (p.329).

Plants wilt and die back
Melons are notorious for rotting at the point where the stem joins the roots. Take care to keep the stems and the soil around them as dry as you can.
- See **Foot and root rots** (p.327).

Kiwifruit

Despite the name "kiwi", these fruits are not actually native to New Zealand. Their original name, Chinese gooseberry, gives a much better indication of where they first came from: eastern Asia. However, New Zealanders renamed them, marketed them aggressively, and began to export them to the rest of the world.

The plants are not hard to grow. In fact, they are very vigorous, and left to their own devices they can grow 9m (28ft) or more. But unless you can give them the right growing conditions it's not so easy to get them to crop.

(top to bottom) **Kiwifruits** are about the size of hens' eggs, with brown, slightly furry skins. Inside, the flesh is bright green with a mass of small, edible, black seeds. **Hardy varieties** have been bred that are virtually hairless. The skins are very smooth and you don't need to peel the fruits before eating them.

Growing kiwifruit

Kiwifruits are deciduous vines and once established are actually hardy enough to survive most winters in cool temperate regions. However, the new shoots and blossom that appear in spring are tender, and easily damaged by even a slight frost. The fruits need a sunny site and a hot summer if they are to ripen properly. You should probably attempt kiwifruits only if you are able to grow dessert grapes outdoors. They are, unfortunately, too large for a greenhouse.

The year at a glance

	spring			summer			autumn			winter		
	M	A	M	J	J	A	S	O	N	D	J	F
plant	▬							▬	▬	▬	▬	▬
summer-prune				▬	▬	▬						
winter-prune								▬	▬	▬	▬	▬
harvest								▬				

Choosing a variety

Some kiwifruits are self-fertile and will pollinate themselves. Others are not, and bear only male flowers or only female flowers. A female kiwifruit must be planted with a male or self-fertile partner in order to produce fruit.

'Jenny' is the best-known modern, self-fertile variety. Amongst traditional, non-self-fertile kiwifruits, the most widely available female plants are 'Hayward' and 'Bruno'. 'Tomuri' is a good choice as a male partner.

So-called hardy kiwifruits are slightly different from the regular type. The fruits are smaller and can be eaten whole, including the skin, like grapes. Varieties include 'Issai' and 'Ananasnaya'.

When and where to plant

Plant November–March during the period of winter dormancy. Kiwifruits grow best in a warm, sheltered corner or against a south-facing wall, away from any danger of frost pockets.

Soil type

Kiwifruits need fertile, free-draining soil with a pH of about 6.5–7.

(top to bottom) **New growth** is very vulnerable to spring frosts, and tender young shoots and buds are easily damaged. Protect with fleece if necessary. **Kiwifruit flowers** are white or cream in colour, fragrant, and can measure up to 4cm (1¹/₂in) in diameter. They may be either male or female.

Planting distances
3–5m (10–16ft) apart.

Routine care
■ WATERING Water generously and regularly throughout the growing season. Ease off in the autumn.
■ FEEDING Apply a general compound fertilizer each February, before growth starts.
■ MULCHING In March spread a layer of organic mulch around the base of the plants.

Pruning and training
Kiwifruits are so vigorous that unless you train and prune them regularly you'll end up with a knotted mass of vine with too much foliage and not enough fruit. There are two approaches to training: one formal, the other informal. Both need strong support systems, as established vines become very heavy.

The formal method is to grow the plants as espaliers, with a vertical central stem from which laterals spread out left and right, supported on horizontal wires about 45cm (18in) apart. The laterals will produce sub-laterals or sideshoots. You can develop these into fruiting spurs if you pinch them back to between five and seven leaves beyond the final fruit during the summer. Then prune them again in winter, this time to two buds beyond the point where the final fruit grew until you picked it. The espalier system is best for self-fertile varieties, where you are growing just one plant.

The informal method allows the vines to scramble up over a pergola or trellis, though it helps if you can train laterals along overhead wires or wooden struts once they reach the top. As with an espalier, pinch out growing tips in summer, and in winter cut back last year's growth in order to develop a system of fruiting spurs. If you are growing varieties that are not self-fertile, plant a male and female together, in the same planting hole if necessary.

Harvesting and storing
Kiwifruits may not ripen until October. However, in some areas you may have to pick them earlier, before they are damaged by the first frosts of the autumn. No matter. They will continue to ripen indoors, gradually becoming softer. In fact, stored in a cool dry place they should keep for a couple of months or more.

Yield
It takes a long time for a kiwifruit to reach its full cropping potential – up to seven years in some cases. At that point, a single vine may produce 10–15kg (22–33lb) of fruit.

What can go wrong
Very few pests and diseases seem to trouble kiwifruit. Drought or irregular watering may cause leaves to fall, and small, underdeveloped fruits are usually a sign of a poor summer – too cold and not enough sunshine.

A kiwi vine climbs up a home-made pergola built from stout wooden poles supporting a metal frame.

Cape gooseberries

Cape gooseberries get their name from the Cape of Good Hope, at the southern tip of Africa, where they were widely grown in the 19th century. They are also known as *Physalis*, which is their botanical name, and are part of the same plant family as tomatoes, aubergines, and potatoes. Their closest relatives are the tomatillo, which is also edible, and the ornamental garden plant, Chinese lantern, which is not.

Cape gooseberries are small, round, orange fruits that grow inside a papery shell or husk, and have a distinctive sharp-sweet flavour that, to some, is an acquired taste. They need a warm climate to crop reliably, and so in cooler regions you will often be advised to grow them in greenhouses. However, if you can grow tomatoes and aubergines outdoors, it's worth giving Cape gooseberries a try.

Fruits ripen in stages from late summmer onwards and, like Chinese lanterns (*Physalis alkekengi*), they are encased in a similar, though less colourful papery husk. You can leave fruits on the plant until deep yellow and fully ripe, as birds don't seem to find them very palatable, but pick them before the first frosts.

Growing Cape gooseberries

Cape gooseberries are perennials, but they are not hardy and won't survive cold winters. It's therefore best to treat them as annuals and grow them afresh from seed every year. They need similar growing conditions to tomatoes. There are no named varieties.

The year at a glance

	spring			summer			autumn			winter		
	M	A	M	J	J	A	S	O	N	D	J	F
sow indoors	▬											
plant undercover		▬	▬									
plant outdoors		▬	▬	▬								
harvest						▬	▬	▬				

PLANTING CAPE GOOSEBERRIES

Prepare your planting site in advance by removing any weeds, digging in some well-rotted organic matter, and raking over the surface of the soil to break up any lumps. Harden off indoor-raised seedlings before planting them out.

1 Dig a hole that will comfortably accommodate the rootball of the pot-grown seedling. Draw the soil around it, firm it down, and water it in thoroughly.

2 Protect with a cloche if the wind is still cold or if there is any risk of overnight frost.

When and where to sow

Sow indoors in about March. Use seed trays or pots filled with standard seed compost and sow at a depth of ½cm (¼in). Either cover and place on a sunny windowsill or use a heated propagator. Germination requires a steady minimum temperature of about 18°C (64°F).

When and where to plant

If you have a sunny, sheltered site, plant out seedlings directly into the ground between April and June. If not, grow them in containers or plant them in a greenhouse border where they can be trained up canes or stakes.

Soil type

Cape gooseberries need fertile, well-drained soil with a slightly acid pH of about 6.5.

Planting distances

■ PLANTS 75cm (30in) apart.
■ ROW SPACING 1–1.2m (3–4ft) apart.

Growing in containers

Transplant seedlings into a pot or container with a diameter of at least 30–38cm (12–15in), and fill it with potting compost mixed with a little sand or coarse grit to improve drainage. Containers can be brought under cover in cold weather and moved onto a warm patio or balcony during summer.

Routine care

■ WATERING Water regularly, but don't overdo it or you'll end up with too much foliage. Plants don't like being waterlogged.
■ FEEDING Feed once or twice with tomato fertilizer when the fruits start to form.
■ PINCHING OUT If the plant seems reluctant

to produce flowers, pinch out the growing tips.

■ STAKING Plants can grow quite tall, and may need staking and tying loosely with string.

Harvesting and storing

As they ripen, the outer husks or lanterns enclosing the fruits become papery and pale brown. Inside, the fruits themselves turn an ever-deepening yellow-orange and their flavour intensifies. In the case of plants grown outdoors, it's often a race to see if the fruits will ripen before the arrival of the first frost. If you have to pick them before they are fully ripe, don't worry; they will go on ripening somewhere dry and sunny indoors. Even ripe fruits can be stored in their husks for several weeks.

What can go wrong

Cape gooseberries are mercifully trouble-free. Outdoors, aphids (see p.334) can be problematic. Under cover, the usual greenhouse pests and diseases may strike, including whitefly (see p.341) and powdery mildew (see p.329).

(above, left to right) **Flowers** may keep appearing until quite late in the summer, so it's not unusual to see both fruits and flowers on a single branch at the same time. **Cape gooseberries** are ready to pick when the green husks have dried out and turned a pale brown colour, and the fruits inside are bright orange-yellow. They get sweeter as they ripen – although they will always have a sharp tang. (below). **Unfold and discard** the inedible papery husks to eat the fruit raw or, if you have a good crop, make jelly.

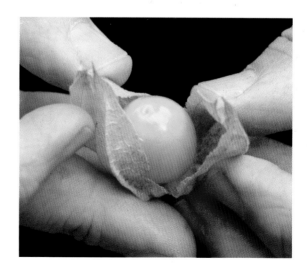

Other tender and exotic fruit

These plants are not for everyone. If you live in a cool temperate region, remember that they are a long way from home. Their natural habitat may be either dry scrub and semi-desert, or hot, humid, subtropical and tropical climates, so growing them under cover will be your only option.

Avocados

Avocado pears are fun to grow, although whether or not you can persuade them to produce any fruit is another matter entirely. Their native habitat in tropical Central America provides them with consistent high temperatures and high humidity. In cool climates they will grow under cover but need heat to stand any chance of fruiting.

■ HOW TO GROW Avocados can be grown from seed. Remove the stone, soak it in hot water, and plant it in a small pot filled with compost. Slicing off the top and dipping it in fungicide sometimes speeds up germination, but you may still have to wait weeks or even months for a shoot to appear. It's easier to buy ready-grown plants grafted onto special disease-resistant rootstocks. You may need more than one to guarantee cross-pollination. Avocados grown under cover need temperatures of 20–30°C (68–86°F), 70 per cent humidity, and regular watering and feeding. Even then, insufficient sunlight, and days that are too short may mean that they never fruit.

Bananas

Wild bananas came originally from southeast Asia, although they are now grown in most tropical regions of the world. In spite of the fact that they are tree-sized, they are not trees at all; they are in fact large stalks or shoots that sprout from underground rhizomes.

■ HOW TO GROW One look at the conditions required to grow a banana that produces fruit will give you an immediate idea of what chance you have: a steady temperature of about 27°C (81°F) during the day and 20°C (68°F) at night, constant humidity of at least 50 per cent, and around twelve hours of bright light every day. Even if you think you can provide this in a greenhouse or polytunnel, bear in mind that banana plants are very large: they can quickly grow to 8m (25ft) in height. Except in the tropics, this is one for the dedicated enthusiast.

Loquats

Also known as Japanese medlars or plums, loquats are orange-yellow fruits about the size of apricots,

with soft, aromatic flesh that may be sweet or sour depending on its ripeness. The trees are evergreen and originate in China, though they are now widely grown in regions with subtropical or Mediterranean climates. Unusually, they flower in the autumn and bear fruit in the spring – so they need mild winters if they are to avoid frost damage.

■ HOW TO GROW Loquats are tolerant, fairly hardy, and easy to grow, though in cool temperate climates they may not ever flower or set fruit unless grown under cover. In warm climates, plant in autumn in a sunny, sheltered spot. Avoid frost pockets. Water and feed young trees during the growing season. Harvest the fruits when they have softened slightly and are fully ripe.

Mangos

Like avocados, growing mangos is something you're more likely to do out of curiosity than as a serious attempt to produce fruit. They are tropical plants native to India and southeast Asia, and will crop only in similarly hot climates. Even the hardiest varieties need average temperatures of about 25°C (77°F) and very high light intensity. Frosts will almost certainly kill them.

■ HOW TO GROW It's possible to grow a mango from seed, if you remove the husk before planting, but once the seed has germinated, it will probably produce a tree that is far too vigorous and won't bear fruit. Instead, buy a young tree grafted on to a dwarfing rootstock. Outdoors, mangos need a sheltered site in full sun, and watering in dry spells.

Under cover, they need heat, light, and – except when in flower – high humidity. During the growing season, water with room-temperature rainwater and feed with liquid tomato fertilizer.

Olives

It's not easy to grow your own olives – at least, not to the point where you can actually eat them. Even if they ripen, they need curing in salt or lye (sodium hydroxide) to remove excessive bitterness, and then storing in oil or brine. And you'd need a small orchard to produce enough to make oil. However, the gnarled, long-lived, evergreen trees are extremely attractive, and in areas with reasonably warm winters, they are worth growing purely for ornamental reasons.

■ HOW TO GROW Plant in free-draining soil in a sheltered, sunny position. In cooler areas, grow trees in containers so that you can bring them under cover in winter. Most varieties are self-fertile, though all are more likely to flower and set fruit if pollinated by a partner. Accustomed to dry, infertile conditions, mature olives will tolerate periods without much water and do not need feeding. Prune

(below, far left to right) **Avocados** have fragrant flowers but the fruits will struggle to ripen in cool, temperate climates. **Bananas** are best grown under cover, but even small varieties are fairly tall. **Loquat** trees may bear fruit if grown under glass. **Mangos** are very big trees so choose a dwarf variety. **Olives** are popular trees and often grown as standards in containers.

them in spring, cutting back old growth and encouraging plenty of new sideshoots on which fruit should be borne the following year.

Papayas

Papayas are tropical fruits that look a little like melons. They originally came from Central America, although they are now grown widely around the world. Confusingly, they are sometimes also called pawpaws, but they are not the same species as the native North American fruit (see right).

■ HOW TO GROW Outdoors, papayas will grow and fruit successfully in hot, sunny, humid conditions. Frosts, cold winds, and waterlogged soil will damage, if not kill, them. Pollination is a challenge, too. Some plants bear both male and female flowers, and will self-pollinate. Others are strictly single-sex, with flowers that are either all male or all female. Worse still, next year they may swap gender. To pre-empt such transsexual behaviour, the safest thing is to plant several trees as neighbours. In cool climates, papayas must be grown in a tall heated glasshouse or polytunnel.

Passion fruits

Of this large family of evergreen vines, purple granadilla is the passion fruit usually grown for its fruits. They are oval and about the size of small plums, with wrinkled purple or yellow skins and yellow-orange flesh. The pulpy, aromatic seeds can be scooped straight from the fruits.

■ HOW TO GROW Passion fruits need frost-free winters and average temperatures of 20–24°C (68–75°F) during the growing season. They may be happy in the corner of a sunny patio or against a south-facing wall, but if not, grow them under cover. Propagate seeds indoors and plant out in May or June (in the same way as melons, see p.297). Train the vines up wires or a trellis. Water plentifully and feed with tomato fertilizer. In winter, cut back last year's sideshoots to within 2 buds of the main stems; they won't fruit again, so you are aiming to encourage new growth that will.

Pawpaws

Also known as prairie bananas and custard bananas, pawpaws are native to North America where they grow widely, often in the wild. They are rare in the UK and elsewhere in Europe. Although not strictly speaking tender plants, in northern regions they produce only a few, unripe fruits even after a warm summer, and are best attempted under cover. When they are ripe, the yellow-green fruits have a creamy flesh with a mild tropical-fruit flavour resembling bananas, mangos, and citrus. But don't eat them when they are unripe because they can cause stomach upsets.

■ HOW TO GROW Plant in the dormant season, in late autumn or early spring. Choose a sheltered site with deep, fertile, free-draining soil. Some varieties are self-fertile, but others may need pollinating by hand. Feed and water regularly, especially in the spring and early summer. Harvest in September or October.

Pepinos

The pepino is a little like a small melon. The fruits are yellow, cream, or green, with juicy, orange-yellow flesh that tastes like a combination of melon, pear, and cucumber. For that reason, they are sometimes known as melon pears. They come from the Andes in South America, and are members of the same family as potatoes and tomatoes.

■ HOW TO GROW Grow pepinos from seed in the same way as tomatoes or peppers. Sow in pots in late winter, either indoors on a sunny windowsill or in a propagator. In cool temperate climates, transplant them into growing bags or containers. They can be put outside once all danger of frost is over and stay there until the autumn when you should bring them under cover to ripen. Support, pinch out, water, and feed them as you would tomato plants.

Persimmons

Japanese persimmons, as their name suggests, are native to Japan, China, and other parts of Asia. They are large trees and can be grown in cool climates, although they are vulnerable to frosts in spring, and need warm temperatures in autumn if the fruits are to ripen. Depending on the variety, fruits are either astringent (they are high in tannin and too bitter to eat until softened or cooked) or non-astringent (they are sweet enough to eat raw when ripe). American persimmons are hardier but tend to produce small, astringent fruit.

■ HOW TO GROW Choose a sunny, sheltered site and plant in fertile, free-draining soil. Avoid frost pockets. Water if there is any danger of the tree drying out. Persimmons can be grown under cover, although they will need very large containers.

Pineapples

Pineapples originate from Central America. It was Christopher Columbus who brought the first fruits back to Europe at the end of the 15th century. They need subtropical or tropical growing conditions: high temperatures, high humidity, rich soil, and lots of light.

■ HOW TO GROW In cool temperate regions, the only way to grow pineapples is in containers in a greenhouse or polytunnel – a large one, since they can eventually reach 4m (12ft) in height. The easiest way to start is with a ripe, shop-bought pineapple. Cut off the top, along with about 1cm (½in) of the flesh – not too much or it will rot. Stand the crown in a flat dish for a week or so to dry out, maintaining a minimum temperature of about 18°C (64°F). Plant it in a 30cm (12in) pot, so that the base of the leaves are at soil level. Now, water regularly, don't let the temperature fall below 20°C (68°F) or rise above 32°C (90°F), feed with liquid tomato fertilizer

(far left to right) **Papayas** are small trees that resemble palms. **Passion fruits** have beautiful flowers as well as delicious fruits with edible seeds. **Pawpaws** are native to North America and unrelated to tropical papayas. **Pepinos** resemble small melons. **Persimmons** store well if you keep a short length of stalk attached. **Pineapples** fruit at the end of a central flower spike.

in spring and summer, keep humidity and light levels high, don't allow the plant to stand in a draught. It may be several years before you get even a modest-sized fruit.

Pineapple guavas

Also known as feijoa, from its botanical name, the pineapple guava is a native of high-altitude parts of subtropical South America. However, it is also happy enough in many cool temperate regions, where it is often grown as an ornamental garden plant. In order to grow pineapple guava for its fruit, the plant needs long, hot summers, and may require protection to ensure not only that late spring frosts don't destroy the flowers, but also that early autumn frosts don't damage fruits that have not yet ripened.

■ HOW TO GROW Pineapple guavas can be grown from seed but it's easier and faster to to buy a young container-grown plant. Plant in a warm, sunny, sheltered spot or in pots that can be brought under cover during winter and when there is a risk of frost. Water regularly throughout the spring and summer. Prune lightly after harvesting.

Pineapple guavas are green-skinned, egg-sized fruits with sweet, aromatic flesh with a pineapple-mint flavour. The flowers are edible, too.

Pomegranates

Pomegranates originate from southwest Asia and are therefore happiest growing in hot, arid conditions. Don't attempt them unless you can give them the right kind of microclimate. In cool temperate regions, your only chance is to try them in containers under glass – although bear in mind that they do not like high levels of humidity.

■ HOW TO GROW Pomegranates can be grown from seed, but it's better to start with a plant raised from a cutting. For container-growing, use a 21–24cm (8–9in) pot filled with potting compost mixed with grit to improve drainage. Water regularly but not excessively in spring and summer, and less often in winter. Feed with liquid tomato fertilizer during the growing season. Maintain a minimum temperature of 10°C (50°F), ensuring the plants get as much heat and light as possible in summer. To grow trees in the open, plant in a sunny, sheltered site. Although self-fertile, crops are better if trees have a partner for cross-pollination. Prune in winter or early spring during the dormant period.

Prickly pears

Prickly pears are cacti, whose natural home is in the arid areas of southern and western USA, Central and South America, and the Mediterranean. The purple or red fruits, which grow on the ends of the cactus's pads, are edible – provided that the spines are meticulously removed first. They are sometimes known as cactus figs or Indian figs.

■ HOW TO GROW In cool temperate regions, prickly pears can be grown only in greenhouses or conservatories. They need a consistent temperature of 18–25°C (64–77°F) and may not survive if it falls below 10°C (50°F) for anything more than short

periods. Soil should be sandy and free-draining, and the air should be kept dry, not humid. Beyond that, the plants have very few requirements. But be patient, they may take several years before they fruit – and don't be tempted to touch them without wearing gloves.

Strawberry guavas

The strawberry guava comes from the same family as the evergreen garden shrub myrtle. It originates from tropical Central and South America, where it can grow to 5m (16ft) in height. There is also a yellow-skinned variety commonly known as lemon guava. So-called tropical or apple guavas are closely related, but the fruits are larger and the plants less tolerant of low temperatures.

■ HOW TO GROW To grow strawberry guavas outdoors you'll need a sunny, sheltered, frost-free site, with consistent daytime temperatures of 24–30°C (75–86°F) throughout the summer. In cool temperate zones, it's wiser to grow the plants in containers, bringing them under cover when necessary. Hand-pollinate, and water and feed regularly in the growing season. In warm climates, guavas may flower continuously and so fruits ripen all year round. In cooler climates, fruits should be ready to harvest between October and December.

Tamarillos

Also known as tree tomatoes, tamarillos come from the same family as tomatoes and aubergines. These fruits are subtropical natives of South America, and are egg-shaped with green skins that slowly turn red, orange, or yellow. They are sweet enough to eat raw only when fully ripe. The skin is unpalatable.

■ HOW TO GROW Tamarillos need lots of sunshine, high temperatures, high humidity, and a sheltered site. They won't tolerate frosts. Plant in rich, free-draining soil but take care to water plentifully during dry spells. In cool climates, grow them in containers under cover.

(below, far left to right) **Pineapple guavas** are small trees with dark green, leathery foliage. **Pomegranates**, which grow on small trees in their native habitat, need a hot summer to ripen. **Prickly pears** are hardier than many other cacti and delicious to eat, but the spines can seriously irritate the skin. **Strawberry guavas** are traditionally cooked and made into jelly. **Tamarillos** grow on shrubby trees in Peru and Brazil, where they ripen reliably. In cooler regions they are unappetising raw and much better eaten cooked.

Fruit doctor

Ask any fruit grower and the chances are they'll claim they suffer more than their fair share of pests and diseases. Why? The answer is probably twofold. First, fruit trees, bushes, and canes last a lot longer than other food crops. In contrast, most vegetables are annuals – there one year and gone the next. So, unless they're grown year after year in the same spot, they are less likely to build up persistent infections or colonies of soil-dwelling insects. With fruit, such problems have time to build up. Second, there's the maturing fruit itself. Few things in the garden attract wasps, flies, birds, and other wildlife, as powerfully as sweet, ripe fruit. It's as irresistible to them as it is to you.

Nets and fences are the ultimate defence against birds and animals. And ensuring good hygiene and providing the right growing conditions are the best way to guarantee healthy plants. Beyond that, it's worth learning as much as you can about what you're up against. This chapter catalogues the pests, parasites, diseases, and disorders that most commonly attack fruit, and its aim is to arm you with the information you need to keep them at bay.

Diagnosis isn't difficult here. Brown rot has completely spoiled these cherries. Remove and destroy them straight away or the fungal spores will spread rapidly and infect other parts of the tree.

What's wrong?

When things go wrong, the cause of the problem is likely to be one of three things: a plant disease; an attack by a pest or parasite; or a disorder triggered by the wrong growing conditions. Attacks by animals, birds, and most insects are the easiest to diagnose. If your fruit bushes are crawling with aphids or pigeons are feasting on your strawberries, then the culprits are there in front of your eyes. Similarly, it should be obvious if your plants have suffered from frost, drought, or sun scorch. However, there's a wide range of fungal, bacterial, and viral diseases, nutritional disorders, and infestations by microscopic mites too tiny to see with the naked eye, that are somewhat harder to diagnose.

Disease or disorder?

Plants that are suffering often display very similar visible symptoms whether they are under attack by pests or suffering from a disease or disorder. Wilting of blossom and new shoots, leaf curling and distortion, and yellowing of foliage are all common early warning signs that something is wrong. Often, such symptoms look like disease but aren't. They are simply the plant's response to being put under stress – perhaps by frost, underwatering, or a lack of certain nutrients. Don't make a diagnosis too hastily. And, most importantly, don't resort to chemicals unless you're sure you have no alternative.

(below, left to right) **Frost damage** occurs when the temperature falls below freezing, causing sap within plant cells to expand and rupture the cell walls. Blossom and young shoots quickly wilt and die back. **Watering** plants in containers is vital during hot weather. They dry out more quickly than those in open ground. **Seep hoses** and drip-feed watering systems water the soil, not the foliage, and are a good investment.

Good or bad growing conditions?

No plant will thrive unless you can give it the right growing conditions. As a fruit grower, this should be your mantra. After all, your primary aim is to grow plants that produce as large a crop of perfect, healthy fruit as possible. A tree or bush that survives but crops poorly is pointless.

Lack of water, exposure to strong winds or frost, insufficient light, waterlogged soil, and mineral deficiencies are all examples of poor growing conditions. Getting things right should be your number one priority – plants that are in good health are much better able to resist disease and attack by pests and parasites.

Remember that many of us try to grow fruit in a climatic zone that is not the same as the plant's native habitat. In cool temperate regions, it will always be a challenge to grow (and ripen) peaches, nectarines, apricots, figs, melons, and grapes outdoors. And even attempting tropical and subtropical crops, such as avocados, mangos, papayas, and bananas requires a heated greenhouse and meticulous control of the microclimate. It's not just a question of temperature – although that is crucial – it's also a matter of humidity, light intensity, and the number of daylight hours.

Friend or foe?

When it comes to wildlife, there's a fine line between what's welcome and what isn't. Birds can be valuable allies, since they keep down the insect population by eating grubs and larvae. But they can be one of your worst enemies, too – pigeons can strip fruit bushes and strawberry beds in just a matter of hours. Insects are the same. Some are positively beneficial – bees, hoverflies, ladybirds, and lacewings, for example. Others are extremely destructive, tunnelling into ripening fruit and feeding voraciously on plant tissue.

Interestingly, it is possible to use insect against insect. Biological controls involve the deliberate introduction of predatory mites or parasitic wasps to kill specific pests, such as whitefly or red spider mites. Using nematodes (microscopic worms) to target slugs, or live bacteria to infect certain caterpillars, also relies on this method of attack.

(below, left to right) **Ladybirds** are most definitely friends. Both adults and larvae feast on aphids. **Greenhouses** provide microclimates that extend the range of plants you can grow – but may also provide the perfect conditions for insect pests. **Beer traps** are an eco-friendly and effective way of keeping wasps away from ripening fruit.

Healthy soil

The soil in which you plant your fruit trees and bushes is vitally important. If it is fertile and well-structured, the chances are that the plants will grow well, stay healthy, and produce good crops. Soils differ widely. Some are light and sandy, others are heavy and clay-like. Some are acid, others are alkaline. And while some are rich in nutrients, others are thin and poor.

Soil structure

All soils consist of minute particles of weathered rock, mixed with water and organic matter from rotted-down remains of plants and animals. It is the size of the particles that largely determines the nature of the soil. Sandy soils are made up of fairly large particles, so they are usually light and gritty to the touch. Clay soils are made up of much smaller particles, so they tend to be dense and heavy, more like dough or pastry. The more organic matter the soil contains the better its structure. It makes clay soils more free-draining and lessens the risk of them becoming compacted or waterlogged. And organic matter makes sandy soils more water-retentive, and counteracts any loss of fertility that may occur when nutrients are washed out by rain.

Soil acidity and alkalinity

All soils have a pH value. It's a measurement of how acidic or alkaline they are. Soils with a low pH are acid, and those with a high pH are alkaline. It's rarely a big issue, as most fruits are fairly tolerant, if anything preferring neutral or perhaps slightly acid soils. The exceptions are blueberries and cranberries: they grow well only in acid soils.

■ ACID SOILS are low in calcium. It is fairly easy to make them more alkaline by adding lime (calcium carbonate) or a lime-rich material, such as mushroom compost.

ACID OR ALKALINE?

1–5	very acid
6	acid
6.5	slightly acid
7	neutral
7.5	slightly alkaline
8	alkaline
9–14	very alkaline

Measuring soil pH is done using a simple test kit. Add soil to the solution in the test tube, shake well, then match the resulting colour against the pH chart provided.

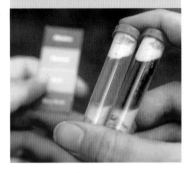

(below left to right) **Clay soil** is sticky when wet and can be rolled into a ball. **Sandy soil** is light, feels gritty, and the particles don't stick together. **To reduce soil acidity,** spread powdered lime over the soil and rake it evenly. Wear gloves and a face mask, and avoid windy days.

■ ALKALINE SOILS are high in calcium, and are often found in chalk and limestone areas. They can trigger a nutrient disorder called lime-induced chlorosis (see p.320). Alkaline soils can be made more acid by adding composted sawdust, composted pine bark or needles, sulphur dust or chips, or loam-based ericaceous compost.

Feeding your soil

Generous crops of fruit year after year make heavy demands on the soil. They take out a lot of nutrients. It should come as no surprise that some of that goodness needs putting back. Feeding your soil will keep it healthy, fertile, and productive. There are two methods. The first is to add organic material in the form of compost or manure. The second is to use fertilizers – either organic or inorganic, whichever you prefer.

Composts and manures

These are natural organic materials made up of decomposed or rotted plant matter and animal waste. When dug into the soil before planting, they improve its structure by breaking up compacted masses so that air can circulate, and roots can grow deeply and spread widely. They improve drainage, too. Clay soils drain more freely, whereas sandy soils retain moisture for longer.

Farmyard and stable manures are ideal soil improvers, if you can find a source for them. They usually comprise straw and animal dung, sometimes with woodshavings or sawdust as well. Leave them to rot down for at least six months before using them. Garden and household compost is decayed plant matter that has been broken down by tiny micro-organisms. You can buy it, but it's easy to make your own.

Once trees and perennial fruits are established, it's best to add composts and manures as a surface mulch. In time, worms will do the work for you and draw it down into the soil.

Fertilizers

These provide a more concentrated, quick-acting, source of nutrients than manures and composts. They are usually sold in liquid, powder, granule, or pelleted form, and may be organic or inorganic. Organic fertilizers are derived entirely from plant or animal material. They include: bonemeal; dried blood; hoof and horn; fish meal; blood, fish, and bonemeal; and seaweed extracts. Inorganic fertilizers are extracted from minerals or are produced using industrial-scale chemical processes.

Key nutrients

All fertilizers contain at least one of the three key elements that plants need from the soil: nitrogen (N, added in the form of nitrates), phosphorus (P, added in the form of phosphates), and potassium (K, added in the form of potash). Many contain a mixture of all three. Some also include calcium, magnesium, and sulphur, as well as trace elements such as boron, copper, iron, manganese, and molybdenum.

(top to bottom) **Spread well-rotted compost** or manure around the plants, taking care not to pile it up against the trunk or stem. Mulching after watering will increase moisture retention. **Farmyard manure** improves soil structure and adds back valuable nutrients. **Garden compost heaps** rot down to produce rich, fertile material that should be dark and crumbly, just like soil.

Common mineral deficiencies

If plants are denied their necessary nutrients, they fail to grow properly and show signs of malnutrition, just like humans. Often, the cause is not that the minerals are actually missing from the soil but that chemical imbalances prevent plants from absorbing them properly – perhaps through lack of water or because the soil is too acid or alkaline.

Boron deficiency

Boron is washed out of light soils by heavy rain. Low levels occur in very dry or recently limed soils.

■ **Symptoms** Shoots may die back and leaves yellow. Apples and pears may be distorted and develop cork-like patches; strawberries are small and pale, and leaves are distorted with yellow tips.

■ **Treatment** Mix borax with horticultural sand and rake it into the soil, if possible before you plant.

Calcium deficiency

Calcium levels are low in acid soils. Even where there is sufficient calcium, plants may be unable to absorb it if the ground is very dry.

■ **Symptoms** Apples develop **bitter pit** (see p.325). Sometimes the flesh becomes "glassy" and semi-transparent.

■ **Treatment** Add powdered lime to soil and rake it in to increase the pH level. Prevent soil from drying out by watering regularly and apply a mulch to retain moisture.

Iron deficiency (lime-induced chlorosis)

It's rare to find soil that is truly short of iron. What tends to happen is that the high levels of calcium in recently limed or very alkaline soils prevent plants from absorbing the iron that is available. For this reason, the disorder is also known as lime-induced chlorosis. It usually goes hand-in-hand with manganese deficiency.

■ **Symptoms** Leaves yellow, starting at the edges then spreading in between the veins, which remain green. Finally, the entire leaf may turn brown and wither. New leaves are affected first. Symptoms are similar to those of both manganese and magnesium deficiency. Tree fruit, such as apples, pears, and peaches, and soft fruit, such as strawberries, raspberries, and blueberries can be badly affected.

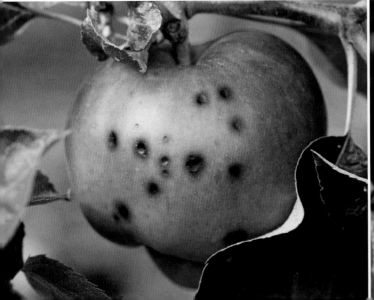

■ **Treatment** Acidifying the soil may help, but it is best to buy special chelated or sequestered iron mixtures, which provide iron in a form that plants are able to absorb.

Magnesium deficiency

Heavy rain will readily wash magnesium out of light soils. Levels may also be low in acid soils or when high-potash fertilizers have been used to increase the amounts of potassium.

■ **Symptoms** Leaves turn yellow between the veins and around the edges because there is insufficient magnesium to produce green chlorophyll. The yellow areas may turn red, purple, or brown. Unlike iron and manganese deficiency, old leaves are affected first.

■ **Treatment** Apply Epsom salts (magnesium sulphate) as a foliar spray or spread it over the soil.

Manganese deficiency

Insufficient manganese is most common on acid, peaty soils or on poorly drained, sandy soils.

■ **Symptoms** Almost identical to those of iron deficiency, with which it is often associated.

■ **Treatment** Avoid adding too much lime to soils where the problem has been identified. Spray affected plants with manganese sulphate solution.

Nitrogen deficiency

Soils without much organic matter are those most likely to have insufficient nitrogen. So, too, are soils in containers. Periods of heavy rain, which wash out nutrients, make the problem worse.

■ **Symptoms** Leaves are pale green or yellow due to insufficient chlorophyll. Some may even turn pink, red, or purple. Older leaves near the base of the plant are the worst affected. Plants are generally smaller and more spindly than they should be.

■ **Treatment** Add lots of well-rotted compost, manure, or other organic material, or some high-nitrogen fertilizer.

Potassium deficiency

This is most likely to occur on light, sandy soils.

■ **Symptoms** Potassium is part of the process by which plants absorb water and photosynthesize. Without enough potassium, leaves curl, go yellow, scorch at the edges, and may have purple-brown spots underneath. Flowering is poor, fruits are small, and plants may be more vulnerable to disease.

■ **Treatment** Add sulphate of potash fertilizer. Composted bracken or comfrey will help restore levels, too.

(below, far left to right) **Bitter pit** in apples is a sign of lack of calcium, often caused by dry conditions. **Chlorosis** is caused by iron or manganese deficiency and produces distinctive yellowing of the leaves in between the veins. **Magnesium deficiency** can show as yellow leaf markings, particularly at the margins. **Potassium deficiency** typically causes leaves to turn brown, scorch, and curl upwards at the edges.

Diseases and disorders

Most diseases that commonly afflict fruit are caused by one of three things: a fungus, a virus, or bacteria. In each case, micro-organisms (or pathogens) invade the plant and disrupt or interfere with its normal, healthy growth. Sometimes the symptoms of infection are minor and can be easily treated – or even ignored – and the plant recovers. But in severe cases a plant may be so badly weakened by disease that it dies.

(top to bottom) **Clean tools** carefully after use. Use a disinfectant solution or spray to kill any bacteria, and dry blades carefully to prevent rust.
When spraying products straight on to the leaves of affected plants, always measure quantities accurately and make up only as much as you need.

How diseases spread

Most fungal infections are spread by spores blown from one plant to another by the wind or transmitted by the splashing of water from a can or hose. Bacteria spread in the same way, although insects and animals can also carry them. Viruses are often transmitted by sap-feeding insects, especially aphids, although they can also be passed on via infected seeds or cuttings.

Preventing disease

Plants are most at risk when they are damaged or have just been pruned. It's often through open wounds that infections enter in the first place. They are also vulnerable in damp, humid, stagnant conditions, where diseases thrive and reproduce.
■ DON'T OVERCROWD plants. Give them enough space for light to get to them and for air to circulate freely.
■ WEED, water, and feed them, and give them the right growing conditions. The healthier your plants, the more resistant to infection they will be.
■ DISINFECT TOOLS before and after use – especially when pruning.
■ CLEAR AWAY all windfalls, fallen leaves, and offcuts from pruning. Burn, instead of composting, any material that you suspect might be infected.

Treating diseased plants

Some fungal diseases can be treated with fungicides, which kill off the fungal spores. They are either "contact", which means they work only on fungal growths that are sprayed directly, or "systemic", which means that they are absorbed into the plant tissue and circulate internally. Fungicides may be synthetic (such as mancozeb) or organic (such as copper-based Bordeaux mixture or sulphur). If you decide to use them, do so with care, and follow the manufacturer's instructions.

Viruses are rarely treatable. Dig up and destroy affected plants. Bacterial diseases are best combated with swift action. As soon as you see any tell-tale signs, remove all infected material and hope that the disease does not spread.

Common fruit diseases

1 Brown rot
The spores of this fungus usually enter fruits whose skins have split or that have been damaged by birds or insects. Brown rot can spread very rapidly (see p.326).

2 Canker
A fungal disease, apple and pear canker (see p.324) enters the wood via cracks in the bark or via pruning cuts. Bacterial canker (see p.324) spreads in the same way, affecting buds, shoots, and leaves, as well as stems and branches.

3 Dieback
When new growth wilts, withers, and dies off, a variety of different infections can be to blame. Perhaps the most common are botrytis (see p.325) and eutypa (see p.327).

4 Leaf spots
Irregular spots, blotches, patches, and discolourations can be hard to diagnose. One of the fungal infections known as fungal leaf spot (see p.327) may be the cause or these may be a symptom of bacterial canker (see p.324).

5 Mildews
Powdery mildew (see p.329) is very common, and affects a wide range of fruit. It's rarely fatal, but it can stunt growth and it's important to prevent it from spreading. Downy mildew (see p.327) is restricted to grapes.

6 Moulds
Grey mould is the type you're most likely to encounter. It is caused by the fungus botrytis (see p.325), and is worse in damp, humid conditions where air cannot circulate freely. Soft fruits tend to be badly affected.

7 Scab
Typically, the symptoms of scab are brown or black fungal growths that appear as patches on leaves and on the skins of fruit (see p.330). Badly infected apples, pears, and plums tend to be stunted and misshapen, and cracked or split.

8 Viruses
Viruses are notoriously difficult to diagnose. Symptoms may include distorted, stunted, or oddly coloured leaves, but often growth is simply poor and crops are disappointing. Particularly susceptible fruits are raspberries, strawberries blueberries (shown here), and blackcurrants.

A–Z of diseases and disorders

Listed here are the diseases that most commonly affect fruit trees, bushes, and other plants. Almost all are caused by fungi, viruses, or bacteria. Some are treatable, others are not. In all cases, good hygiene and the right growing conditions will help keep plants healthy, and swift action will prevent infections from spreading. In addition to the conditions listed here, plants may sometimes suffer from disorders that look very like diseases but are actually caused by a lack of essential minerals in the soil (see pp.320–21).

American gooseberry mildew

This notoriously destructive disorder is caused by a fungus that thrives in still, non-circulating air. It tends to be worse on fruit bushes fed with high-nitrogen fertilizer, as it stimulates new growth that is particularly vulnerable.

■ **Crops affected** Gooseberries, blackcurrants.

■ **Symptoms** Initially, powdery white patches appear on shoots and leaves, then on the fruits themselves. New shoots may become misshapen and fail to grow properly. Eventually, the skins of the fruits may turn brown and felt-like or leathery and, although the mildew can be removed and the fruits eaten, they are not very tempting.

■ **Treatment** Cut out and destroy all affected areas, taking care not to leave any diseased foliage or fruit on the ground, or the fungus will overwinter and reappear next year. Space bushes well apart and prune them to open up their centres and to allow air to circulate freely. If necessary, spray with a fungicide in spring.

In future, grow resistant varieties and use a general rather than nitrogen-rich fertilizer.

Apple and pear canker

Cankers may be either bacterial or fungal. It is the fungal form that attacks apples and pears. Spores enter via pruning cuts, cracks in the bark, and the small scars left when leaves fall in autumn. **Scab** makes a tree more prone to attack, too (see p.330). Canker can be very destructive if not treated.

■ **Crops affected** Apples, pears.

■ **Symptoms** Areas of bark discolour, hollow, and split or crack in concentric, flaky rings. The infected site swells up, and growth ceases around it. Fungal growths may appear – creamy white in spring and summer, and red in autumn and winter. Whole branches may die off.

■ **Treatment** Prune out and destroy all infected wood, removing whole branches if necessary, and treating cuts with special wound paint. Spray with a copper-based fungicide, such as Bordeaux mixture.

Apple scab

■ See **Scab** (p.330).

Arabis mosaic

■ See **Strawberry virus** (p.331).

Bacterial canker

This is a serious disease that needs prompt action to prevent it spreading and killing the tree. The bacteria usually enters in the autumn, via cracks in the tree's bark, wounds, or pruning cuts, although it can also attack new shoots and foliage in spring. When leaves are infected, the disorder is sometimes called bacterial leaf spot. Young trees are most at risk – especially if the weather is damp and windy.

■ **Crops affected** All stone fruit – apricots, cherries, nectarines, plums, peaches.

■ **Symptoms** Bacterial canker causes small dark spots in leaves that turn into round holes. The leaves subsequently yellow, wither, and die. Buds do not open, branches die back, and areas of infected bark become sunken and may ooze orange resin or gum.

■ **Treatment** Immediately prune out and destroy all infected wood, removing whole branches if necessary, and treating cuts with special wound paint. Sterilize any tools you've used. In late summer and early autumn, spray with a copper-based fungicide, such as Bordeaux mixture.

Bacterial leaf spot
■ See **Bacterial canker** (p.324).

Bitter pit
This is a calcium-deficiency disorder. It occurs when apple trees – particularly large, heavy-cropping varieties – are unable to absorb sufficient calcium from the soil. As a result, fruit cells die and rot. The deficiency is often caused by the roots being too dry.
■ **Crops affected** Apples.
■ **Symptoms** Small, round, dark spots or sunken pits appear on the skin of apples, and sometimes in the flesh, too. The fruit may taste slightly bitter.
■ **Treatment** Mulch around trees and, if necessary, water to keep up moisture levels in the soil. Use a general rather than a nitrogen-rich fertilizer.

Blackberry cane spot
Sometimes called purple blotch, this fungus is very similar to raspberry cane spot (see p.329).
■ **Symptoms** From about May, round, purple, or brown spots appear on leaves. The spots turn grey-white in the centre but remain purple around the edges. On the canes they are more elliptical in shape and may grow into blotches up to 1cm (½in) long. Tiny black specks of fungal growth may be visible in the white centres. In the case of serious infections, leaves and canes may die.
■ **Crops affected** Blackberries, hybrid berries.

■ **Treatment** Cut down and destroy all infected canes. As a preventative measure, try a copper-based fungicide.

Blackcurrant reversion disease/virus
■ See **Reversion disease** (p.330).

Blossom wilt
This disease is caused by a fungus very closely related to the one responsible for brown rot.
■ **Crops affected** Apples, apricots, cherries, plums, peaches, pears.
■ **Symptoms** New blossom turns brown, withers, and dies. So, too, do new leaves.
■ **Treatment** Remove and destroy infected blossom before the fungus spreads to leaves and stems.

Blueberry stem blight
A fungus that usually infects plants via wounds, perhaps caused by pruning cuts or insect damage.
■ **Crops affected** Blueberries.
■ **Symptoms** Clusters of leaves turn brown, wither, and die but do not fall immediately. Instead they remain on the affected stem, rather like brown "flags", in contrast with surrounding healthy green foliage. Eventually, they do drop, the stem dies back, and the infection can quickly spread.
■ **Treatment** Cut out and destroy all affected stems, right back to the point where there are no longer any brown patches visible in the wood.

Blueberry virus
Blueberries can be afflicted by a number of different viruses,

including "mosaic" and "ringspot". They are not always easy to diagnose, and can be hard to eradicate.
■ **Crops affected** Blueberries.
■ **Symptoms** Yellow-green, red, or pink mottling or mosaic patterns appear on leaves, new shoots may die back, and plants grow and crop poorly.
■ **Treatment** Symptoms can vary in severity from year to year. If plants are badly infected, remove and burn them. Always buy certified virus-free plants.

Botrytis
Also known as grey mould, *Botrytis cinerea* is a fungus. The spores are spread in the air or by rain or water splash, and usually get into plants through wounds or damaged areas. Infections are worse in wet summers.
■ **Crops affected** Worst affected fruits include apples, strawberries, blackberries, raspberries, gooseberries, grapes, and figs.
■ **Symptoms** As its common name suggests, fluffy grey, off-white, or grey-brown mould appears on the stems of plants, on leaves, on fruits, and on flowers. Plants with badly infected stems may yellow, wilt, and die (see **Gooseberry dieback** p.328).
■ **Treatment** Remove and destroy any affected parts of the plant. Don't leave any infected plant material lying around, as the spores will survive if they are transferred to the soil. Ensure plants that survive attacks have space for air to circulate freely around them.

Brown rot

This particular form of rot is caused by a fungus. The spores often find their way under the skin of fruits via damaged areas left where birds and insects have been feeding, though they can also be spread by rainwater.

■ **Crops affected** Apples, apricots, cherries, plums, peaches, pears.

■ **Symptoms** Initially, the fruit develops soft, brown, rotten patches. As these spread, white, crusty spots or pustules appear, often in circular patterns. Eventually the fruit shrivels up and either falls to the ground or remains on the tree in a dessicated state.

■ **Treatment** Pick off and destroy all infected fruit, including windfalls. Prune out any stems or branches that have also become infected, as the fungus is able to overwinter and survive from one year to the next.

Cane blight

■ See **Raspberry cane blight** (p.329).

Cane spot

■ See **Blackberry cane spot** (p.325) and **Raspberry cane spot** (p.329).

Canker

■ See **Apple and pear canker** (p.324), **Bacterial canker** (p.324), and **Mulberry canker** (p.328).

Cherry leaf blight

■ See **Fungal leaf spot** (p.327).

Cherry leaf scorch

Despite its name, this disorder has nothing to do with extremes of heat or light. It is caused by a fungus.

■ **Crops affected** Cherries, and occasionally apricots.

■ **Symptoms** Initially, leaves develop irregular yellow patches. They turn increasingly brown, wither, and die, but instead of falling to the ground remain in place on the tree over winter. Infections are rarely fatal, although they are difficult to eradicate and are likely to recur.

■ **Treatment** Cut off and destroy infected foliage and branches. No appropriate fungicide is available.

Chlorosis, lime-induced

■ See **Iron deficiency** (p.320).

Cluster cup rust

■ See **Gooseberry rust** (p.328).

Coral spot

This is a waterborne fungus that grows on woody stems and branches. If it is allowed to spread it can be lethal.

■ **Crops affected** Currants, figs, and other trees and bushes.

■ **Symptoms** Pink or orange spots or pustules appear on the bark, often around a wound or ragged pruning cut.

■ **Treatment** Prune out and burn all infected wood.

Coryneum blight

■ See **Shot-hole disease** (p.331).

Crown rot

A soil-inhabiting fungus causes the crowns of strawberry plants to rot and the leaves to wilt. Badly infected plants die. The problem is worse in warm weather and with strawberries grown under cover.

■ **Crops affected** Strawberries.

■ **Symptoms** Young leaves in the middle of the plant wilt and may turn yellow. Lifting affected plants and cutting through the crown will show it to be brown and rotten.

■ **Treatment** There is no cure. Dig up and destroy diseased plants, and do not replant strawberries on the infected site. If possible, choose resistant varieties in future.

Cucumber mosaic virus

This is a serious, widespread virus that can wipe out plants completely.

■ **Crops affected** Melons, cucumbers, courgettes, and squashes.

■ **Symptoms** Leaves become misshapen and stunted, and develop yellow, mosaic patterning. Flowers may not appear. Any fruits that do form are small, hard, and inedible. Plants may die.

■ **Treatment** There is no cure. Dig up and destroy all affected plants.

Dieback

Dieback can be caused by a number of different infections. See also **Botrytis** (see p.325), **Eutypa** (see p.327), and **Gooseberry dieback** (p.328).

■ **Crops affected** Most tree and soft fruit.

■ **Symptoms** New shoots and leaves wilt, dry up, and turn brown. If the infection spreads, branches gradually die off and ultimately the whole plant may die.

■ **Treatment** Cut off and destroy infected foliage and branches. If necessary, spray with an appropriate fungicide. If the whole plant is affected, uproot and destroy it.

Downy mildew
This type of mildew is caused by a range of different fungi that thrive in damp, humid conditions.

■ **Crops affected** Grapes.

■ **Symptoms** Pale green, yellow, or brown patches develop on the upper surface of leaves, with off-white, fluffy mould on the underside. As the patches spread, the leaves die. Once the disease takes hold and the plant is weakened, **Botrytis** (see p.325) may follow.

■ **Treatment** Remove and destroy infected leaves. Discourage the onset of the disease by ensuring good air circulation and avoiding over-watering.

European pear rust
■ See **Rust** (p.330).

Eutypa
Dieback can be caused by a fungus called *Eutypa lata*. In the case of grape vines, the infection may take hold following pruning.

■ **Crops affected** Gooseberries, grapes, redcurrants.

■ **Symptoms** New shoots and leaf growth may be weak or stunted. Older leaves wither, dry up, turn yellow or brown, and fall off. Branches gradually die off completely. In the end, the whole plant may die.

■ **Treatment** Cut off and destroy infected foliage and branches. If necessary, spray with an appropriate fungicide. If the whole plant is affected, uproot and destroy it.

False silver leaf
This is a less serious condition than the true fungal disease, silver leaf.

■ **Crops affected** All tree fruit.

■ **Symptoms** Leaves develop a silvery sheen, and some may turn brown at the edges. Symptoms are similar to those of **silver leaf** (see p.331), but the diagnosis is more likely to be false silver leaf if the entire tree is silvered, and if no brown staining can be seen in the centre of branches when cut through. The probable cause is that the tree is under stress – due to drought, malnutrition, or heavy attack by insects or other pests.

■ **Treatment** Feed and water regularly, and in spring spread an organic mulch around the base of trees.

Fireblight
This is a serious bacterial disease that infects trees via their flowers, is transmitted by rain splash, and may in time be lethal.

■ **Crops affected** Apples, pears.

■ **Symptoms** Flowers turn brown, wither, and die. Then leaves do the same. As the disease spreads, stems and branches are affected too. Peeling back a strip of bark may reveal fiery, orange-red markings on the wood.

■ **Treatment** Prune out and destroy all infected wood – or dig up and burn the entire tree.

Foot and root rots
These rots are caused by a range of different fungi. They live in the soil and in standing water.

■ **Crops affected** Soft fruit, citrus, melons, and, in particular, container-grown plants.

■ **Symptoms** If the base of the plant stem is infected, it will darken and the tissues will start to shrink and die. Leaves and stems above will wilt, go yellow or brown, and die. Infected roots may turn black or brown, and break up or rot.

■ **Treatment** Once the disease has taken hold, there is no remedy. Immediately remove and destroy infected plants – and the soil in which they are growing.

Fungal leaf spot
A range of different fungi attack the leaf tissues. Some target only specific types of crop. The disease is likely to be worse in wet summers. See also **Bacterial canker** (p.324).

■ **Crops affected** Blackberries, currants, gooseberries, raspberries, strawberries. Two particular species can cause leaf spot or leaf blight in cherries and quinces, too.

■ **Symptoms** In May or June, leaves develop small brown or grey spots where tissue has died. The spots may spread and join up, and leaves turn yellow before falling off. Young shoots, stems, and canes may be affected as well. On raspberries, tiny pinprick-sized black or brown growths are the tell-tale sign that the disease is fungal rather than bacterial leaf spot.

■ **Treatment** If you catch it early, the disease is unlikely to be fatal. Remove and destroy infected leaves. Don't leave any lying around at the end of the year, or the spores may survive the winter.

Gooseberry dieback

Dieback is usually caused by a fungal infection, either grey mould **botrytis** (see p.325) or **eutypa** (see p.327).

■ **Crops affected** Gooseberries, with similar problems on currants and raspberries.

■ **Symptoms** Leaves wither, dry up, turn brown, and fall off. The bark on stems may crack, and branches gradually die off completely. In the end, the whole plant may die.

■ **Treatment** Cut off and destroy infected foliage and branches. If necessary, spray with an appropriate fungicide. If the whole plant is affected, uproot it and destroy it.

Gooseberry mildew

■ See **American gooseberry mildew** (p.324).

Gooseberry rust

A fungal growth also known as cluster cup rust. Serious infections often start after a dry spring, and then worsen during the summer, finally damaging the fruits themselves.

■ **Crops affected** Gooseberries, and less often, currants.

■ **Symptoms** Dark orange or red blisters (or pustules) appear on leaves and may spread to fruits and to stems – where the tell-tale signs are tiny cup-shaped hollows with yellow outer rims.

■ **Treatment** Cut off and destroy infected foliage. If necessary, spray

with an appropriate fungicide. Do not grow gooseberries near sedges, which act as hosts to the fungal spores.

Grey mould

■ See **Botrytis** (p.325).

Honey fungus

The term covers a range of fungi that can attack all fruits, and other plants too.

■ **Crops affected** All tree and bush fruits, and strawberries.

■ **Symptoms** A warning sign may be wilting leaves or poor foliage, but in some cases a plant may die surprisingly quickly and unexpectedly. Peel back the bark at the base of the trunk or stem, or inspect the roots, and you may find white fungus that smells of mushrooms. Sometimes, honey-coloured toadstools grow around the base of infected trees.

■ **Treatment** Dig up and destroy infected plants, including their root systems. Healthy plants have more resistance.

Leaf spot

■ See **Bacterial canker** (p.324) and **Fungal leaf spot** (p.327).

Lime-induced chlorosis

■ See **Iron deficiency** (p.320).

Mildew

See **American gooseberry mildew** (p.324), **Downy mildew** (p.327), and **Powdery mildew** (p.329).

Mulberry canker

A fungal form of canker that attacks mulberries. It can be most troublesome after a wet spring.

■ **Crops affected** Mulberries.

■ **Symptoms** Young shoots wither and die back, as cankers encircle the stems. Spores may be visible on sunken or swollen areas of bark.

■ **Treatment** Prune out and destroy all infected wood.

Peach leaf curl

This fungus is the bane of any gardener who grows peaches and nectarines. However, disastrous though it may appear, it is not usually fatal.

■ **Crops affected** Peaches, nectarines.

■ **Symptoms** Leaves curl, blister, and turn orange-red or even purple. If left in place, they develop an off-white, powdery mould, go brown, and drop. New leaves that open subsequently are unaffected, though the tree may have been weakened by the initial loss of foliage.

■ **Treatment** Remove and destroy infected leaves at once. Spray with copper fungicide in winter – though not when the buds open – and cover with a temporary rainproof sheet to prevent spores from spreading the disease.

Pear rust and Plum rust

■ See **Rust** (p.330).

Pear scab

■ See **Scab** (p.330).

Pear stony pit virus

The virus makes infected fruit inedible. It is more likely to affect older, established trees, but it is contagious and should be dealt with before it spreads.

■ **Crops affected** Pears.
■ **Symptoms** Pears become misshapen, pitted, and lumpy, with surface dimples. Inside, they may be hard and woody.
■ **Treatment** There is no cure for the virus. Dig out and burn badly infected trees.

Pocket plum

A fungal infection that causes fruits to become distorted and hollow, and to drop early. They are inedible.
■ **Crops affected** Plums, gages, bullaces, damsons.
■ **Symptoms** Young fruitlets become misshapen and elongated, like miniature, empty bananas. They shrivel like prunes, and do not contain stones. White spores may form on them before they eventually drop to the ground.
■ **Treatment** Remove and destroy all affected fruit to prevent the fungus from overwintering.

Powdery mildew

This mildew is caused by a range of different fungi that thrive in dry soil. The spores spread in the air and via rain or water splashes.
■ **Crops affected** A wide range of fruit, including apples, plums, peaches, strawberries, raspberries, blackberries, currants, gooseberries, grapes, and melons.
■ **Symptoms** A white powdery coating of mildew appears on leaves – usually on the upper surface, but sometimes on the underside as well. It may turn slightly purple. Leaves go yellow and fall off. Fruits such as grapes may split or burst open before rotting. The plant's growth is

impaired, and it may even die.
■ **Treatment** Remove and destroy infected leaves. Spray with a fungicide, and try to prevent the onset of the disease by ensuring good air circulation and watering regularly.

Purple blotch

■ See **Blackberry cane spot** (p.325).

Quince leaf blight

This disease is caused by a fungus similar to those responsible for other forms of **fungal leaf spot** (p.327). It is likely to be worse in wet weather.
■ **Crops affected** Quinces.
■ **Symptoms** Leaves develop small red or brown spots, which gradually spread and turn black. The remaining leaf tissue goes yellow and withers, and leaves that have died fall early. Infected shoots may die back completely, and fruits themselves may be spotted and misshapen.
■ **Treatment** Prune out affected areas, and destroy infected leaves and fruits. Don't leave any lying about on the ground. Appropriate fungicides are not available.

Raspberry cane blight

Cane blight is caused by a soil-borne fungal infection that gets into the stems via wounds made by insects, pruning, or frost.
■ **Crops affected** Raspberries.
■ **Symptoms** Bark splits and peels just above soil level, and canes become brittle and may die.
■ **Treatment** Cut down and destroy all infected canes. Spray remaining canes with a copper-based fungicide.

Raspberry cane spot

Cane spot is a fungus that targets many cane fruits. It is not uncommon.
■ **Crops affected** Raspberries, blackberries, hybrid berries.
■ **Symptoms** Purple spots or elliptical patches with white centres appear on canes and leaves – also on flowers and sometimes fruit. There may be fewer berries than normal and some may be misshapen. In bad cases, leaves may fall, and canes may split and die. Blackberries and hybrid berries may be affected by this and also by the very similar **blackberry cane spot** (p. 325).
■ **Treatment** Cut down and destroy all infected canes.

Raspberry spur blight

Like cane blight, raspberry spur blight is a fungal disease – but a less common and slightly less serious one. Damp weather increases the risk of it spreading.
■ **Crops affected** Raspberries, hybrid berries.
■ **Symptoms** Leaves develop brown blotches and purple patches appear around new buds on new canes. Towards autumn, they turn from purple to dark brown, then silvery-grey with visible black spores. Next year's crop will be poor, and new buds and shoots on infected canes may wither and die the following spring.
■ **Treatment** Cut down and destroy all infected canes. Thin out any overcrowding.

Raspberry virus

Actually, a number of different viruses can attack raspberry canes. Once established, they are

extremely difficult to eradicate.
- **Crops affected** Raspberries, blackberries, hybrid berries.
- **Symptoms** Yellow-green mottling or mosaic patterns appear on leaves, which may also curl downwards at the edges and become smaller than normal. Plants grow and crop poorly. The symptoms can be confused with those of **raspberry leaf and bud mite** (see p.338).
- **Treatment** Remove and destroy all infected plants. Do not grow cane fruit in the same position again.

Red core
A fungus that lives in the soil and attacks the roots of strawberries. It tends to be worse on heavy soils prone to waterlogging.
- **Crops affected** Strawberries.
- **Symptoms** Early signs usually become visible in late spring or early summer: stunted growth, and discoloured foliage – red-orange inner leaves and brown, dry outer ones. Berries are undersized and may ripen earlier than normal. Roots are dark-coloured with a red rather than white central core.
- **Treatment** There is no cure. Moreover, the disease is easily spread and can persist in the soil for years. Dig up and destroy diseased plants, and do not replant strawberries on the infected site.

Reversion disease
Also known as blackcurrant reversion virus, this disease is widespread and results in lower than normal yields of berries. It is thought to be transmitted by **blackcurrant gall/big bud mites** (see p.335).

- **Crops affected** Blackcurrants.
- **Symptoms** Diagnosis is difficult as the only symptom may be smaller leaves, with some yellowing and thinner than normal veins, and fewer flowers than on uninfected plants.
- **Treatment** Dig up and destroy diseased plants. Inspect bushes regularly and remove any swollen buds in order to control big bud mites. There is no other cure.

Rust
Rusts, which vary in colour from yellow through orange to brown, are all caused by fungi. They thrive in damp conditions. The rust that most commonly affects pears is known as European pear rust. See also **gooseberry rust** (p.328).
- **Crops affected** Blackberries, raspberries, gooseberries, pears, plums.
- **Symptoms** Bright-coloured, rust-like patches of spores appear on leaves and stems.
- **Treatment** Cut off and destroy infected foliage. If necessary, spray with an appropriate fungicide.

Scab
Scabs are fungal growths that can spread rapidly in damp, humid conditions.
- **Crops affected** Apples, cherries, nectarines, peaches, pears, plums.
- **Symptoms** Dark-brown scabs appear on the skins of fruits, and may spread to cover most of the surface. Badly infected apples and pears are small and distorted, and may crack and rot. Plums may split and ooze gum. Leaves and stems may be affected too.

- **Treatment** Cut out infected wood, remove infected fruit, and collect up and destroy fallen leaves. If necessary, spray with an appropriate fungicide. In winter, prune apple and pear trees to increase air circulation.

Shanking
This is a disorder that affects grapes, and one that may be caused by poor soil, or too much or too little water.
- **Crops affected** Grapes.
- **Symptoms** Not all the grapes in a bunch ripen properly. And they take on odd colours: black grapes may be red, and green grapes may be translucent. Stalks shrivel, and grapes wither and taste watery, sour, and unpleasant.
- **Treatment** Remove affected fruit. To rest the vine, reduce cropping for a couple of years by removing more flower trusses than usual. Feed and water regularly, and if necessary top dress and mulch the soil.

Shot-hole disease
A disorder that can affect both leaves and fruit. It is usually the result of a fungal infection sometimes known as Coryneum blight, but can also be a symptom of **bacterial canker** (see p.324).
- **Crops affected** Apricots, cherries, nectarines, peaches, plums.
- **Symptoms** Small, red-brown leaf spots appear on foliage. The centres of the spots decay to leave holes in the leaves. Fruits may be covered with similar spots, which may be corky, slightly sunken, or they may ooze gum.
- **Treatment** If the disease is

fungal and you catch it early, it is unlikely to be serious. Remove and destroy infected leaves, stems, and fruit. Otherwise, treat as for bacterial canker.

Silver leaf

This is a serious fungal disease that takes its name from a silvery sheen that develops on affected leaves. The fungus attacks via fresh wounds in the bark and pruning cuts.

■ **Crops affected** Plums and cherries. Also peaches, nectarines, and less often, apples and pears.

■ **Symptoms** Infected leaf tissues have a silvery sheen, and leaves may turn brown at the edges. Sure signs of silver leaf are that infected wood is stained brown inside and that branches and stems die back progressively. Purple, white, or brown fungus may appear through the bark on dead wood. Silver leaf is sometimes mistaken for the much less serious **false silver leaf** (see p.327).

■ **Treatment** Remove and burn badly infected trees. Otherwise, prune out all affected (stained) wood. In future, prune only in June, July or August, when the fungus is less likely to attack, and always be scrupulous about sterilizing tools.

Sooty mould

■ See **Aphids** (p.334).

Stony pit virus

■ See **Pear stony pit virus** (p.328).

Strawberry green petal

Named after the abnormally green flowers it produces, this destructive virus is spread chiefly by insects called leafhoppers.

■ **Crops affected** Strawberries.

■ **Symptoms** Flowers are smaller than normal, and petals are green instead of white or pink. Leaves turn yellow or red, and fruit may be misshapen or may simply not develop at all.

■ **Treatment** There is no cure. Remove and burn badly infected plants. In future, you may want to use an insecticide to eliminate leafhoppers.

Strawberry virus

Numerous different viruses affect strawberries, including yellow edge and arabis mosaic. They are spread by insects – particularly strawberry aphids, but also by mites, leafhoppers, and eelworms.

■ **Crops affected** Strawberries.

■ **Symptoms** Some or all of the following symptoms may be present: stunted growth, leaves distorted, crumpled, or crinkled, yellow edges, yellow spots and blotches, yellow streaks or mosaic patterning.

■ **Treatment** There is no cure. Remove and burn badly infected plants. Renew strawberries regularly. Depending on the variety, grow them afresh each year or for no longer than four years at the most. Rotate the position of crops as you would with vegetables.

Verticillium wilt

A fungus that persists in the soil as well as in dead plant matter and weeds.

■ **Crops affected** Strawberries.

■ **Symptoms** Usually in summer, plants wilt, older leaves turn red or brown, and young leaves go yellow. There may be black streaks on leaf stems. In severe cases, plants may die.

■ **Treatment** There is no cure. Remove and burn badly infected plants. Replant new, certified disease-free strawberry plants elsewhere – but not on a site where potatoes or tomatoes have been grown previously.

Virus

■ See **Blueberry virus** (p.325), **Raspberry virus** (p.329), **Reversion** (p.330), and **Strawberry virus** (this page).

Yellow edge

■ See **Strawberry virus** (this page).

Pests and parasites

All gardeners have a love-hate relationship with insects, birds, and animals. Some are easy to love: for example, bees and other pollinating insects, without which flowers would not be fertilized and fruit would not set. Others are harder to feel affection for: birds that strip buds and ripe fruit, animals that damage the bark of young trees, or grubs and larvae that tunnel into developing fruits, spoiling the crop and rendering it inedible.

(top to bottom) **Hang pheromone traps** in trees, in May for apples, and in June and July for plums. The female pheromone in the traps attracts male moths, which then get stuck to an adhesive sheet inside, preventing them from breeding. With luck, the result of this enforced birth control will be noticeably fewer codling moth and plum fruit moth caterpillars. **Sticky grease bands** prevent female winter moths, who are unable to fly, from climbing tree trunks and laying their eggs during winter. Fit them to tree stakes as well, so moths can't cross over via tree ties.

How to deter pests

Birds are a notorious problem. In winter they eat fruit buds, and in summer they eat the fruit itself. They are particularly fond of raspberries, currants, and strawberries, but few types of fruit are entirely safe. Let's be honest: scarers don't really work, however ingenious they are. Birds get accustomed to them very quickly. The only guaranteed solution is to use nets or build a fruit cage.

Animals – primarily, rabbits, badgers, and deer – both damage plants, and eat the fruit. Only fences provide sure protection, provided they are sufficiently strong and tall, or sunk deep enough underground.

You can combat insect pests in a number of ways. Physical barriers such as grease bands prevent them invading and laying their eggs, and sticky traps will catch them, hopefully before they are able to mate. Regular inspection may allow you to remove and destroy them by hand. And keeping your plot clean and free of weeds, fallen leaves, and other plant debris offers them fewer places in which to set up home.

Using insecticides

The sale of insecticides to home gardeners is tightly controlled. In recent years, many well-known, widely used products have been withdrawn, and more look set to be banned in the future.

Insecticides are classified as either organic or synthetic. The ingredients of organic insecticides are derived wholly from plant or animal organisms, and include fatty acids, insecticidal soaps, winter washes made from plant oils, and pyrethrum (which is derived from flowers). Synthetic insecticides are non-organic; bifenthrin is one of the few permitted for use by fruit growers.

If you decide to use an insecticide, follow these rules:

■ USE INSECTICIDES only on food crops for which they are explicitly stated to be appropriate, and follow the manufacturer's instructions.
■ WEAR GLOVES and, if necessary, a mask and goggles.
■ DON'T SPRAY when flowers are open or shortly before you harvest.
■ SPRAY EARLY in the morning or late in the evening, when bees and other beneficial insects are less likely to be harmed.
■ DON'T SPRAY when it is windy.

Common fruit pests

1 Birds
Birds will eat most soft fruits unless they are protected by nets. They are partial to tree fruit, too. Once they have punctured the skins, insects will join in as well, and rot soon sets in on anything they leave behind.

2 Aphids
Often referred to as simply blackfly or greenfly, there are hundreds of different species of aphid, most of which target specific crops.

3 Moth caterpillars
Winter moth caterpillars hatch in spring from eggs laid earlier in winter, and immediately start feeding on young shoots and leaves. They can cause severe defoliation. Codling moth and plum fruit moth caterpillars tunnel into the fruit.

4 Grubs and larvae
The larvae of various species of sawfly feed on apples (on which they leave ribbon-like scars), gooseberries, and plums. The cherry and pear slugworm is a sawfly, too. Other grubs include those of raspberry beetles, leatherjackets, and pear midges.

5 Mites
So small they are often invisible to the naked eye, mites usually live and feed inside buds, leaf tissue, or fruitlets, preventing them from developing properly. Different species infest blackberries (shown here), blackcurrants, pears, strawberries, and grape vines.

6 Red spider mite
Glasshouse or polytunnel infestations of spider mite can be very destructive. Foliage becomes discoloured and wilts, and may be covered with silk webbing. In hot summers, spider mites colonize outdoor plants, too.

7 Scale insects and mealybugs
These flat, shell-like insects, sometimes covered in sticky white wax, are usually found on plant stems and on the ribs of leaves. They feed on sap and are widespread on plants grown under cover.

8 Wasps
In mid- to late summer, when many fruit crops are ripening, wasps may make holes in soft-skinned fruits and feed on harder-skinned fruits that have already been damaged by birds.

A–Z of pests and parasites

Sadly, fruit trees and bushes spend much of their lives under attack from insect, bird, and animal predators, particularly as fruits ripen and become increasingly irresistible. But knowledge is power. If you can recognize what you're dealing with, you'll be a lot more effective at combating it. It pays to know as much as possible about the life cycle, feeding habits, and behaviour of all potential pests and parasites, from aphids to winter moths.

Aphids

Blackfly and greenfly are the most common type of aphid, although amongst the hundreds of different species, many other colours are found, too. Aphids are tiny, sap-sucking insects that multiply at an incredible rate – when just a week old, young aphids are themselves ready to breed.

■ **See** Currant blister aphid (p.336), **Mealy plum aphid** (p.337), **Plum leaf-curling aphid** (p.338), **Rosy apple aphid** (p.339), **Woolly aphid** (p.341).

■ **Crops affected** A wide range, many of which are targeted by aphid species specific to particular plant types, such as cherries, plums, currants, and gooseberries.

■ **Damage** A heavy infestation causes leaves to curl and distort, and can stunt growth. The sticky honeydew that aphids excrete fosters black, sooty mould.

■ **Treatment** Organic controls include pyrethrum and insecticidal soap sprays, and for trees and bushes a plant-oil based winter wash. Ladybirds (which feed on the honeydew), lacewings, and other insects can act as natural predators. Otherwise, spray with an inorganic insecticide such as bifenthrin.

Apple leaf miner

Small moths lay their eggs underneath young leaves in spring. Tiny caterpillars hatch and feed inside the leaves, tunnelling their way through "mines" in the leaf tissue, leaving long, winding trails that become gradually wider until they exit.

■ **Crops affected** Apples, pears, cherries.

■ **Damage** The tracks are unsightly but the damage is not usually serious.

■ **Treatment** Not normally necessary.

Apple sawfly

White maggots hatch from eggs laid when trees are in blossom and then tunnel into young fruitlets to feed. On exiting, they leave a hole filled with excrement or "frass", similar to that left by a codling moth maggot. Of the two, sawfly grubs tend to attack earlier in the summer than codling moths.

■ **Crops affected** Apples.

■ **Damage** Young fruitlets fall early. Apples that survive and ripen may have ribbon-like scars on their skins.

■ **Treatment** Destroy all affected fruits. If necessary, spray as soon as blossom drops with bifenthrin.

Apple sucker

Tiny, aphid-like insects feed inside buds and on newly opened flowers.

■ **Crops affected** Apples.

■ **Damage** Blossom turns brown and may be misshapen or even destroyed. The damage is similar to that caused by frost.

■ **Treatment** If necessary, spray trees with bifenthrin or pyrethrum before flower buds open.

Apple blossom weevil

The brown adult weevils lay their eggs in flower buds. When the young larvae hatch, they feed inside the developing buds, preventing them from opening properly.

■ **Crops affected** Apples, and occasionally pears, quinces, medlars.

■ **Damage** Buds may burst, but flowers do not open properly and the closed outer petals turn brown and die. This is sometimes known as "capped" blossom. Fruitlets do not form at all.

■ **Treatment** Infestations are rarely so severe that they destroy the tree's entire crop.

Badgers

■ **See** Deer and other animals (p.336).

Big bud mite
■ See **Blackcurrant gall mite** (this page).

Birds
Pigeons, bullfinches, magpies, jays, and blackbirds are amongst the birds most likely to pose a problem.

■ **Crops affected** All stone and soft fruit.

■ **Damage** Birds can strip trees and bushes of young buds, and may eat ripening fruits.

■ **Treatment** Bird-scarers of all kinds are always worth trying, but birds are smart and will soon ignore them. Nets and fruit cages are the only guaranteed solution.

Blackberry mite
These are microscopically small mites that overwinter on plants, and emerge in the spring to feed on blossom and young fruitlets. As they do so, they release a chemical that stops the fruits from ripening properly. The condition is sometimes known as redberry disease, and the culprits as redberry mites.

■ **Crops affected** Blackberries, hybrid berries.

■ **Damage** Fruits fail to ripen fully. While some parts of an affected berry turn black as normal, other parts remain red and hard. The problem increases in hot weather, and is worse towards the end of the season.

■ **Treatment** There are no chemical controls. Try cutting out and burning affected canes in an attempt to prevent the mites from overwintering, and thus break their life-cycle.

Blackcurrant gall midge
Also known as blackcurrant leaf midge or even blackcurrant leaf curling midge. Tiny, white or orange maggots hatch from eggs laid inside new, young, unfurled leaves. They feed on the leaves during the course of spring and summer, preventing them from opening and thus stunting new growth.

■ **Crops affected** Blackcurrants.

■ **Damage** Leaves are distorted, fail to open properly, and may die.

■ **Treatment** There is no cure. Try resistant varieties.

Blackcurrant gall mite
Also known as big bud mites, these microscopic insects spend the winter living and feeding inside buds, moving on when they open in spring. A single infested bud may contain a colony of several thousand mites.

■ **Crops affected** Blackcurrants.

■ **Damage** Infested buds swell up, do not develop properly, and will probably die and fall in the summer. Worse, big bud mites can spread a virus called **reversion disease** (see p.330).

■ **Treatment** Inspect bushes carefully throughout the autumn and winter, and pick off and destroy any swollen buds. Uproot and burn badly infested plants.

Blackcurrant leaf midge, blackcurrant leaf curling midge
■ See **Blackcurrant gall midge** (this page).

Blackcurrant sawfly
■ See **Gooseberry sawfly** (p.336).

Blackfly
■ See **Aphids** (p.334).

Brown scale
■ See **Scale insects** (p.339).

Capsid bugs
These are small, flying insects that feed on the sap in leaves, shoot tips, flower buds, and fruit. Their saliva infects and kills plant tissue. Adult females lay eggs in the autumn, which hatch in spring, causing maximum damage from late spring into summer. Capsid bugs are hard to spot and fly off if disturbed.

■ **Crops affected** Apples, currants, gooseberries, raspberries, strawberries.

■ **Damage** New leaves and shoots are deformed, established leaves have red-brown spots and small brown-edged holes, and may appear tattered. Apples have raised scabs on their skin.

■ **Treatment** If necessary, spray with bifenthrin after blossom has fallen.

Caterpillars
■ See **Codling moth** (this page), **Plum fruit moth** (p.338), **Tortrix moth** (p.340), **Winter moth** (p.341).

Cherry blackfly
■ See **Aphids** (p.334).

Cherry slugworms
■ See **Slugworms** (p.340).

Codling moth
The small female codling moths lay their eggs on fruits in June and July. On hatching, the larvae tunnel into the fruit, all the way to the

core, eating as they go. After about a month, they depart, leaving an exit hole. Similar holes are created by apple sawfly grubs, though they are likely to attack young fruitlets earlier in the summer.

■ **Crops affected** Apples, pears.

■ **Damage** Fruits are riddled with tunnels, and inedible. They may fall early from the tree.

■ **Treatment** In May, hang pheromone traps to attract and trap male moths, preventing them from mating (see p.332). If necessary, spray with bifenthrin in June and July.

Currant blister aphid

The pale yellow aphids hatch in spring and colonize the undersides of leaves, where they feed on the sap. In summer, they fly off but return in autumn to lay eggs that will overwinter on the bushes.

■ **Crops affected** Blackcurrants, redcurrants, whitecurrants.

■ **Damage** Leaves are distorted and puckered, with raised, bubble-like blisters that are yellow on blackcurrants, and red on red- and whitecurrants. The blisters are unsightly, but rarely affect the crop.

■ **Treatment** In midwinter, spraying with a plant-oil based winter wash on a mild, dry, non-windy day may prevent eggs hatching. Otherwise, in spring before symptoms develop, treat young foliage with an organic insecticide spray such as pyrethrum.

Deer and other animals

In rural areas, deer, rabbits, and badgers can cause much damage.

■ **Crops affected** All tree and soft fruit.

■ **Damage** Young shoots are eaten, and a ring of bark may be completely stripped from around immature trees. Later in the summer, ripening fruit becomes a target.

■ **Treatment** Tree trunks can be ringed with mesh guards made from metal or tough plastic (see p.38), but ultimately fences are the only real deterrent – high ones for deer, ones that extend below the ground for rabbits, and even electric ones for badgers.

Eelworms

These are microscopic nematodes that feed on plant tissue and live in the soil or plant debris. In strawberries, so-called leaf eelworms and stem eelworms cause similar damage.

■ **Crops affected** Strawberries.

■ **Damage** Leaves are crumpled and distorted, stalks may be unusually short and thick, or uncharacteristically long and red in colour. Growth is stunted. Though you'll be unable to see them with the naked eye, badly infested plants can contain millions of eelworms.

■ **Treatment** There is no cure, although regularly clearing debris and weeds will reduce the risk of infestation. Remove and burn affected plants, and do not use the same site again for strawberries for five years or more.

Fruit tree red spider mite

■ See **Red spider mite** (p.339).

Fruit tree tortrix moth

■ See **Tortrix moth** (p.340).

Glasshouse red spider mite

■ See **Red spider mite** (p.339).

Glasshouse whitefly

■ See **Whiteflies** (p.341).

Gooseberry sawfly

Rather than the sawflies themselves, it is actually their larvae that do the damage. They hatch in spring and summer from small, green eggs laid on the leaves, often deep in the middle of the bush. As they grow, their appetites increase and they quickly eat their way out along the stems, devouring new foliage as they go. By the time you spot them they may well have stripped most of the leaves back to the veins. The common gooseberry sawfly is the most prevalent. It can grow up to 20mm (¾in) long, and has a pale green body with black spots and a black head. The blackcurrant sawfly is a closely related species.

■ **Crops affected** Gooseberries, blackcurrants, redcurrants, whitecurrants.

■ **Damage** Leaves may be stripped clean, leaving no more than a skeleton of ribs and veins. Fruit is not affected, although the plant may have been badly weakened.

■ **Treatment** From May onwards, inspect plants regularly and carefully, especially deep in the centre of bushes. Pick off and destroy eggs and larvae, or spray several times with pyrethrum.

Greenfly

■ See **Aphids** (p.334).

Leaf miner

■ See **Apple leaf miner** (p.334).

Leatherjackets

These are actually the larvae of the crane fly, commonly known as the daddy longlegs. Their parents notwithstanding, the larvae have no legs – though they can grow up to 4.5cm (1³/₄ in) in length and have a voracious appetite.

■ **Crops affected** Blackberries, raspberries, strawberries.

■ **Damage** Stems and roots may be eaten through, causing plants to wilt and die.

■ **Treatment** Collect and destroy the larvae if they come to the surface after rain – provided birds don't beat you to it. Insecticides have limited success, but a parasitic nematode is available, and slug pellets can be effective.

Mealybugs

Female mealybugs are small, flat, pale-coloured insects that cover themselves and their eggs in a fluffy, sticky, white wax. They feed on sap. Males don't feed – and don't live long either.

■ **Crops affected** In temperate climates, crops grown under cover such as figs, grapes, melons, citrus, and other tender fruit.

■ **Damage** Heavy infestations can weaken plants.

■ **Treatment** Paint the bugs with brush dipped in methylated spirits, spray several times with insecticidal soap, or employ a special predatory ladybird called *Cryptolaemus montrouzieri*.

Mealy plum aphid

These greenfly hatch in spring from eggs that overwinter on plum trees. They form colonies on the undersides of leaves, where they secrete a white, mealy wax with

which they cover themselves.

■ **Crops affected** Plums, gages, bullaces, damsons.

■ **Damage** Leaves are not misshapen, but they do become covered in sticky honeydew, on which grey or black sooty mould tends to grow. Heavy infestations can stunt growth and spoil fruits. However, most of the aphids leave to colonize other plants during June and July, only returning in the autumn.

■ **Treatment** In midwinter, when trees are dormant, spray with a plant-oil based winter wash. Choose a mild, dry, non-windy day. In spring, young foliage can be sprayed with pyrethrum, insecticidal soap, or an inorganic insecticide, such as bifenthrin.

Moths

■ See **Codling moth** (p.335), **Plum fruit moth** (p.338), **Tortrix moth** (p.340), **Winter moth** (p.341).

Pear leaf blister mite

The mites are microscopic insects that live within the tissue of the tree's leaves, releasing a damaging toxin as they feed.

■ **Crops affected** Pears, and occasionally apples.

■ **Damage** Initially, pink or yellow-green blisters appear on the leaves, either side of the central rib. They turn darker as the summer progresses. Crops are unlikely to be affected.

■ **Treatment** Pick off and destroy affected leaves.

Pear leaf midge

Also known as pear leaf-curling midges, these tiny grubs hatch

from eggs laid by flies on the edges of young leaves and, as they begin feeding, prevent the leaves from opening properly.

■ **Crops affected** Pears. Related species also attack apples and plums.

■ **Damage** Leaves remain tightly curled. They turn red then black, and die off. Similar symptoms may be caused by the **tortrix moth** (see p.340).

■ **Treatment** Spraying is not normally effective. Pick off infected leaves and destroy them.

Pear midge

Adult midges lay eggs in new buds in spring. When the eggs hatch, small creamy white maggots start feeding on the young flowers and fruitlets.

■ **Crops affected** Pears.

■ **Damage** Young fruitlets containing pear midge maggots blacken, swell, and fall.

■ **Treatment** Pick off and destroy infested fruitlets. If necessary, spray small trees with bifenthrin shortly before flowers open.

Pear slugworms

■ See **Slugworms** (p.340).

Pear sucker

Small insects about 2mm long that feed on sap from buds, flowers, and leaves. They excrete sticky honeydew, just like aphids.

■ **Crops affected** Pears.

■ **Damage** Blossom goes brown and dies, leaves are covered with sticky honeydew, which in turn may develop grey sooty mould, and fruitlets may be misshapen and drop prematurely.

■ **Treatment** If necessary, spray with an insecticide such as bifenthrin after blossom has fallen.

Phylloxera

Phylloxera are small insects, related to aphids, that feed on the sap of vines. It is thought that insect populations came to Europe from North America, where phylloxera originated, in the 19th century. This invasion had devastating results for the wine industry, the French in particular.

■ **Crops affected** Grapes.

■ **Damage** Visible signs on leaves and roots include rounded, protective galls or swellings that the insects create around themselves. The plant usually dies.

■ **Treatment** There is no treatment, although, due largely to grafting of European cultivars onto naturally resistant North American rootstocks, phylloxera is currently under control.

Plum fruit moth

A relative of the **codling moth** (p.335), plum fruit moths also lay eggs in summer. Once hatched, pink caterpillars tunnel into the fruit.

■ **Crops affected** Plums, gages, bullaces, damsons, and less frequently, peaches.

■ **Damage** Caterpillars feed around the stone in the centre of the fruit, then eat their way out, leaving excrement as they go. Fruits may rot and fall.

■ **Treatment** In June and July, hang pheromone traps to attract and trap male moths, preventing them from mating (see p.332). If possible, destroy any affected fruit before the caterpillars leave and move on to overwinter.

Plum leaf-curling aphid

The aphids are small and yellow-green in colour. They suck the sap from the plant tissue of new leaves. Eggs are laid in the autumn and overwinter on the trees, hatching early in the new year ready for young to feed on buds as they burst and new leaves emerge. In May, the adults depart leaving further growth undamaged.

■ **Crops affected** Plums, gages, bullaces, damsons.

■ **Damage** New, young leaves are tightly curled and distorted. Their growth will be stunted.

■ **Treatment** In midwinter, when trees are dormant, spray with a plant-oil based winter wash. Choose a mild, dry, non-windy day. In spring, young foliage can be sprayed with an approved systemic insecticide – but not when the tree is in blossom.

Plum sawfly

White maggots about 1cm (½in) long hatch from eggs, laid in spring when trees are in blossom, and then tunnel into young fruitlets to feed. They leave a small hole ringed with black excrement or "frass".

■ **Crops affected** Plums, gages, bullaces, and damsons.

■ **Damage** Young fruitlets fall early, before they have ripened.

■ **Treatment** Destroy all affected fruits to prevent the maggots overwintering in the soil. If necessary, spray trees with bifenthrin a week or so after blossom drops.

Rabbits

■ See **Deer and other animals** (p.336).

Raspberry beetle

Adult beetles lay their eggs on flowers in summer. On hatching, the pale creamy-brown grubs feed on the ripening berries, burrowing inside.

■ **Crops affected** Raspberries, blackberries, hybrid berries.

■ **Damage** Berries may be small and have dried, shrivelled patches around the stalk. After picking, the grubs may crawl out from inside.

■ **Treatment** Effective insecticide sprays are no longer available. Remove nets, and hoe around canes in spring and autumn to bring pupae in the soil to the surface for birds to eat.

Raspberry cane midge

Tiny pink–red grubs or larvae no more than 4mm in length bore just beneath the surface of canes in summer and autumn.

■ **Crops affected** Raspberries, blackberries, hybrid berries.

■ **Damage** Cracks and splits caused by the grubs increase the risk of infection by **Raspberry cane blight** (see p.329).

■ **Treatment** As for raspberry beetle.

Raspberry leaf and bud mite

Tiny mites suck the sap from the undersides of leaves, causing discolouration and distortion.

■ **Crops affected** Raspberries.

■ **Damage** Pale yellow blotches appear on the upper surfaces of leaves beneath which mites have been feeding. New leaves may become distorted. Symptoms are similar to those of raspberry virus – though usually less serious.

■ **Treatment** There are no insecticides available. Cut down autumn-fruiting varieties at the end of each year so the mites have nowhere to overwinter.

Raspberry moth

Caterpillars are pink-red and may be about 1cm (½in) long.

■ **Crops affected** Raspberries, blackberries, hybrid berries.

■ **Damage** In April and May, caterpillars that have overwintered tunnel into new shoots and buds to feed, often causing them to then shrivel and die.

■ **Treatment** Cut off and destroy affected shoots. Cut down autumn-fruiting varieties after harvesting, instead of waiting until February, so the mites have nowhere to overwinter.

Redberry disease and redberry mite

■ See **Blackberry mite** (p.335).

Red spider mite

There are two types: fruit tree red spider mite and glasshouse or two-spotted red spider mite. In hot summers, the latter are found outdoors as well as under cover. The mites live and lay eggs on the undersides of leaves, and feed on sap. Like actual spiders they have eight legs, and are tiny – less than 1mm long. Fruit tree spider mites are dark-red, and glasshouse spider mites are yellow-green in spring and summer, turning orange-red in autumn and winter.

■ **Crops affected** Tree fruit such as apples, plums, peaches,

nectarines, apricots, and less commonly, cherries and pears. All soft fruit, especially strawberries and blackcurrants. Tender fruit grown under cover such as figs, melons, and citrus.

■ **Damage** Leaves become dull and mottled, go silvery-bronze or yellow-white, and may wilt, turn brittle, and fall. Plants may eventually be covered with fine, white, silk webbing.

■ **Treatment** Under cover, spray with water regularly to increase humidity. A predatory mite *Phytoseiulus persimilis* is available as a biological control. If necessary, spray with bifenthrin or insecticidal soap.

Rosy apple aphid

Two different species attack apples. One is active in early spring and can stunt new growth; the other, sometimes called rosy leaf-curling aphid, colonizes the inside of tightly curled leaves.

■ **Crops affected** Apples.

■ **Damage** Leaves are curled and distorted, sometimes turning yellow or red. Fruits may be small and misshapen.

■ **Treatment** Organic controls include pyrethrum, insecticidal soap sprays, and natural predators such as ladybirds. Or spray with an inorganic insecticide such as bifenthrin, before the leaves curl up.

Sawfly

■ See **Apple sawfly** (p.334), **Gooseberry sawfly** (p.336), and **Plum sawfly** (p.338).

Scale insects

All scale insects have distinctive, shell-like coverings, rather like

small turtles. Some secrete a white, waxy substance. Of the numerous types of scale insect, those most often affecting fruit are woolly currant scale, brown scale, and soft scale.

■ **Crops affected** Tree fruit, citrus, vines, and soft fruit bushes, both outdoors and in greenhouses.

■ **Damage** Scale insects colonize trunks and branches of trees, and stems of bushes. The white, fluffy, waxy secretion and sticky honeydew that some insects produce can host grey sooty moulds. Light infestations rarely cause damage, but severe ones can weaken shrubs.

■ **Treatment** In midwinter, when outdoor, deciduous plants are dormant, spray with a plant-oil based winter wash. Other approved insecticides are likely to be effective only in June and July, when young insects hatch from eggs protected beneath the adult females' shells.

Slugs and snails

The tell-tale trail of slime, and the sight of decimated, spoiled plants is the bane of every gardener's life.

■ **Crops affected** Strawberries are particularly at risk, but sometimes blackcurrants, raspberries, hybrid berries, and melons may be attacked too.

■ **Damage** Slugs may start feeding on tender new shoots of strawberry plants, though they will reserve their biggest onslaught for the ripe fruits.

■ **Treatment** Employ baits (upturned grapefruit halves, beer traps) and barriers (sharp gravel, crushed eggshells, copper bands). Keep down weeds to minimize hiding places. Introduce the parasitic nematode *Phasmarhabditis hermaphrodita.* If necessary, resort to slug pellets.

Slugworms

Also known as pear and cherry slugworms, these are not in fact slugs at all, but sawfly larvae which cover themselves in slimy black mucus.

■ **Crops affected** Cherries, pears, and less often, plums.
■ **Damage** The larvae usually feed on the upper surfaces of leaves, eating away the tissue and leaving brown, skeleton-like patches of exposed veins.
■ **Treatment** If necessary, spray with an insecticide such as bifenthrin or pyrethrum as soon as evidence is apparent.

Soft scale

■ See **Scale insects** (p.339).

Spider mite

■ See **Red spider mite** (p.339).

Strawberry beetles

Two species feed on strawberries: strawberry seed beetles and strawberry ground beetles. Both are black and can be up to 2cm (³/₄in) long. They feed at night, but may be found under leaves and straw during the day.
■ **Crops affected** Strawberries.
■ **Damage** The beetles feed on the flesh of ripening strawberries and cause the same sort of damage as slugs and birds, but closer inspection may show that they have carefully removed and eaten the seeds from near the surface, especially on the undersides of the berries.

■ **Treatment** There are no approved insecticides available. Remove old foliage as soon as plants have finished cropping, and keep strawberry beds clean, tidy, and free of weeds so that the beetles can't overwinter.

Strawberry blossom weevil

These tiny weevils hatch and feed inside new strawberry flower buds, usually preventing them from opening, and sometimes killing them.
■ **Crops affected** Strawberries.
■ **Damage** Flower buds fail to open. If the weevils eat through the stalks, the buds droop, shrivel, and may drop off.
■ **Treatment** There are no approved insecticides, although attacks are rarely so severe that they ruin an entire crop.

Strawberry mite

The microscopically small mites are too tiny to see with the naked eye. They feed on new leaves, preventing them from developing normally and stunting the plant's growth – usually quite late in the season. Infestations may be worse in hot, dry summers.
■ **Crops affected** Strawberries.
■ **Damage** Leaves are small, crumpled, and distorted. They may turn brown and dry out.
■ **Treatment** There are no approved insecticides available. Remove and destroy affected plants, and replant elsewhere with new, certified disease-free plants.

Sucker

■ See **Apple sucker** (p.334) and **Pear sucker** (p.337).

Thrips

These are small, slender insects that eat into the surfaces of leaves and feed on the sap. They can damage flower petals, too.
■ **Crops affected** Citrus fruit – as well as a wide variety of other plants, under cover and outdoors.
■ **Damage** Leaves may display yellow streaks or silvery patches, and tiny specks of black excrement may be visible.
■ **Treatment** If necessary, spray with bifenthrin or pyrethrum.

Tortrix moth

There are several species. The fruit tree tortrix moth spins silk in order to curl young leaves around itself. The summer fruit tortrix feeds on ripening fruits, sometimes out of sight under cover of a leaf that it has attached to the fruit with silk.
■ **Crops affected** Apples, blackcurrants, cherries, pears, plums, raspberries, strawberries.
■ **Damage** Leaves are stunted and growing shoots are sometimes damaged. Fruit may be spoiled.
■ **Treatment** Remove affected leaves by hand. If necessary, spray with bifenthrin or pyrethrum before leaves become curled.

Vine leaf blister mite

Also known as vine erinose mites, these are microscopic insects that live and feed on leaves.
■ **Crops affected** Grapes.
■ **Damage** Blisters appear on the surface of leaves. Underneath, patches of dense, fine white hairs form, which gradually discolour and produce yellow, red, or brown felt-like patches. Sometimes, the patches appear on the upper surfaces, too.

■ **Treatment** There are no approved insecticides available, but the damage is usually unsightly rather than truly harmful. Remove and destroy affected leaves if you wish, but beware of stripping off too many.

Vine weevils
Adult weevils are black beetles up to 1cm (½in) long when fully grown. They don't fly but are agile climbers. They usually hide during the day, and come out to feed only at night. More destructive are their fat, white, underground larvae that feed on plant roots.
■ **Crops affected** Strawberries, grapes, and other tender fruit grown under cover.
■ **Damage** Leaf edges are notched where adults have fed on them. More seriously, roots can be so damaged by larvae living in the soil, that young plants may be killed.
■ **Treatment** Search out, pick off, and destroy adult weevils – at night, by torchlight, if necessary. As a biological control, try introducing the pathogenic nematode *Steinernema kraussei*.

Wasps
Wasps tend to be a pest only in mid- to late summer. Earlier in the year, young insects are likely to act as beneficial predators, feeding on caterpillars and other grubs.
■ **Crops affected** Most ripe fruit crops.
■ **Damage** Wasps create holes in fruit as they feed on the flesh.
■ **Treatment** Don't tamper with wasps if you can avoid it. Nests should be dealt with by professionals. The best deterrent is

perhaps to set up a bait of sweet, rotting fruit, or a pot of jam or sugary liquid to lure them away from your most valued crops.

Weevils
■ See **Vine weevils** (this page).

Whiteflies
Glasshouse whiteflies are tiny, moth-like flies with wedge-shaped, white wings that colonize the undersides of leaves, where they also lay their eggs.
■ **Crops affected** Grape vines, citrus, melons, and other tender fruit grown under cover.
■ **Damage** The young suck sap from leaves causing them to yellow and stunting plant growth. They secrete honeydew which fosters black, sooty mould.
■ **Treatment** If necessary, spray with insecticidal soap, pyrethrum, or bifenthrin. Use yellow sticky traps, or the parasitic wasp *Encarsia formosa*.

Winter moth
It's not so much the moths as their voracious caterpillars that do the damage. These hatch early in spring from eggs laid on branches the previous autumn, and begin feeding on new leaves, flowers, and even on young fruitlets. Unchecked, they are capable of stripping leaves. The caterpillars of the winter moth are pale green with yellow stripes, and can grow to 2.5cm (1in). The brown mottled umber moth and the March moth are very similar in behaviour. All may move with a distinctive arching of their bodies.
■ **Crops affected** Apples, cherries, pears, plums.

■ **Damage** Leaves may be stripped clean, leaving no more than a skeleton of ribs and veins. Severe attacks may produce malformed fruits, and seriously weaken the tree.
■ **Treatment** In October, tie sticky grease bands around trunks to prevent the flightless adult females from crawling up and laying eggs. In spring, inspect small trees carefully and remove caterpillars by hand. If necessary, spray immediately after bud burst but before blossom opens with bifenthrin or pyrethrum.

Wireworms
These are the soil-dwelling larvae of click beetles. The worms are orange-brown and up to 2.5cm (1in) long.
■ **Crops affected** Raspberries, strawberries.
■ **Damage** The stems of young plants may be severed, and roots may be eaten into.
■ **Treatment** Search the soil around damaged crops and destroy any wireworms you find.

Woolly aphid
A sap-sucking aphid that lives on apple branches and covers itself with a white woolly secretion.
■ **Crops affected** Apples.
■ **Damage** Leaves and fruit may be misshapen, and swollen galls may form on stems. If these split, canker may enter.
■ **Treatment** Brush off insects or prune out bad infestations. If necessary, spray with bifenthrin.

Woolly currant scale
■ See **Scale insects** (p.339).

Index

Page numbers in *italics* indicate an illustration. Page numbers in **bold** refer to a main section or entry.

Acknowledgments

Author's acknowledgments

Thanks to the following: Anna Kruger and Alison
Gardner, who have brought their customary skill,
professionalism, and patience to the production
of what's now our third book together; Jo
Whittingham for her eagle eye and valuable
suggestions; Alison Donovan, Helen Fewster,
Esther Ripley, and the team at Dorling Kindersley;
Barbara Wood, my plot neighbour at The Royal
Paddocks Allotments, Hampton Wick, who has
been as helpful, wise, and generous as ever; a host
of friends who have allowed the unforgiving eye
of my camera lens free rein of their gardens and
orchards – Charles and Annabel Rathbone, Mic
and Julia Cady, Fiona MacIntyre and Nigel Waters,
Christopher and Linda Davis, and Janice and Nick
Maris; the staff at RHS Wisley, RHS Rosemoor, and
the National Fruit Collection at Brogdale Farm in
Kent; members of the RHS Fruit Group; and finally
Jim Buckland and Sarah Wain of West Dean
Gardens in Sussex, who have restored and run
one of the most beautiful kitchen gardens in the
country. If you've never visited, do so at once.
It's an inspiration. www.westdean.org.uk

Index Michèle Clark

Picture credits

Dorling Kindersley would like to thank
Alan Buckingham for new photography:

(Key: a-above; b-below/bottom; c-centre; f-far;
l-left; r-right; t-top)

1, 4tl, 4tr, 5tl, 5tc, 8br, 9, 13tl, 13c, 13cr, 13bc, 13br,
15cl, 15cr, 15bl, 15bc, 15br, 16tl, 16tr, 21cr, 24bl,
24bc, 25tl, 25bc, 25br, 27tl, 27tr, 27bc, 27br, 30bl,
32tl, 32tr, 34bc, 35, 36t, 36c, 36b, 37t, 37c, 37bl,
37bcl, 37bcr, 37br, 38tl, 38tcl, 38tc, 38tcr, 38tr,
39bl, 39bc, 39br, 40, 42tl, 42cl, 42tr, 42b, 43t,
43ctl, 43bl, 43br, 43cr, 44t, 44bl, 45t, 45ctl, 45ctr,

45cbl, 45cbr, 46tr, 46b, 47t, 47c, 47b, 48t, 48ctl, 48cbr, 48br, 49tl, 49tr, 49c, 49b, 50, 51t, 54tr, 54cr, 54cl, 54bl, 54bc, 54br, 55l, 55c, 55r, 61t, 63c, 64l, 64c, 64r, 65l, 65c, 65r, 66, 67bl, 67br, 68, 69tl, 69tc, 69tr, 69br, 70, 71bl, 72t, 74/5, 75tr, 76tc, 76tr, 76bc, 76br, 77tl, 77bl, 77bc, 77r, 78tl, 78tcl, 78tcr, 78bl, 78br, 79tr, 80, 82tl, 82cl, 82b, 83t, 83bl, 83br, 84t, 84cr, 84bl, 84br, 85t, 85b, 87br, 88tl, 88ccl, 88cr, 89, 90/1, 92t, 93t, 93b, 95, 96br, 97b, 98, 99ct, 99b, 100tl, 100tc, 100bl, 100bc, 100br, 101tc, 101bc, 101br, 102, 104tl, 104cl, 104cr, 104b, 105cr, 106cl, 106br, 106br, 107t, 107ct, 107cb, 107b, 108, 109tr, 109cl, 109clc, 109bcr, 109bl, 109bcl, 110, 113tl, 113tc, 113tr, 115cr, 115br, 116bl, 116br, 118tc, 118bc, 118br, 119tl, 119bl, 119bc, 120, 122tl, 122tr, 122b, 123t, 123c, 123br, 125cl, 125c, 125cr, 129bl, 130tl, 130tcl, 130tcr, 130tr, 131cl, 131cr, 133tr, 134bl, 134bcl, 134bcr, 134br, 135tl, 135bl, 135br, 138tr, 138b, 139, 141t, 141c, 141b, 143tl, 143tr, 143c, 143b, 146b, 147t, 149tr, 151t, 151cl, 157t, 157ctl, 157ctr, 157cb, 158l, 158r, 159, 160bl, 160bc, 160br, 161, 162l, 162r, 164t, 164b, 166, 168tc, 170r, 172br, 173tl, 173tc, 173tr, 175tl, 175tr, 177tl, 177bl, 177tr, 177bcr,

179, 181tr, 181br, 182, 184t, 184bl, 185ct, 186tr, 188, 189br, 192tl, 193tl, 193tc, 194br, 195bl, 195br, 196, 198ctr, 198bl, 199bl, 200, 201bl, 201bc, 201br, 202t, 203tl, 203tcl, 203tcr, 204, 205r, 206ctl, 207c, 207cb, 207b, 208, 210cl, 210bl, 210br, 211tr, 211b, 212, 214br, 215tr, 215ct, 215cb, 215b, 216cr, 217tl, 217tc, 217bl, 217bc, 217r, 218, 220cl, 220b, 223tl, 224bl, 225tl, 225tc, 225br, 227cl, 227br, 228bl, 228tr, 228bc, 228br, 229bl, 229bc, 230, 232tl, 232ctl, 232cbr, 232br, 234tl, 234tc, 234tr, 235tl, 235bl, 236tr, 237tl, 237tc, 237bc, 237br, 240tl, 242bl, 242bc, 243tl, 243tc, 243tr, 243br, 245t, 245ct, 245cbl, 245cbr, 245b, 248cl, 248cr, 248bl, 249tl, 249tr, 249ct, 250, 254tl, 254tc, 254tr, 257tr, 258, 260tl, 260tr, 265, 266br, 267c, 267b, 268, 274tl, 274tc, 277bl, 280tl, 280tc, 280bl, 280bc, 280br, 281br, 283, 284, 286tr, 286bl, 287t, 287cl, 293br, 293bl, 294, 297tl, 297tr, 297bl, 297br, 298tl, 298cl, 298cr, 298bl, 298br, 303tr, 303br, 304, 305, 306bl, 306br, 307tl, 307tr, 307br, 308bc, 309br, 310br, 315, 317bl, 320br, 321bl, 323tl, 323tr, 323ctl, 323ctr, 323cbl, 323cbr, 323br, 333tl, 333tr, 333ctl, 333cbl, 333cbr, 333br

Alan Buckingham © **Dorling Kindersley**

5tr, 8bl, 13tl, 13tr, 15c, 27bl, 43cbl, 44br, 45b, 46c, 48ctr, 48bl, 53tr, 54tl, 54c, 78bc, 79tc, 79bl, 79bc, 79br, 82tr, , 83c, 88ccr, 93ct, 93cb, 101bl, 105t, 105br, 109crc, 118bl, 119br, 124, 128, 134tl, 172bl, 173br, 184cl, 184br, 193tr, 198br, 203tr, 207t, 207ct, 210cr, 211c, 220t, 224tr, 225tr, 229br, 232tr, 232bl, 240bl, 320bl, 321br, 323bl, 332tl, 333ctr,

Dorling Kindersley would like to thank **Peter Anderson** for new photography:

2/3, 6/7, 11, 13bl, 15tl, 15tr, 17bl, 18, 20, 21t, 21b, 25tr, 25bl, 26c, 26bc, 26br, 39tl, 39tc, 39tr, 44cl, 61br, 62, 72bl, 73, 78cr, 87tl, 92bl, 92r, 96t, 96bl, 97tc, 97tr, 105cbl, 106t, 111, 112tl, 112tc, 116tc, 116tr, 117br, 126, 132, 133c, 133ca, 132t, 132cb, 133b, 144, 146car, 147cb, 150, 151cb, 151b, 152, 154, 157b, 170l, 176, 180, 185bc, 198cl, 199t, 211tl, 220cra, 221bl, 223tr, 235bcr, 235br, 238, 240ca, 240tr, 240br, 246, 248t, 249bl, 255, 272, 273bl, 275, 299, 300bl, 300br.

The publisher would like to thank the following for their kind permission to reproduce their photographs:

4 **Blackmoor Nurseries**: (tc). 13 **Blackmoor Nurseries**: (tc). 15 **Corbis**: Ed Young/AgStock Images (tc). 17 **The Garden Collection**: Torie Chugg/Sue Hitchens, RHS Hampton Court 05. 19 **Alamy Images**: Wildscape/Jason Smalley. 22 **Dorling Kindersley**: Alison Gardner (bl). 23 **Dorling Kindersley**: Alison Gardner (t). **The Garden Collection**: Liz Eddison/Prieure Notre-Dame d'Orsan, France (bl). 29 **Photolibrary**: Mayer/Le Scanff/Garden Picture Library. 46 **R.V. Roger Ltd.**: (tc). 53 **Blackmoor Nurseries**: (bl). 56 **Dorling Kindersley**: Alison Gardner. 71 **Photolibrary**: Claire Higgins/Garden Picture Library (br). 77 **Dorling Kindersley**: Alison Gardner (cb). 91 **Sarah Wain, West Dean Gardens**: (tl) (tc) (tr). 101 **FLPA**: Nigel Cattlin (clb). 112 **Reads Nursery**: (br). 122 **Garden World Images**: Trevor Sims (cr). 123 **Victoriana Nursery Gardens**: Stephen Shirley (bl). 136 **Getty Images**: Inga Spence. 138 **Blackmoor Nurseries**: (ca) (cb). Ron Ludekens: (cr). 146 **Blackmoor Nurseries**: (tr). **GAP Photos**: (ca). 147 **Photolibrary**: Paroli Galperti/Cuboimages (cla). 155 **Sarah Wain, West Dean Gardens**. 168 **Alamy Images**: John Glover (tr). **Photoshot**: Michael Warren (tl). **Ron Ludekens**: (c). **Science Photo Library**: (cr). 169 **Photolibrary**: Martin Page/Garden Picture Library (br). 177 **Dorling Kindersley**: Alison

Gardner (cl). 184 **Photoshot**: Photos Horticultural (cr). 185 **GAP Photos**: (clb). **Photoshot**: Michael Warren (tl). 191 **Dorling Kindersley**: Alison Gardner (tl). 194 **FLPA**: Nigel Cattlin (bl). 198 **Alamy Images**: Greg Wright (crb). **Photoshot**: Photos Horticultural/Michael Warren (tr). 199 **Photoshot**: Photos Horticultural/Michael Warren (cla). **Scottish Crop Research Institute**: (clb). 210 **Photoshot**: Flowerphotos/Jonathan Buckley (tr). 221 **GAP Photos**: Dave Bevan (tl); J S Sira (bc). **R.V. Roger Ltd.**: (cl) (cb). 240 **Blackmoor Nurseries**: (crb). 242 **Corbis**: Image Source (br). 248 **Tadeusz Kusibab**: (br). 249 **Tadeusz Kusibab**: (cb). **Thompson & Morgan**: (bc). 252 **Dorling Kindersley**: Alison Gardner. 253 **Garden World Images**: John Swithinbank (r). 257 **Dorling Kindersley**: Alison Gardner (cla) (tl). 259 **R.V. Roger Ltd.**: (cr) (br). 261 **Garden World Images**: Trevor Sims. 262 Corbis: Mark Bolton (c). **Photolibrary**: Garden Picture Library/Michel Viard (br). **Thompson & Morgan**: (tr). 263 **Alamy Images**: John Glover (cl). Corbis: Gallo Images/Martin Harvey (bl); Tania Midgley (tl). **Photoshot**: JTB (c). 266 **Alamy Images**: Hendrik Holler/Bon Appetit (tr). **Corbis**: Ed Young/AgStock Images (bc) (cr). **GAP Photos**: Richard Bloom (tc). **Garden World Images**: Trevor Sims (c). 267 **Blackmoor Nurseries**: (tl). 281 **Dorling Kindersley**: Alison Gardner (clb). 286 **Corbis**: Ed Young/AgStock Images (br). **The Garden Collection**:

Derek Harris (ca). **Photolibrary**: Garden Picture Library/David Cavagnaro (tc). 287 **Corbis**: AgStock Images (bl); Bill Barksdale/AgStock Images (cb). 288 **Photolibrary**: Garden Picture Library/Friedrich Strauss. 290 **Photolibrary**: Garden Picture Library/Michele Lamontagne. 293 **Dorling Kindersley**: Alison Gardner (cl). 296 **Corbis**: Bill Barksdale/AgStock Images (tc). 302 **Corbis**: AgStock Images (t). **Getty Images**: Visuals Unlimited/Inga Spence (crb). 308 **Corbis**: Bill Ross/Surf (bl). **Garden World Images**: Liz Cole (br). 309 **Corbis**: Douglas Peebles/Encyclopedia (bl). 310 **Corbis**: Melinda Holden/Comet (bc); Douglas Peebles/Encyclopedia (bl). 311 **Corbis**: Jose Fuste Raga/Encyclopedia (br); David Samuel Robbins/Documentary (bc). **Garden World Images**: Trevor Sims (bl). 312 **Garden World Images**: Flora Toskana (bl). 313 **Corbis**: Stefano Amantini/Atlantide Phototravel/Latitude (bl); DK Limited/Encyclopedia (bc); Michelle Garrett/Documentary Value (br). 316 **Garden World Images**: (bl). 333 **Dorling Kindersley**: Alison Gardner (bc)

Jacket images: Front and spine: **Photolibrary**: Amanda Heywood. Back: **Dorling Kindersley**: Peter Anderson tr; **GAP Photos**: Pernilla Bergdahl cr; Geoff Kidd bl; Zara Napier fcr; S&O fcl; Friedrich Strauss cl. Front Flaps: **Dorling Kindersley**: Peter Anderson

All other images © Dorling Kindersley
For further information see: www.dkimages.com

Fruit nurseries and suppliers

Bernwode Plants
Kingswood Lane, Ludgershall,
Buckinghamshire HP18 9RB
Tel: 01844 237 415
www.bernwodeplants.co.uk

Blackmoor Nurseries
Blackmoor, Liss, Hampshire GU33 6BS
Tel: 01420 477 978
www.blackmoor.co.uk

Chris Bowers & Sons
Whispering Trees Nurseries,
Wimbotsham, Norfolk PE34 3QB
Tel: 01366 388 752
www.chrisbowers.co.uk

Brogdale Farm
Home of the National Fruit Collection,
Brogdale Road, Faversham,
Kent ME13 8XZ
Tel: 01795 536 250
www.brogdale.org
www.brogdalecollections.co.uk

D.T. Brown
Bury Road, Newmarket,
Suffolk CB8 7PQ
Tel: 08453 710 534
www.dtbrownseeds.co.uk

The Citrus Centre
West Mare Lane, Pulborough,
West Sussex RH20 2EA
Tel: 01798 872 786
www.citruscentre.co.uk

Deacon's Nursery
Moor View, Godshill,
Isle of Wight PO38 3HW
Tel: 01983 840 750
www.deaconsnurseryfruits.co.uk

Dobies
Long Road, Paignton, Devon TQ4 7SX
Tel: 08447 017 625
www.dobies.co.uk

Global Orange Groves UK
Horton Road, Horton Heath,
Wimborne, Dorset BH21 7JN
Tel: 01202 826 244
www.globalorangegroves.co.uk

Keepers Nursery
Gallants Court, East Farleigh,
Maidstone, Kent ME15 0LE
Tel: 01622 726 465
www.keepers-nursery.co.uk

Marshalls/Unwins
Alconbury Hill, Huntingdon,
Cambridgeshire PE28 4HY
Tel: 01480 443 390
www.marshalls-seeds.co.uk
www.unwins.co.uk

Mr Fothergill's
Gazeley Road, Kentford,
Suffolk CB8 7QB
Tel: 08453 710 518
www.mr-fothergills.co.uk

Ken Muir
Rectory Road, Weeley Heath,
Clacton-on-Sea, Essex CO16 9BJ
Tel: 01255 830 181
www.kenmuir.co.uk

Reads Nursery
Hales Hall, Loddon,
Norfolk NR14 6QW
Tel: 01508 548 395
www.readsnursery.co.uk

Ready to Grow
Online sales only
www.readytogrow.co.uk

R.V. Roger
Malton Road, Pickering,
North Yorkshire YO18 7JW
Tel: 01751 472 226
www.rvroger.co.uk

Thompson & Morgan
Poplar Lane, Ipswich, Suffolk IP8 3BU
Tel: 08442 485 383
www.thompson-morgan.com

Thornhayes Nursery
St Andrews Wood, Dulford,
Cullompton, Devon EX15 2DF
Tel: 01884 266 746
www.thornhayes-nursery.co.uk

J. Tweedie Fruit Trees
Maryfield Road Nursery,
Terregles, Dumfriesshire DG2 9TH
Tel: 01387 720 880

Victoriana Nursery
Challock, Ashford, Kent TN25 4DG
Tel: 01233 740 529
www.victoriananursery.co.uk

Walcot Organic Nursery
Lower Walcot Farm, Walcot Lane,
Drakes Broughton, Pershore,
Worcestershire WR10 2AL
Tel: 01905 841 587
www.walcotnursery.co.uk

Welsh Fruit Stocks
Bryngwyn, Kington,
Hereford HR5 3QZ
Tel: 01497 851 209
www.welshfruitstocks.co.uk